DESMOND J. KEENAN

THE CATHOLIC CHURCH IN NINETEENTH-CENTURY IRELAND

A SOCIOLOGICAL STUDY

GILL AND MACMILLAN

BARNES & NOBLE BOOKS
Totowa, New Jersey

First published 1983 by
Gill and Macmillan Ltd
Goldenbridge
Dublin 8
with associated companies in
Auckland, Dallas, Delhi, Hong Kong,
Johannesburg, Lagos, London, Manzini,
Melbourne, Nairobi, New York, Singapore,
Tokyo, Washington

7171 1196 2

First published in the USA 1983 by
Barnes & Noble Books
81 Adams Drive
Totowa, New Jersey, 07512
ISBN 0-389-20426-9

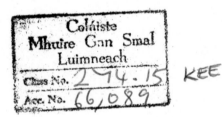
Origination by Galaxy Reproductions Ltd
Printed in Great Britain by
Biddles Ltd, Guildford and King's Lynn

To the Memory of
Archbishop Daniel Murray

Victrix Causa Diis Placuit: Sed Victa Catoni
(The victorious cause pleased the gods;
the vanquished, Cato)

Contents

Acknowledgments

I am indebted to the archbishops of Armagh, Dublin and Cashel and to the bishops of Dromore and Clogher for access to their diocesan archives. The personal kindness and attention of the present bishop of Dromore, Most Rev. Dr Brooks, who allowed me access to his house and provided assistance and hospitality at a time which was personally inconvenient to himself, is gratefully remembered, as is the unfailing courtesy and attention of the Dublin diocesan archivist, Dr Kevin Kennedy. My thanks are due also to the abbot and community of Mellifont Abbey, Co. Louth, who allowed me access to their theological library.

The thesis on which this book is based was first considered and pondered over at the time of the Ulster Workers' Strike in 1974. Thanks are due to innumerable unknown people who made academic research possible in Ulster in the intervening years. I would, however, especially like to thank the crews of the 'Enterprise Express' who, through thick and thin, kept open the rail line with Dublin where much of the research was conducted.

I would like to thank Professor J. A. Jackson of Trinity College, Dublin, formerly of Queen's University, Belfast, for his advice and encouragement, and especially for first suggesting to me in his own quiet way that I might like to proceed to post-graduate research.

My academic debts are many but Professor Roy Wallis, Ms E. Carlisle, Mr A. E. C. W. Spencer, and Dr J. Whyte of Queen's University, Belfast deserve particular thanks. Mrs J. Press, M.A., of the Rupert Stanley College of Further Education, discussed almost every point in the book with me.

Note on References

References are grouped, usually at the end of each paragraph, and the principal sources for that paragraph only are cited. Reference is made in parentheses to the numbered sources in the bibliography. Thus, for example, (*184*, 19; *344*) indicates that page 19 of item no. 184 in the bibliography (de Freine's *The Great Silence*) together with item 344 (Murray's *Irish Annual Miscellany*) are the principal sources for the material in the preceding paragraph.

Introduction

In the year 1700 the Catholic Church in Ireland might have seemed on the verge of extinction. In the year 1900 it was at the centre of a worldwide sphere of prestige and influence. How did this come about?

It is now possible to trace with some degree of confidence the stages of this transformation. Surprisingly, the starting point was a penal law designed to eliminate the Catholic Church by cutting off the supply of priests. In 1703 an act was passed requiring the parish clergy to be registered and friars and bishops to depart the kingdom. To ease the blow, registered priests were allowed to have an abode and a masshouse, and to conduct services. It was expected that they would not be replaced when they died and that the people would gradually go to the churches of the Establishment. The law in fact proved relatively easy to avoid. Priests registered, and bishops registered as priests, and not all Protestants were of the persecuting kind. As long as the clergy respected the Protestant character of the kingdom and did not attack the Established Church they were in little danger. Difficulties there were, but, despite poverty, a parish and diocesan system was kept going all over Ireland. The Irish took no part in the Jacobite movements in 1715, 1719 and 1745.

In this latter year, at the request of the Catholic Lord Taaffe, George II personally authorised the Carmelite friars to open a church in Dublin. In 1751 the Catholic bishop of Ferns was summoned before the Irish Privy Council on charges of treason. He stated openly that there were twenty-four Catholic bishops in Ireland in regular communication with the pope, that he himself ordained priests, and that there were friars in the country. He also acknowledged that he collected money for the purpose of petitioning parliament. The charges were dismissed (*245; 446*).

From this date the Catholic Church functioned publicly. Synods of bishops were held and the Catholic Association openly pursued civil and religious liberty for Catholics. Towards the end of the period the Irish government negotiated openly with the hierarchy with regard to the construction of the Royal College of Maynooth. Except in the Protestant areas of the north east, the structures of the Church and the religious belief and morale of the people had come through unscathed. Unlike England or Scotland, or even France, there were no areas which had lost religion or had gone over to the heretics, except of course in the special conditions of the north east. Protestantism was of course much more strongly established in rural areas of the south than it is at the present day, but there were strong Catholic parishes in all areas. By 1800, when this book opens, the Catholic Church was in a healthy state all over Ireland. It then launched itself into a phenomenal development in many different aspects of religious life, not only throughout Ireland, but spreading on the tides of empire to the furthest parts of the globe. This book describes the process.

It developed in two stages. Between 1800 and 1850 there was a great period of innovation. Between 1850 and 1920 there was a period when the new developments were consolidated but in which innovations were few. Strangely, this latter period was one of creativity in Irish secular society, which saw the development of the republican (Fenian) movement, home rule, the language movement, the new tactics of the Land League, Sinn Féin, the IRB and IRA, the socialist and trade union movements, the dairy co-operative movement, and the Gaelic Athletic Association. Though priests were associated with these in varying degrees, they were essentially secular movements. There is some slight indication that Ireland at this period was tending towards a secular society.

Towards the end of the nineteenth century there were indications of a revival of creativity in the Irish Church, not always in a healthy direction. The great drive against drink was reorganised, censorship of books introduced, and formal processes of juridical procedures in canon law instituted. There was also a tendency towards a sacramental rather than a devotional spirituality.

But the great revival, the drive to totally Catholicise the Irish state, coincided with the struggle to achieve national independence. The first major sign of the new spirit was the setting up of the Maynooth Mission to China, but Fr Willie Doyle, before his death on the Western Front, had begun to popularise the 'purchase' of the 'Black Babies'. 'Pudsy Ryan' of the *Far East* (Maynooth Mission to China) became a household figure. Mission periodicals multiplied and were distributed by promoters throughout the country. Vocations multiplied, colleges were founded, new orders set up. The focus of the campaign was now the pagan blacks in British Africa. As the religious orders were now heavily committed to the foreign missions, the precise details of information from the mission fields depended on what missionary magazines one subscribed to.

The missionary effort was matched by developments at home. The Legion of Mary was founded and soon launched its own missionary effort. Manifestations of Catholicism took on an ostentatious character, as for example in the famous Eucharistic Congress in 1932. There were various holy years and marian years, with drives to put crosses on every crossroads. There was public rejection of atheistic communism. Public pilgrimages, especially to Lourdes, became common, at first by boat and train, but later almost universally by Aer Lingus. The 'perpetual novena' became popular.

The priests withdrew from overt politics but their influence on public affairs remained considerable. The debacle over the 'Mother and Child' scheme became famous. The clergy became closely involved in social issues and began to study sociology. 'State corporatism' was advanced as a theory on how best Christian ethics could be applied in a modern state. The period is well described by Dr J. Whyte. It lasted until the Second Vatican Council and perhaps beyond. It is the Catholic Ireland we know (*538*).

The period 1700 to 1900 therefore separates itself into various stages relatively clearly marked: 1704 to 1750, the period of the registration of the clergy; 1750 to 1800, a period when Church life could be practised openly; 1800 to 1850, a period of development and innovation; 1850 to 1900, a period of consolidation. The Church in the twentieth century acquired various characteristics of its own which were lacking in the earlier periods.

The ordering of the material in this book depends on the characteristics of the two phases in the nineteenth century. First, the Church is fully described as it was at the beginning of the century. Then the various changes that came about in the course of the century are described. The state of the Church at the end of the century is not described for it is merely a combination of the two earlier parts. The state of the Church at any of the intervening points can be roughly estimated by determining for one's self how far the process of change had progressed. The changes themselves are grouped loosely under two major headings, those which were the result of the exertions of private individuals, priests, laymen or nuns, and those which by and large dealt with the affairs of the whole Irish Church and were more properly the affairs of the bishops. The material is dealt with in chronological order as far as possible, each new development being treated when it manifested itself. This results in the fact that most of the examples are drawn from the first half of the century, for events in the second half were largely repetitive. The major events in the second half of the century are, however, all commented on. No attempt is made to write a history of the Church in the nineteenth century but rather to examine it sociologically. A concluding chapter summarises the results and significance of the investigation. Technical details of the methodology are given in an appendix. Catholic technical terms except the most common are explained, but as befits a book aimed at the general reader Catholic religious jargon is avoided.

The story of the development of the Catholic Church in the nineteenth century in Ireland is now described fully for the first time with material drawn from the widest possible sources. If some of the conclusions I arrive at differ from those given by earlier researchers, the evidence is all presented and the reader can judge.

1
The Social Environment of the Catholic Church in Ireland

General Background

Following the Act of Union in 1800, Ireland was part of the United Kingdom of Great Britain and Ireland. Although about three-quarters of the population of Ireland was Catholic, they were excluded from all positions of importance.

The union of the parliaments had transferred the power of legislation from Dublin to Westminster; but in all other respects, powers still rested with the people who had formed the government before the Union, both centrally and locally (*32*, 286).

Catholic Emancipation, which would have allowed Catholic landowners to sit in parliament, had been virtually promised at the time of the Union but never put into effect. What the passing of an Emancipation Act would mean was expressed in a letter from the Attorney-General, William Saurin, to Lord Norbury:

> ... that however they may think otherwise, the Catholics would, in spite of them, elect Catholic members, and then have the nomination of the Sheriffs, and, in many instances, perhaps of the Judges; and that the Protestants would be put in the background as the Catholics were formerly, I think he would bring the effect of the measure home to themselves, and satisfy them that they could scarcely submit to live in the country if it were passed (*177*, 80).

If, in addition to Emancipation, the Act of Union were to be repealed then the Catholics would have an overwhelming majority in parliament. From 1793 Catholics had been allowed to vote, and the franchise was relatively extensive, for it included those who held a freehold lease at two pounds a year or more, the 'forty-shilling freeholders'. But as these freeholders were tenants, whose leases would come up for renewal sooner or later, it was not in their interest to vote against the wishes of their landlords. So until 1829 the Catholic franchise was ineffective in securing any direct influence for Catholics, partly because no Catholics could be elected to parliament, and partly because it would have been inexpedient for a Catholic voter to oppose his landlord. (It should be noted that many landlords were guided by their tenants and a majority of Irish MPs voted for Emancipation.)

With regard to the government of the country, Catholics had to deal with the parliament in Westminster, for the king with the Westminster parliament constituted the government of the realm. They also had to deal with the Irish administration centred in Dublin Castle, which consisted of a lord lieutenant, or viceroy, and a chief secretary, along with an Irish civil service. Up to 1820, that is during the Portland, Percival and Liverpool administrations, little was done by the lord lieutenants to remove Orange influence from the Irish administration. After that date it was largely neutral as between Catholics and Orangemen. The Irish government under the Act of Union was of course appointed by the government of the United Kingdom. The distinction between the Irish government and the British government is important, for the Irish officials could take no steps in Rome without first convincing the prime minister of their necessity.

Besides the government, there were the two main Protestant bodies, the Established Episcopal Church, which in 1861 included about 12 per cent of the population, and the Presbyterians, who had about 9 per cent of the population (*300*, 18). The great mass of these were concentrated in the north east of the island and were numerically weak over much of the rest of the island.

The Established Church was the official church of the Protestant state. Its organisation embraced the whole island, even in those areas where it had few adherents. It was the legal continuation of the medieval church in Ireland and inherited many of the rights of that church. It could, and did, exact tithes from the entire population, and not merely from its own adherents. Whenever a matter had to be referred to an ecclesiastical court, as for example in the probate of wills, it was referred to the court of the Established Church.

Like the Catholic Church it was organised in dioceses and parishes. As the Catholic Church and the Established Church were both continuations of the same medieval Irish Church, the organisation of the two churches was originally identical. Comparison therefore between the two organisations is often instructive. There were several distinct trends among the Protestant clergy. Some of them were politically minded and supported the Protestant Ascendancy. Others were 'Low Church' or 'Evangelical' in tendency, being inclined to neglect the prescribed forms of doctrine and worship. Some were very anti-Roman, while others were prepared to work harmoniously with the Catholics. In the course of the nineteenth century there was considerable re-organisation and modernisation in the Established Church (*176; 258; 316; 315; 304; 305; 54; 55; 4*).

The interests of the government, either in Dublin or Westminster, and the Established Church were by no means identical. The government was chiefly interested in promoting civil harmony, while the Irish bishops acted as a pressure group in parliament or the Irish privy council.

The Presbyterians were based largely in Ulster, and came into little contact with the Catholics in other parts. For most of the century they were preoccupied with their own internal affairs and held aloof from politics. They made little common cause with the Catholics, except briefly in the tenant right campaign of the 1850s. The common anti-popery element in both persuasions finally aligned them with the Established Church (*300; 272; 71; 419; 274*).

Within both strands of Protestantism the 'Evangelical Movement', which was noted for its anti-popery, was characterised by an emotional anti-ritualistic approach to religion, with a great emphasis on reading the Bible, and a tendency to blur doctrinal and juridical distinctions between Protestant bodies. In Ireland, the 'New Dissent' as it was also called, was represented by the Methodists, and was also influential within the Established Church (*176; 316; 41; 600*).

By the Whig Settlement of 1690, Protestants were given exclusive access to public offices in the three kingdoms. This was unremarkable in the Europe in the time. As Castlereagh remarked, the political situation in Europe was stabilised for a century and a half after the Peace of Westphalia (1648) just on that principle. But the fact that the bulk of the Irish did not conform to the Established Church, together with the growing tolerance of the Age of Enlightenment, brought changes. However, if liberal or tolerant ideas were allowed, most of the Protestants in official positions in Ireland could expect to lose their jobs. By no means all Irish Protestants opposed Catholic political claims, but those who did were estimated to control about 40 per cent of Irish seats in parliament around 1820.

The Latin Patriarchate

The Catholic Church in Ireland belonged to the Holy Roman Catholic and Apostolic Church under the leadership of the pope. This comprised a group of churches or rites, including 'Eastern' or 'Uniate' churches. More immediately the Irish Church belonged to the 'Western' Church or Latin Patriarchate. In theory this meant recognising the ultimate authority of the bishop of Rome as Latin Patriarch, but in practice it came to mean much more. It meant the use of a common language, Latin, as the medium of study and communication, the Latin rite as the basis of worship, the Latin canon law as the basis of control, the Latin Bible and the Latin Church Fathers as the sources of authority, and the use of common forms of religious practice and devotion. Much of this Latin culture was common to the Protestant Churches as well.

In Rome the pope had an ecclesiastical civil service to deal with the affairs of the various churches, both Latin and others, as well as with princes and heads of state. These civil servants were organised into congregations, or departments. A congregation consisted of several cardinals under a prefect, who was assisted by an official secretary and other minor officials. Irish affairs, irregularly, were dealt with by the

Congregation of Propaganda whose proper function was to supervise the foreign missions to the pagans. This arrangement ceased in 1908.

The *Congregatio de Propaganda Fide* (the Congregation for the Propagation of the Faith) was usually referred to as Propaganda or the Propaganda, or 'Rome', for it, with few exceptions, was the only Roman body which dealt with Church affairs in Ireland. It was set up in 1622 to deal with the pagan missions or with areas which lacked a hierarchy. It had all the powers to deal with matters in its own territories which were shared out among the other Roman congregations. Normally, the acts of Propaganda were the acts of that body even if approved by the pope. Rarely did the pope act himself, and still more rarely act infallibly. (Similarly, the acts of a king's minister or department were the acts of the minister, not of the sovereign.)

Almost all communication with Rome was channelled to Propaganda. But there were exceptions. Anyone could write to the pope about anything. Secondly, all communications regarding heresy, including Protestantism, went to the Holy Office. These latter archives are not available. It is impossible to say how important this communication was.

Thirdly, communications with Rome by individuals or by governments who were not Catholics were properly made to the papal Secretariat of State. In 1815 the foreign secretary, Lord Castlereagh, and the papal secretary of state or foreign minister discussed the setting up of diplomatic relations between the Vatican and the Court of St James. Castlereagh advised against it because of anti-popery feeling in London. There never in fact was any difficulty in communicating between London and Rome over Canadian and Irish bishoprics for example, or the accreditation of missionaries to the colonies. (A priest in this latter case just took his official papers to the Colonial Office.) An informal link was set up by appointing a secretary of legation to the Court of Tuscany, in Florence, to attend to Roman affairs. While the link of the crown with Hanover lasted (until 1837) the Hanoverian diplomatic service could be used. Prince Metternich in the next decade offered the services of the Austrian Chancellery, but it does not seem to have been necessary. The government, despite *Praemunire*, which applied to it also, just appointed a minister *ad hoc* (*62; 268*).

In the days after Waterloo British members of parliament visiting Rome, as well as English peers, and there were many of them, were always presented to the pope. All through the century this scared the Irish nationalists who suspected some British plot. In fact, neither the British parliament nor the Vatican took Irish affairs as seriously as the Irish did. The earnest, religious and serious-minded Gladstone was probably the one exception. The Foreign Office was of course little concerned with Irish affairs. The British government was only interested, as far as the Irish Church was concerned, in excluding violently anti-Union priests from being made bishops. How systematically they pursued this objective, or how frequently the papal Secretariat of State brought such matters to their notice, is difficult to determine.

Propaganda could refer particular questions to other congregations such as the Court of Ecclesiastical Affairs. The condemnation of the 'Plan of Campaign' in 1888, being a moral question, came from the Inquisition or Holy Office through Propaganda in the form of a reply. The precise nature of the authority of Propaganda in Ireland was not defined, and was subject to dispute. The pope, though he rarely did so, could act *motu proprio*, i.e. without being asked, or personally, thus acting himself with his own personal authority, not that of the congregation. Gregory XVI did this over national education in 1839. Propaganda was not a court of law, but acted largely as a conciliating body (*139*).

There is a continuing significance in a verdict made about medieval relationships with the papacy:

> It cannot be sufficiently emphasised that throughout its medieval history the system of papal provisions is a judicial and not an administrative system; and the rescript of provision approaches much nearer to the judicial writ than to the administrative order (*179*, 13).

When E. R. Norman, referring to Archbishop Cullen of Dublin's relations with Rome, remarks that 'as usual, Rome was merely reacting to information imparted to it by Cullen himself', he was stating a principle of wider application.

The next peculiarity concerned the appointment of bishops. Though Ireland had a properly constituted hierarchy it was not allowed to elect its own bishops. Technically, the appointments to bishoprics and some other offices in Ireland were 'reserved' to the Holy See, so that the pope could 'provide' the see with a bishop. But in fact, except in extremely rare cases the pope appointed someone who was requested by the various parties in Ireland who were recognised to have an interest — the diocesan chapter, the metropolitans and bishops of the province, the monarch, or indeed the local Irish chieftains. (It was of course open to any Catholic to write to the pope about anything: on the varied sources from which suggestions or petitions for appointment might come, see *535*.) Excessive, or too overt lobbying in Rome *on one's own behalf* was, by the 1820s, the surest way of defeating any hopes one might have. The Irish Church recognised that the pope had the 'naked right' of appointing (and also removing) bishops without consulting the local Church (*578; 535; 553*).

The full doctrine of the 'Primacy of Peter', i.e. that the pope has immediate and ordinary jurisdiction in every part of the Church, was not defined until 1870. The Irish Church, of course, held this doctrine in the sense usually understood before 1870. It had no peculiar tenets on the topic. It was a *Roman* Catholic Church.

Close attention to papal *actions* in Ireland throughout the nineteenth century shows that the various popes, whatever their personal views, did not overstep the limits of papal authority as it existed in the pontificate of Pope Martin V, immediately after the Council of Constance. On 6 April 1415, the Council of Constance passed the decree *Sacrosancta* which declared the pope subject to a general council. But Martin V did not give any general approval to the decrees of Constance, and indirectly condemned *Sacrosancta* by forbidding an appeal from the pope to the council. On the other hand he complied with the other decree of Constance, the decree *Frequens*, calling for frequent ecumenical councils. The Council of Florence, 1439, dealing with the Greeks, produced merely a vague theological formulation, a plenary power of feeding, ruling and governing the whole Church. This remained the state of the relationship until 1870. The pope and the curia might favour those who favoured papal claims and look with disfavour on those who were 'conciliarist' in tendency, but Rome could not act unilaterally to change the relationship (*246; 192*).

A priest in the diocese of Meath in 1820, when writing to a friend, says that he did not understand why Maynooth was not held in respect in Rome. It was true one of the professors held the French anti-Roman opinion on papal infallibility, but another of them (MacHale) held the opinion of Bellarmine, and the matter was an open one. The views of Dr Doyle, Dr Murray and Dr Higgins on the limits of papal authority were somewhat gallican or conciliarist. Their views of the papal claims did not disqualify them from being chosen bishops (*385; 170; 332*).

A strongminded pope with centralising tendencies could do much in an administrative manner to make Rome the actual centre of the Latin Church, but the state of juridical relationships remained unchanged. According to O'Reilly, Dr O'Finan, the Bishop of Killala, was not *obliged* to follow a directive of the Holy See.

The pope, according to Doyle, was regarded as the 'executive authority' in the Catholic Church, and so strictly speaking the Irish Church had to deal with the pope only on such matters as the general councils allocated to him. According to Dr Murray, Catholics admitted that papal bulls were entitled to respect and if not contrary to the law of God or Irish usages were entitled to obedience, as coming from a superior. According to Doyle, if the pope was enforcing a discipline already settled he was entitled to respect, otherwise the Irish Church would treat the bulls as they did the Quarantotti Rescript. According to Dr Higgins, if the pope promulgated a dogma, and it were received by a majority of bishops, then it was infallibly true from the consent of the Church. Rome, for its part, never seems to have acted unilaterally to change the internal discipline of a national church without its consent (*Dublin Evening Post*, 28 August 1817, concerning veto; *170; 332*).

Even when there was no question of juridical rights, as in

the matter of the Queen's Colleges, appeal could still be made to Rome. The point in such a case was to get a 'condemnation' by the authority of the Holy See on the grounds that some practice was either sinful, or dangerous to faith or morals. The pope's advisors, and in the case of national education, the pope himself, gave a decision on the moral lawfulness of a particular practice. Papal infallibility was not invoked. In 1855 Archbishops Cullen and Dixon prohibited the teaching in Maynooth of the old opinions such as were expressed by the Irish bishops in 1825. Theologians who felt inclined to hold what became the minority opinion in the First Vatican Council were allowed no scope, so debate in Ireland was not merely curtailed: it was abolished. The two Irish bishops who sided with the minority at that council did so on the grounds of the inexpediency of defining. They were Moriarity of Kerry and MacHale of Tuam, to whom may be added the Limerick-born bishop of Little Rock, Arkansas. All three finally accepted the definition.

But in practice, when a decision was made by Rome it was accepted by the Irish Church after the matter was fought to the last and Rome insisted. The adage which came down from antiquity, *Roma locuta est: causa finita est* (Rome has spoken: the case is closed), was simply applied. The characteristic notes of Jansenism, its 'respectful silences', its 'interpretations', its 'appeals to a general council' were not found. More than one archbishop eventually took refuge in a respectful silence when the case went against him, but it was just that. It was not a contemptuous way of saying the pope did not know what he was talking about. (Theologically, in a non-infallible decision, a Catholic who does not accept it can maintain a respectful silence, but may not preach or act against the decision.)

Decisions came in the form of 'replies' or 'responses', again underlying the appellate nature of the relationship between Ireland and Rome. So it is always instructive to enquire who referred the matter to Rome and furnished the information. Such information was not always correct, and Rome, knowing this, usually replied in the vaguest and most general terms. This was not evasiveness on Rome's part, but common sense. Formal categorical decisions were usually arrived at after a very prolonged investigation over several years.

Primate Curtis, writing to Dr Plunket of Meath, said:

> I have the honour of transmitting to your lordship the enclosed copy of Cardinal Fontana's circular letter to the four archbishops, which was received in our meeting of the 29th ultimo. In my letter of the 10th instant to His Eminence I mention some particulars in which the information given to the Sacred Congregation appears incorrect concerning heterodox proselytizing schools, as they have been silenced and put down already in many places by Catholic schools, which the prelates endeavour to erect and encourage as the best antidotes against such attempts (Curtis to Plunket, 28 October 1819, *97*, III, 429f; *Codex Juris* Canon 1374, *Fontes*, litt. encycl. (ad Ep. Hiberniae) 18 September 1819).

An incident in the life of John Dillon at the end of the century reflects the extreme difficulty Rome had in understanding the Irish political factions. The secretary of state, Cardinal Rampolla, began an audience with him by asking if he knew the Duke of Norfolk, the English Catholic leader. Dillon explained he was Irish. 'Then doubtless you are a friend of Archbishop Walsh', said Rampolla. Dillon's reply was frosty. A resident apostolic delegate was clearly a necessity (*301*).

A routine matter on which Propaganda wanted information was that of the unsuitability of candidates for episcopal office, for the problem from Rome's point of view was to keep out manifestly unsuitable or inappropriate candidates. Rome cross-checked by obtaining the opinion of the bishops separately. But in a matter where episcopal opinion itself was sharply divided the system broke down. As Larkin notes, even in the 1880s Rome had little detailed knowledge of the Irish priests (*270; 535*).

Communication with Rome presented no difficulty. Political obstacles to communication with Rome were non-existent. In theory any act of foreign jurisdiction or any appeal to a foreign jurisdiction was contrary to the law of the realm. But in practice, the government recognised the 'titular' bishops even though it was known that they were exercising a foreign jurisdiction.

In the 1840s Dr O'Higgins thought that the pope could be in breach of a statute of *Praemunire* if he attempted to deal with a *political* affair, i.e. the question of repeal. Croke was of the same opinion later. Dr Murray freely admitted that ordinary bulls came as 'communications from one gentleman to another'. There was no question of the government intercepting them or prohibiting them. Such bulls were essentially private and the civil courts steadfastly refused to recognise them or their effects (*62; 170*).

By the Quarantotti Rescript in 1814 Rome was prepared to concede the rights of the *veto* and the *exequatur*, the *veto* being the right to prohibit an appointment, the *exequatur* being the right to prohibit the promulgation of some bull or brief. As the Irish Catholic bishops in no way claimed any secular jurisdiction whatsoever in the ecclesiastical courts, or as lay magistrates in the secular courts, and abandoned all claim to sit in parliament, claims to the *veto* and *exequatur* were really unnecessary. In fact, when Peel and Wellington finally brought in the Catholic Emancipation Bill, all such claims were dropped. The statutes of *Praemunire* were not repealed. It was a commonplace among all Irish Catholics all through the century that Catholics did not and could not receive *political* directives from the pope (*139*).

Later in the century decisions in the O'Keeffe case had a peculiar effect. As E. R. Norman put it: 'two government boards and a Dublin court had accepted that an ecclesiastical censure could apparently be given what amounted to a legal effect'. But at no time in the nineteenth century was a bishop likely to be summoned to court and charged with exercising foreign jurisdiction.

The promulgation of the papal brief *Dominus ac Redemptor* in 1773 is interesting as it shows that the mere promulgation of a papal edict in Rome was not sufficient to make it obligatory in the whole world. In Prussia, Frederick the Great refused to execute this brief suppressing the Jesuits, and Catherine the Great of Russia refused the *exequatur*. As the British dominions were under Propaganda, that congregation was instructed to forward copies of the brief to the bishops of the territories under its care. Propaganda, accordingly, sent copies to the nuncio in Brussels who sent on copies to the individual bishops in Holland, England, Scotland and Ireland.

In England, the vicar apostolic in London thought written communication in this matter too dangerous, so he decided to communicate by word of mouth the contents of the brief to each individual Jesuit as he met him. With regard to the Jesuits in North America, he sent copies, not of his brief, but of the formula of submission. This was a very special case, but it warns us not to assume that every papal communication was automatically promulgated in Ireland. In the eighteenth century the archbishop of Dublin still did not promulgate the decree *Tametsi* of Trent. On the other hand, if the pope wished to communicate with Ireland he had no difficulty in doing so (*412*).

Relations between the British government and the papacy were not strained; in fact the reverse was true.

> Certainly, for three hundred years, with the exception of one very brief period, there have never existed such friendly relations between the Holy See and the Crown of Great Britain as under the seventh Pius. An admiration for this empire, and an affection even for it, seemed instinctive both in the pope and in his minister. . . . More than once was England ready to receive him on board her ships of war and give him an asylum (*542*, 107).

The too friendly relations between the pope and the British government form the background to the veto controversy which so stirred the patriotic clergy in Ireland.

The precise nature of papal jurisdiction in the eyes of the civil law is interesting. From 1751 onwards the Irish government officially knew that papal jurisdiction was being exercised in Ireland. (Strictly speaking only the bull of appointment and the exercise of special faculties constituted the papal jurisdiction, for the bishop, once appointed, governed in his own right.) But the matter had to be tested in the courts. Early in the century local authorities like corporations or grand juries were empowered to appoint and pay Catholic chaplains for Catholic prisoners. Some Orange corporations, as in Dublin, deliberately kept appointing suspended priests, but Archbishop Troy refused faculties. (Troy's legal defence, incidentally, was that the local clergymen had always attended, and he thought they should get the stipend, and he had no wish to interfere in disputes between clergymen, which was a safe stance.)

One priest thus refused faculties appealed to the courts, and the Lord Chief Justice, ever courteous and correct, replied as follows. The court did not recognise any such person as Archbishop Troy or any authority residing in him. The plaintiff had failed to take up his post, not from any recognisable cause such as illness, and so could not be paid the salary. The plaintiff might recognise authority in Troy but the court could not. The case was dismissed and the grand jury was ordered to make another appointment (*Saunders' Newsletter*, 1815). The fairness of the courts was recognised by the Catholics.

Later in the century, in the O'Keeffe case, the court gave the verdict against Fr O'Keeffe on the grounds of the consensual nature of ecclesiastical jurisdiction. Bishops were able to make decisions which were binding in law at least as to certain effects because the members of the Church were considered to have agreed to be bound by the rules of the Church just as in any club, society or union.

The definition in 1870 of papal primacy and infallibility made very little practical difference. Cardinal Newman explained to Gladstone that though the pope had direct authority over dogmatic questions, his authority over political and social ones was merely indirect, i.e. whenever a point of moral teaching was involved. There was thus no direct exercise of papal authority or infringement of *Praemunire*. Archbishop Croke in fact considered a letter of the papal secretary of state, Cardinal Rampolla, as 'unconstitutional', i.e. against the British constitution(!). In any case, after 1870 the canon law and the weight of precedents changed very slowly (*267*).

Religion in Irish Society

I have examined a considerable number of Irish periodicals to discover the amount of attention devoted to strictly religious matters compared to secular concerns. Despite extensive statistical manipulation of the data, the only significant point to emerge was that in non-religious periodicals (i.e. ones in which less than three-quarters of the space was devoted to religious matters) references to religion show no statistically significant change in frequency between 1815 and 1914.

References to religion as a percentage of all references

Period	%
1815-25	27.8
1830-49	27.1
1850-59	27.8
1865-75	23.8
1895-1914	23.1

The decline in the last period was accounted for almost entirely by a decline in references to religion in periodicals from north east Ireland, which were mainly Protestant.

This, however, seems an important conclusion, for if Irish society was becoming more secular we would expect the number of references to religion to fall. On the other hand, if there was a major revival in religion during the century, we would expect the number of references to religion in the periodical literature to rise. Neither of these hypotheses is verified.

It is reasonable, therefore, to be sceptical about any theories which claim that there was a religious revival (or decline) in Ireland among Catholics in the course of the nineteenth century. These figures refer to the 'social prominence' of religion in Irish society. It is possible, though not proven by the figures, that Irish *society* tended to become more secular as the twentieth century approached.

2
Beliefs

Official Beliefs
   It has been stated that beliefs in the Irish Church in the
pre-Famine period differed significantly from those of the
Roman Church. David Miller, for example, sees Irish religion
as being what he calls a 'Model One' religion, that is, one
suited to a pre-literate society.

> Analysed in terms of a simple but useful typology pro-
> posed by Elizabeth K. Nottingham, pre-famine Irish
> peasant religion had not completely made the transition
> from what she calls Model One, the religion of a 'pre-
> literate society', to Model Two, that of a 'changing pre-
> industrial society'. . . .
> Perhaps because of the incomplete imposition of Roman
> discipline upon the Irish Church in the Middle Ages and,
> later, the difficulties created for the Church by the Penal
> Laws, rural Ireland's transition from Model One to Model
> Two had been protracted over a number of centuries.

Thomas Wall too refers to 'native Irish faith and piety' in
those parts where Irish was spoken. Commenting on Dr
Douglas Hyde's *Religious Songs of Connaught* he says, 'In
the *Religious Songs*, as in a reservoir, one may plumb the
depths of native Irish faith and piety. . . . With the loss of the
language the religious mould of the Irish mind was, as it were,
shattered. . . .*(327; 513)*.
   We will examine first the official expositions of religious
belief. The primary sources for this are the various catechisms.
These were very numerous and went through innumerable
editions, revisions, abridgments and expansions. Uniformity
characterised them. In their exposition of Catholic doctrine

they followed a common plan derived from the *Roman Catechism*. They contained four parts in varying order. These parts were (1) an exposition of the Apostles' Creed, (2) an explanation of the Ten Commandments, (3) a section on prayer, with an explanation of the Lord's Prayer and (4) an explanation of the sacraments. All matters of belief could be treated in the exposition of the Creed. All aspects of Christian *morals* could be treated under the heading of the Commandments, all matters of *rites* and *Church order* or *discipline* under the sacraments, and *personal devotion* under the heading of prayer. The exposition of the belief system was common to both Gaelic and English catechisms. There were no distinctive Gaelic catechetical traditions and no survivals of medieval catechisms, just as there was no survival of medieval missals or breviaries.

The second characteristic of the system of instruction was its sober, rational character. It lacked any enthusiastic or mystical element, or emotionalism, wild millenarian expectations or campfire revivalism. The keynote was rather that of the apostle, *sobrie, juste, et pie vivamus in hoc saeculo* (let us live sober, upright and godly lives in this world), but without the manifestations of the outpouring of the Spirit in the Corinthian churches. A set of beliefs was put before the Catholic, defining for him his position in this world, and how he stood with regard to the next one. A set of steps was proposed to him by which he could escape hell and gain heaven. Then, as man could not attain a supernatural end unaided, an exposition was given of the supernatural helps available, and how to obtain them.

No mention is made of the emotional or experiential side of religion. The mild mysticism of the *Imitation of Christ* was apparently unnoticed (*cella frequentata dulcescit*, the cell continually dwelt in groweth sweet), even though the theme of sweetness in prayer was a commonplace since the time of Saint Augustine. Even in England, in the post-Reformation period, a classic of the interior life, Augustine Baker's *Sancta Sophia*, could be written. The dry, formal character of the official body of teaching should be kept in mind when the growth of 'devotions' in the nineteenth century is being studied.

The fourfold schema appears clearly in sermons, instructions and even in the layout of books. The synodal address at the Synod of Cashel in 1813 follows the schema, as does *The Sincere Christian*, one of the works of the Scottish bishop, Dr George Hay, whose writings were popular in Ireland. The sermons of Archbishop Murray are little more than expansions in expository or hortatory form of some part or other of the catechism. Though a rigid adherence to the schema is not a characteristic of the widely-read sermons of Dr O'Gallagher, yet his individual sermons, such as those on the Four Last Things — Death, Judgment, Hell and Heaven — can without any difficulty be fitted into the schema.

Butler's *Catechism* was an almost literal translation of one used on the continent. It was reproduced in many forms. There was an *Abridgment of the Christian Doctrine* by Dr Michael Blake, which was a short version of Butler, and also a *Small Catechism*, a brief selection of almost literal extracts from Butler. The Gaelic Catechism was a literal translation of the revised and enlarged Butler.

Independent of the Butler family of catechisms was that of Andrew Donlevy, published in Paris in 1742, in Gaelic and English, the English version being a translation of the Irish version. No matter which was the original version, the Gaelic catechisms were almost identical with the corresponding English versions. The standard, or Maynooth, catechism adopted by the bishops in 1882 for the whole of Ireland followed the same pattern as the others.

The language of the catechisms was theological. In even a very simple catechism we find 'Three Persons, really distinct, being only one God, having but one and the same divine nature, and they are from all eternity' (*81*). Three *Persons, really distinct, being* one God, *having* one nature, and *being* from all *eternity* are philosophical concepts derived from the medieval schools. Though severely criticised from a pastoral point of view by Archbishop Walsh, his proposal for a new format at the National Synod in 1900 fell through, and the Butler-Maynooth format survived until Vatican II.

So, as far as the *formal* belief system at least is concerned, there is little to support the theory of a unique or lost Celtic spirituality.

Some commentators, however, create a false impression of the uniqueness of the lost (Gaelic) heritage, for they seem to insist that the Irish prayers and religious poems were quite unique both in form and content. I would suggest that there are few, if any, prayer or poem forms in the Irish tradition which do not find parallels in the general European tradition . . . (*391*, 583).

Unofficial Beliefs

We can begin by noting that there was little unbelief or doubt. Carleton mentions one ex-soldier quoting his former sergeant that religion was only priestcraft, 'the whole lot of that and more along wid it is all priestcraft'. Only occasionally do we hear of young men like O'Connell when in London becoming lukewarm in their beliefs. A general knowledge of 'French opinions' was fairly common in Ireland, whether the ideas came from non-commissioned officers, or from upper English servants and there was no censorship until the very end of the century. Non-Catholic literature, whether religious or other, was freely available, but there was no concerted campaign against 'evil literature' or 'evil plays' until the end of the century. Forbes at mid century commented on the intensity of the belief of the peasantry.

With the option of Protestantism freely available, we will not expect to find occult sects of heretics like the Vaudois or Waldenses. Nor were there any Jansenists tenaciously holding on to condemned beliefs while at the same time saying they were loyal members of the Church. Specific oaths against Jansenism were not required. The Gallican or Jansenist affair of the 'Petite Eglise' received little notice in Ireland. In fact, if the bishops had not been negotiating with the British government at the time the matter might have passed unnoticed (*73*).

Carleton gives the most complete account of popular beliefs and superstitions and in these there is a mixture of non-Christian but harmless beliefs. There were beliefs in fairies, ghosts and other malign influences, against which holy water, holy pictures, the tattooing of images of the crucifixion and other charms and spells were regarded as efficacious. Some believed that fasting and prayer conferred a peculiar efficacy to holy water, but also believed that a certain moral licence was allowable to those who prayed and fasted much. The devil was believed not to be able to drink holy water and so could in this way be detected. It is difficult to say that the Catholics in those days were more super-stitious than in our own.

Croker is another excellent source, this time from the South. With regard to the doctrine of Purgatory he reports:

> the general belief of the Irish peasantry is somewhat at variance with the representations of their pastors: the priest describes it as a place of fire, but the people imagine it to be a vast and dreary extent strewn with sharp stones, and abounding with thorns and brambles.

But on the other hand Lover records a belief which does not really square with the above:

> There is a belief among the peasantry in this particular district that the ghost of the last person interred in the churchyard is obliged to traverse, unceasingly, the road between this earth and Purgatory, carrying water to slake the burning thirst of those confined in that 'limbo large'.

There are many other beliefs outside the official Christian beliefs, and as Croker remarked, they were generally of a harmless nature. The people believed in faries and fairy mounds, fairy blasts and bewitched children, charms and spells. According to Croker they believed in the 'evil eye' but not in 'second sight'. In general, as Croker also remarks, Irish beliefs were very like those of the English in Elizabethan times (*161; 75; 24; 206*).

Patterns and religious pilgrimages were popular, and could be held for the most orthodox reasons. But other reasons for holding them were sometimes given. One enquirer at least was informed that the patterns and pilgrimages were carried out as a preservative against *Geasa Dravidacht*, sorceries of the druids. This belief can be interpreted in a perfectly orthodox manner, by assuming that the druids were invoking the power of Satan and the cattle-owners the power of the saint. The rites at the holy wells were also supposed to preserve the cattle from the murrain, and keep the fairies in good humour. These are the only places where an interpretation is given of a rite. Presumably patterns were held to honour a Christian saint (*528; 75*).

. The popular beliefs of any kind did not contradict official beliefs at any point, except perhaps on Purgatory. This *could* have come about by accident. Celtic religion *might* have been in perfect harmony with revealed Jewish religion. The mixture of Christian and non-Christian in nineteenth-century Ireland *could* have been the result of the 'incomplete imposition of Roman discipline' (*327*). On the other hand, it *could* equally have been the result of a successful effort, beginning with St Patrick, to purge any elements directly contradictory to official formulations, and leave only those which were harmless. A study of the Irish Church in the nineteenth century must content itself with noting facts, not with speculating on their origins. In assessing the relative importance of official and unofficial beliefs, it is useful to remember that a similar mixture of beliefs persisted in Ireland until our own times.

The Church's Self-Image and Definition of the Situation

This deals with how the members of the Church saw their Church and its relation to the surrounding world. Some part of the belief might have been theological, but not necessarily. Some part of it might have been fact, but this is not necessarily so either. For example, members of the Church might be convinced that they were about to be persecuted, whether or not there were any objective grounds for such belief. The study of such beliefs is very important for, as the sociologist W. I. Thomas pointed out, 'If men define situations as real they are real in their consequences.'

All the Christian Churches regard themselves as the one true Church founded by Christ. This belief distinguishes the Christian Churches from all other religious bodies. The view that God was in Christ reconciling the world to himself and that He founded a Church to bring that salvation to men ultimately sets the boundaries of the Christian religion. Catholics took it for granted that they belonged to the one true Church. The visible sign of the one true Church for them was adhesion to the pope as head of the Church. The pope was the visible centre of unity and the touchstone of orthodoxy. The fifth-century anti-Arian slogan, attributed not implausibly to Saint Patrick, *Sicut Christiani ita ut Romani sitis* (As you are Christians so be ye also Romans), reflected a profound Irish sentiment. It kept the Irish loyal through persecution. Individual acts of individual popes throughout the century provoked the most strenuous resistance but there never was any question of schism, let alone heresy. Archbishop Murray's letter to Rome in 1839, when it was expected that his views on national education would be condemned, expressed what his panegyrist called his 'apostolic candour and firmness' and at the same time his 'profoundest submission'. Replying to the Cardinal's advance warning, he refused to retract his opinion until there was a definite condemnation. This however he was prepared to obey, but would weep in silence to the end of his days (Meagher). This seems to have been the common attitude of the Irish bishops. There was no uncritical ultramontanism at any time.

The next feature of the self-image was that of the persecuted Church. This was graphically illustrated in a picture in the *Catholic Penny Magazine* in 1834. In it there is a picture or sketch representing the Church. Like the Church in the Book of Revelations it is four square and is founded on a rock. At its front is the unmistakeable colonnade of Bernini in St Peter's, Rome. Round it the tempest blows and the waves lash.

The same concept of a Church battered by the storms of persecution appears in the sermons of the famous Catholic controversialist, the Rev. T. Maguire, who assured his hearers that the gates of hell would never prevail against the Catholic Church (*Catholic Directory* 1840, 157). The conception, though strongly held and felt, was vague as to detail. In the parliamentary enquiry in 1825, Lord Palmerston asked if the ordinary people had any idea how the penal laws affected them. (The bulk of the penal laws were of course directed against the upper and middle classes.) The answer was no:

I do not think they have any definite notions upon that point. They look upon themselves as contrasted with the Protestants of their own rank and as degraded compared with them.

Do they fancy they are more degraded than they really are?

I think so, for they are not fully aware of the extent of the repeal of the penal code.

Have they traditions in the country of what happened in those times [the time of the English conquest] ?

They have traditions and tales about the massacre and execution of priests, the priest hunters, and the difficulty they had heretofore; they were obliged to resort to bogs and morasses for that purpose. They have also recollections of the liberty and what they conceive the privileges they enjoyed formerly, compared with their present degraded state (*170*, 53).

Palmerston also asked what Emancipation, which only affected the higher orders, meant to the lower orders. Dr Magaurin of Ardagh replied, 'I know if they were ·asked what Emancipation meant perhaps they would not be able to define it, but they have a feeling they belong to an excluded caste. . . .' Dr Magaurin was not able to give precise details on the traditions of the peasantry, but he thought they had many traditional stories regarding the sufferings of their ancestors, of how the priests retired to the mountains, and the people followed them, and the places they said mass were still venerated, but Magaurin himself was unable to name any of the spots. Magaurin's vagueness is, I think, worthy of note. He was not being evasive: he had no reason to be. But he was careful not to exaggerate or to present second-hand evidence. A mixture of romanticism and nationalist propaganda makes evidence on these points from later in the century rather suspect. It is quite possible that such evidence came from printed 'romantic' sources rather than from any genuine oral tradition. We must not exaggerate the amount of positive evidence available from authentic contemporary data.

But there is little doubt that there was a feeling of oppres-

sion. According to Dr Doyle, too, the sense of grievance of
the peasantry was marked and more strongly felt by the
lower orders, even if they were vague about the actual
details of the oppression. The peasantry had a lively recol-
lection of the penal code: 'They mention it in the traditionary
tales of the history of their country; and those recollections
are revived when any instance of abuse or violence occurs'.

> *Do they feel that their religion was persecuted in
> former times?*
> They know it was. . . .
> *Do they refer to the periods during the reigns of Queen
> Anne and George I* [this was the period when the penal
> code was enacted]?
> They have not those distinct historical recollections;
> they talk of Elizabeth frequently, they talk of the invasion
> of the Spaniards in 1601, and of Lord Tyrone coming
> down to assist them, and the massacres of that period.
> *Do they recollect anything of Cromwell, or know any-
> thing from tradition?*
> They have Cromwell's Bridge, and there are many places
> pointed out by the name of Cromwell (*170*).

There is considerable point in Disraeli's statement:

> The Irish had a strange passion for calling themselves a
> conquered people. He failed to see when or where they
> had been conquered. It might be urged that they had been
> conquered by Cromwell. What of that? Had not Cromwell
> previously conquered England? Why should his eloquent
> and imaginative friends [the Irish members] try to extract
> a peculiar grievance out of a common misfortune? (*375,*
> 16)

England too was conquered by Normans, Tudors and Parliam-
entarians, without developing the same definition of the
situation. Why then did the Irish Church, apparently alone
among either Catholic or Protestant churches in Europe or
America, have this self-image? There is always the possibility
that Ireland's history was notably more tragic than that of
any other comparable country, but this still does not get over
the difficulty that the objective situation must be recognised

and defined as tragic. L. M. Cullen, for example, notes that Irish historians failed to note and define the great famine of 1740-41 as a national catastrophe, the way a later generation defined the famine of 1845-9.

One possibility is that the Irish definition of the situation was influenced by millenarianism. The belief that one was a member of a righteous persecuted group was central to millenarianism. There is some evidence that millenarian doctrines were known in Ireland (*75; 170; 99*; Appendix C). In this supposition, the part of the millenarian belief that one belonged to a just, or righteous, persecuted, suffering group would simply be applied by the Irish to their situation. On the other hand, however, there is a patriot tradition of grievance against England, stretching back through Swift, even to medieval times. The grievance is lucidly· set out in the 'Remonstrance' of the native Irish addressed to Pope John XXII (*125*, 239).

Another facet of the self-image to emerge was expressed in the phrase 'Catholic Ireland'. The population of Ireland was in fact about three-quarters Catholic. The phrase was used in a number of ways. W. J. Fitzpatrick cites 'all Catholic Ireland acting as one man', and 'the earnest efforts made by Catholic Ireland'. Bernard O'Reilly (1890) refers to the 'ancient idiom of Catholic Ireland'. According to Dr MacHale, referring to the co-operation of leading Catholics in running the national schools, it was no wonder that the famine occurred when such scenes were enacted in Catholic Ireland (*176*, 167). A paper was published in Ireland and the name given to·it was *Catholic Ireland*. Irish and Catholic became interchangeable terms. The Irish Dominican preacher, Fr Tom Burke, said in 1872:

> Take an average Irishman. I don't care where you find him — and you will find that the very first principle in his mind is, 'I am not an Englishman, because I am a Catholic'. Take an Irishman wherever he is found all over the earth, and any casual observer will at once come to the conclusion, 'Oh; he is an Irishman, he is a Catholic'. The two go together.

'Can he forget that the nationality of Ireland means simply the Catholic Church?' Thus Cardinal Cullen in his anger wrote against Judge Keogh (*266; 345*).

The expression 'Catholic Ireland' may have been a popular-isation of Daniel O'Connell's, for he often quotes it. The only example of earlier use I came across was in a resolution passed in Kilkenny in 1808 (*60*, II, 367).

At the parliamentary enquiry in 1825, Fr Collins, explaining the word 'Sassenach', said:

> The true meaning of it is Englishman. There is no Irish term for Protestant. They first knew a Protestant in the person only of the Englishman, and therefore they have identified it with him; nor have they any Irish terms for Catholics. They say Catholickey in Irish, but when they contrast a Protestant with a Catholic, Erinech (Irishman) is the term for a Catholic (*170*, 61).

There was in fact an Irish term for Catholics (*Catholickach*, pl. *Catholickaigh* = *Catholickey*: my spelling harmonised with that of the parliamentary record, and in the adjectival form *Cathoilice* in Donlevy). But according to Fr Collins *Erinech* was the preferred name for Catholics. In the phrase 'Catholic Ireland', politics is clearly blended with religion.

So far, we have seen the image of the suffering persecuted group, and the image of an entirely Catholic island. There was a third element. This was a view of an alleged glorious and holy past. (It is worth noting that the political image of Ireland exactly parallels the religious image.)

> Was it not therefore shameful, if not disgraceful, for Catholic Ireland to be without a record of what has been dearer to her than any earthly treasure — ardent faith, abundant charity, and enlightened piety (*Directory*, 1838)?

> We cannot but observe with what diligence the ancient bishops of Ireland cultivated the Irish language, those holy prelates, etc. (*Ancient Ireland*, 1835).

> The labours of the Irish clergy in the service of the Church, their zeal, their piety, their disinterestedness, their exertions in promoting religious education are justly celebrated. The faith, too, of our people is known to

all. . . . Their attachment to their clergy, their charity towards the poor, and resignation under the most awful privations and overwhelming calamities can never be sufficiently admired (*123*, I, 3).

No courtly arts, no crooked intrigues, no cunning schemes of a wily and tortuous diplomacy were suffered to enter their councils . . . no compromise with a hostile government in the nomination of their chief pastors . . . no compromise in the education of their priesthood in bartering the affections of their flocks for the gold of the government (*399*, I, 176).

And on the subject of the persecutions,

The queen of martyrs on this earth, Ireland, for three hundred years, like the heroic mother of the Maccabees had stood erect, whilst her children fell around her (*178*, 52).

Fortunate Ireland! cherished, protected land! in ancient days known to Christendom as an Island of Saints; in this our day, recognised throughout the same Christendom as a nation heroic in their attachment to the faith, invincible in their moral power to preserve it. . . . (60, II, 434).

This concentration on Ireland's innocence and Ireland's wrongs seems to be connected with the growing antagonism between the churches, between the tenantry and the clergy and the Established Church, between the tenantry and the landlords, and indeed between repealers and unionists. Dr Doyle noted that the trumpet of the last judgment, if sounded, would not produce a more perfect stillness in any assembly of the Irish peasantry than a strong allusion to the wrongs they suffer. Thomas Wyse noted that it was found necessary to hold separate meetings of Catholic and Protestants during the agitation for Emancipation. 'The fact was the popular Catholic orators could not abuse the Protestants freely when there were some of them around.' The deterioration of relationships between Catholics and Protestants seems to date from this period. W. R. le Fanu identifies it with the Tithe War in the 1830s: 'It is hard now to realise

Good relationship between the churches.

the suddenness with which kindness and goodwill were changed to insult and hate.' Although Wyse puts the breakdown a few years earlier, Carleton tends to agree with le Fanu, noting that the early years of the century were comparatively harmonious:

> We may observe by the way that although there was a due admixture of opposite creeds and conflicting principles, yet even then, and the time is not so far back, such was the cordiality of heart and simplicity of manners, when contrasted with the bitter and rancorous spirit of the present day that the very remembrance of the harmony in which they lived is at once pleasing and melancholy.

Patrick Kennedy, writing of Wexford, also describes the harmonious relations between Catholics and Protestants, as did Dr Murray: 'We at present use the word heretic very sparingly: we choose rather, as it is an offensive word, to say "our dissenting brethren", or "our separated brethren", or something of that kind.'

Murray forbade the Sisters of Mercy to display religious emblems like crucifixes or beads in the street. Doyle wished to avoid anything that offended Protestant sensibilities, things like a clerical dress, or external shows, or processions through the streets. The absence of such emblems from Catholic schools presented no difficulty to him. He was not prepared to deny the validity of Anglican Orders (Rome did not pronounce on this until the time of Leo XIII) and actively considered the re-unification of the churches, being prepared to resign from his own see if that would help re-unification (*170*, 402; *175*, I, 323).

It is interesting to note a comment made about the early part of the century by David Croly. According to him, only the friars kept up those peculiarities of Catholicism which offended Protestants, things like habits, cords, scapulars, Agnus Deis and the bread of St Nicholas, while the secular clergy avoided such things. According to Croly, the Catholic Church had gone so far in purifying its liturgy and correcting its breviary, cutting down on holy days and fast days that a *rapprochement* between Catholics and Protestants seemed feasible.

In the nineteenth century Protestants, whether of government, landlord or religious background formed the 'black'
counterpart to the 'white' concept of a stainless church.
In the following century these gave way to 'pagan England'
(*388*).

Even at the highest ecclesiastical level, the change in
Catholic attitudes was marked. Under Archbishop Murray
relationships between the Catholic archbishop of Dublin
and the Protestant archbishop, Whately, were friendly. But
under Cardinal Cullen relations between the archbishops
was to say the least cool. The following excerpts give an
idea of Cullen's style: 'Proselytising schools . . . mere nurseries
of infidelity and hypocrisy'; 'snares laid for their perversion
in so many proselytising and ragged schools'; 'revealing the
designs of Protestant missionaries'; 'seduced for the purpose
of educating as Protestants'; 'into the hands of a Protestant
government' (*176; 123; 367*).

There is much to justify the adjective 'suspicious', at least
in Akeson's characterisation of Cullen as the essence of
'suspicious, persistent, and industrious mediocrity' (*3, 253*).
Under Dr Cullen, Dublin priests were discouraged from
associating with Protestants and the gentry; this proscription
extended to Catholic nobles as well as to those, like Judge
Keogh, whom Cullen disliked.

It would seem, therefore, that beginning about 1770
there was a gradual improvement in relationships between
the main churches in Ireland, but that in the 1820s a
deterioration set in leading to mutual hostility, especially
marked on the Catholic side, which accompanied a Catholic
definition of Ireland which excluded Protestantism. As was
said of Fr Tom Burke: 'His definition of Irish nationality
excluded everything not Catholic and everything English: it
banished not only the Protestant but the Anglo-Irish' (*387*).

Was there a particular social milieu or geographical area
in which this definition of the situation originated and from
which it spread to the rest of Ireland? According to Gustave
de Beaumont,

I do not believe that there is any country where a conquest
of so distant a date has left impressions at once so old and

so vivid. . . . Since that time, Connaught has not ceased to be the great focus of Catholic Ireland. Nowhere is the remembrance of the civil wars so vivid — nowhere are the Englishman and the Protestant detested with a hatred more religious and more national.

Another quotation from de Beaumont can be used to sum up the political definition of the situation, from the point of view of the Catholics.

The Radical Party is composed of all that do not belong to the Tory Party; as it is supported on the foundation of the Catholic population entirely devoted to it we find it sometimes called the Catholic or Nationalist party; it has for its roots old Ireland Celtic and free; and for its head young Ireland enfranchised; for its soul the Catholic religion; for its banner liberty. Its grievances and its hatreds rest on six hundred years of oppression; its hopes on half a century of victories; the sanctity of its cause on a series of oppressions surpassing all belief.

The Catholics and the nationalists had very similar definitions of their situations, so it is not surprising if they became confused with each other. Set against de Beaumont's theory, however, is the fact that O'Connell more than once accused the Connaughtmen of not pulling their weight in the struggle for Emancipation in the 1820s. Munster and Leinster provided him with most support.

The very real belief and fear of many churchmen that the Catholic religion was in imminent danger of being subverted or overthrown either by Protestants or by freethinkers, or by 'moderate' or 'Castle' Catholics duped by them, explains the tenacity with which these churchmen persisted in their political activities (270).

Protestants were not guiltless in bringing about the estrangements. As Dr Doyle put it:

This party (the Catholic party) is kept in a state of constant excitement; they are goaded by the Orangemen, they are insulted by the press, they are taunted with insult by the education societies, the distributors of bibles, and itinerant saints, they are stripped naked and almost

starved by the squirearchy and church; the legislature does
not attend to them, the government do not protect them,
the judges etc. . . . (*149*, 118).

The sentiments of the extreme Protestants can be found
expressed in any issue of the *Immortal Memory Magazine*,
the *Protestant Register* and similar periodicals: Catholics are
not interested in civil liberty but only in gaining power;
they are interested in restoring conditions as under James II;
any girl who becomes a Protestant can expect to be assailed
by a Catholic mob; Catholics wish to extirpate heretics; the
priest Kenny preaches on images and indulgences; miraculous
frauds, etc. (*Immortal Memory Magazine*, 1825).

But as O'Farrell remarked of the self-image of holy Ireland
in the next century, Irish Catholics preferred to live with a
self-image of noble, holy beauty than with reality. Realism,
as a literary style, was not popular. The belief in 'Catholic
Ireland' did not replace an earlier belief. Rather the crystallis-
ation of this belief marked a transition of society from the
pragmatic to the ideological.

3
Ecclesiastical Structures

The Structures of the Irish Church

The Irish Church saw itself as a separate unit within the Latin Church. The point is worth noting because there was no official structure corresponding to this idea of unity. The evidence for this view is varied but consistent. The bishops tended to meet regularly to settle common problems, but not in conjunction with the bishops or vicars apostolic of England and Wales or Scotland. The Catholic Directories tended to list dioceses, parishes, clergy etc. on an all-Ireland basis. When interrogated, clergy referred to matters concerning the Church in Ireland as a whole and not to part or parts of Ireland, or Ireland as part of the Roman Church in the United Kingdom.

This sense of national unity in the Irish Church dated from at least the twelfth century when national synods reconstructed the hierarchy and in doing so excluded claims of Canterbury to jurisdiction over the Norse see of Dublin. Even the wardenship of Galway, cut off from the province of Tuam on the original basis of language and rite, was part of the system. Attempts were made to hold separate episcopal meetings in the four provinces under their own archbishops, but this was abandoned in favour of national meetings.

To what extent or how did the Irish Church see itself as a unit? We should recall that the Catholic Church contains many traditional elements in addition to its formal, rational structure. National institutions in the Church are something of an anomaly. In the post-Tridentine period, especially, bishops dealt directly with the pope, though some local functions were reserved to archbishops.

First, there was no formal, legal, permanent structure

of any kind embracing the whole island, except perhaps the office of primate. Secondly, the Irish bishops of the Roman Catholic branch no longer sat in parliament, so there was no other regularly recurring event which required the Irish bishops to meet. Thirdly, no meeting of the Irish bishops had any legal standing in canon law, and hence they were not collectively authorised to do anything, to buy or sell anything, or in any other way act as a corporate body. Only national synods could deal with affairs of the Irish Church as a whole, but these were convened very infrequently, the most recent one prior to the nineteenth century apparently being that convoked by Archbishop Rinuccini in the 1640s.

When Dr Doyle was questioned about how a national synod could be convoked he replied:

> The metropolitans agreeing with each other, or the Primate, that is, the archbishop of Armagh (though we do not recognise him having a jurisdiction over us) still we would, through respect for his office, assemble, if he called us together . . . as to the jurisdiction of the Primate of All Ireland over the entire Church of Ireland, that, I might say, has ceased altogether (*170*, 398).

There was in fact no way of compelling any bishop to attend, to stay, or to accept the decrees that might be issued.

By the nineteenth century the office of primate was largely honorific. France had several primates, though only the archbishop of Lyons exercised national jurisdiction. Although Ireland had two primates, the archbishop of Armagh was referred to as 'the primate' throughout the nineteenth century, the claims of Dublin being quiescent at this period. The status of the office itself in canon law was rather unclear, and corresponded to that of 'exarch' in the Eastern Church, being a rank intermediate between metropolitan and patriarch. Possible rights of primates could have been to convoke or to preside over national synods or councils, to crown the sovereign, to hear appeals from the metropolitan, and to have rights of precedence. It is not clear if these rights belonged to all primates as such, or if some or all of them were given to the individual primatial sees on their creation.

The office of primate might best be regarded as an unsuccessful attempt at setting up or elaborating an ecclesiastical organisation in the Latin Church. It is worthy of note, and a comment on the respective importance of the offices of primate and apostolic delegate, that Dr Cullen objected strenuously to being made archbishop of Armagh and primate but apparently had no objection to having his name on the *terna* from Dublin, even though he was already primate, or to being made an apostolic delegate. The one office had real power; the other had none. The apostolic delegate was a 'national' appointment. The office differs from that of nuncio, in that the nuncio is directly accredited to the national government, whereas the apostolic delegate is the pope's representative to the members of the Church in the national area.

Nevertheless, in the first part of the nineteenth century, when the government wished to consult the 'Catholic Church', the office of primate came to have some importance. Even so, its role was overshadowed by that of the annual conference of bishops, over which the primate did not necessarily preside. Cullen's attempt to get a genuine central authority in the Irish Church, namely an apostolic delegate, was resented by some of the bishops, and not merely by MacHale (*73; 367*).

Until the end of the eighteenth century, there had been only a vague, though doubtless very strong, idea of a 'national Church', and there was at least some intermittent structure corresponding to it. Yet the idea of a national Church only came to the fore if there was a question of dealing with an outside body, whether the British government or the pope. Thus, Dr Doyle could refer to 'our rights as a national Church' or to 'the Church of Ireland'. The Churches of the Three Kingdoms remained national Churches, even when they belonged to one state (*170*).

This sense of belonging to a national body did not, however, mean that there was a corresponding structure for dealing with national affairs. MacHale's astonishment when Cullen made enquiries about the suffragans in the province of Tuam appears to be genuine, and he referred to Cullen's 'most curious letter' because the archbishop of Armagh was taking it on himself to deal with matters in another province (*399*).

But from the end of the eighteenth century the affairs of the Irish Church were harmonised to some extent by the bishops themselves who met regularly in conference. This conference had no legal basis, nor was it approved by Rome, which was apparently not even aware that the bishops were meeting. The conference had no powers, no precedents to follow, or any rights that I have been able to trace. The very fact of its meeting was opposed to traditional practice, for it was not usual for groups of ecclesiastics to meet in what amounted to a private caucus without informing those others who had a right to be called to a synod — *convocatis de jure convocandis* — those having been duly summoned who had a right in canon law to be summoned. Nevertheless, the bishops' conference developed slowly but steadily into a formal structure for governing the Irish Church.

The conference first began with meetings of the four archbishops or metropolitans about the year 1788. Regular meetings of bishops within a province had begun about 1750; *ad hoc* meetings of the four archbishops may have begun even earlier, and were only placed on a regular basis in 1788. The question of state aid towards the construction of a seminary for future Irish priests seems to have been the point which brought all the bishops together for the first time. Thereafter they met again in 1795 (eighteen bishops), 1798, 1800, 1808, 1809 and thereafter almost annually. There were meetings of the episcopal trustees of Maynooth in 1799, and apparently several meetings of the four archbishops in 1800, 1801, 1804, 1805 and 1807. It is clear that matters of great national importance, like a national seminary and the veto, brought about the custom of having all the bishops assembled.

I do not think that there was any real interruption in the series of meetings once they had begun to assemble regularly to discuss the veto. In fact, the question of nomination of bishops (domestic nomination), with or without a veto, continued throughout this period and was only settled by the rescript of 1829. Meetings were held annually from 1810 to 1816 and again in 1819. Although no references to meetings in 1817 and 1818 have yet been uncovered, it would be unwise to conclude that none took place: there is some circumstantial evidence of a meeting in the former year at least. It would appear that a new series began in 1820: Dr Cullen, writing in 1854, noted that such meetings were held from 1820 to 1849 without interruption (73).

Being considered gatherings of equals, the members first elected a president or chairman of the assembly for each day and a secretary from among their number. The chair was usually taken by one of the archbishops, apparently most often by the archbishop of Dublin, in whose arch-diocese the meetings were held. We have no clear idea how the meetings were conducted, though apparently there was a formal agenda. When a topic was introduced a speaker could speak several times and there could be a real debate; this seems clear from the rules drawn up by Cullen, who objected to the practice. Motions were formally proposed and seconded and put to the vote. If necessary, committees could be set up to consider matters and to report to the main body. The conference could also mandate some of its members to act in its name.

The fact that motions concerning the date of the next meeting were put shows that there was some flexibility with regard to the date. In 1844, during a period of great strain within the hierarchy, it was agreed that special meetings could be called at the behest of five or more bishops. The conference kept a minute book from 1829 to 1851, but apparently only formal motions were recorded in it, so that it does not necessarily reflect the true nature of the business transacted. There may have been much routine business which did not require formal motions. Three specimens of what seem to be agendas, all apparently from the late 1840s, begin with a consideration of the affairs of the Irish colleges abroad; one mentions the state of the college of Maynooth, and twice the college of All Hallows is mentioned. The only one of these which is dated is that of 1849, and in this case the conference was abandoned. Indeed it is reasonable to assume that the administration of the Irish colleges abroad, and responsibility for their property, was the core business, or as it were *raison d'etre*, for the meetings of the body of bishops (73; 549).

This however leads to a puzzle. How could the Irish bishops, who had no collective existence, deal with foreign property, with appointments to Irish colleges abroad, and even have dealings with foreign governments? Either the bishops were regarded as having a moral right to speak, as in the similar case where as a body they dealt with the British government, or such rights were granted to some or all of the Irish bishops in specific bulls or rescripts, those for example concerning the foundations of the colleges. Bishops in general could not be given such rights in law, but only a specific bishop, group of bishops or synod.

Matters which were dealt with by the bishops were the establishment of a uniform discipline in the Irish Church, a reduction in the number of holy days, a national uniformity in the number of indulgences, a uniform method for selecting bishops, a single policy on sacred persons and places in political activities, national addresses to the pope, joint petitions to parliament, or joint protests to parliament, the launching of a national Catholic book society, the state of Irish ecclesiastical students from various dioceses studying on the continent, and the right of Irish bishops to ordain *titulo missionis* — the 'title' of mission. None of these matters involved the exercise of jurisdiction. With regards to the affairs of the colleges, the decisions of the bishops may only have had the force of recommendations to the appropriate authorities.

The system worked as long as the members agreed, or agreed to differ. But when there arose a party in the episcopate which wanted to enforce a majority decision there was only one way to do this and that was by holding a synod. When Cantwell, bishop of Meath, and MacHale, archbishop of Tuam, proposed that the meeting of 1849 should be adjourned in order to conform with the the wishes of the Holy See that in future the meetings should be held synodically, there is no evidence that this was other than a tactical move to deal with a specific problem, the controversy over the Queen's Colleges. Both Cantwell and MacHale were in agreement a few years later against Cullen that a petition to the Holy See from the conference of Irish bishops required the individual assents of all the Irish bishops (*399; 268*);

Archbishop, later Cardinal MacCabe, agreed with the former.

However, the efforts of MacHale, Cantwell and others to secure an appointment to the see of Armagh favourable to their own view on the Queen's Colleges in fact led to the appointment of an archbishop with very different views. Cullen wanted the meetings to be held in a more 'synodal' form. The only authority which could implicitly interfere with episcopal rights was the Holy See. Therefore, the Holy See should itself convoke such meetings, and appoint an apostolic delegate to preside over them, and the decisions submitted to the Holy See would thereafter be binding on all the bishops. Such a form of meeting would place enormous influence in the hands of the permanent apostolic delegate, especially if the latter enjoyed the confidence of Rome. Dr Cantwell in 1856 admirably summed up the situation in a letter to MacHale. 'My only hope now is the appointment of (Cardinal) Brunelli to the Prefectship (of Propaganda) and the removal of Barnabó from the secretaryship' *(399; 73)*. Cantwell did not get his wish, for Barnabó was made prefect. However in 1880 Dr Moran of Ossory was still trying to get Cullen's *Desiderata* adopted and some new rules were adopted in 1882 *(268)*.

The further developments of the episcopal conference is outside the limits of this study. The full development can best be seen in an up-to-date copy of the *Irish Catholic Directory*, where it can be seen that the conference of Irish bishops has developed many agencies, and serves as a form of national ecclesiastical administration in many fields. It may be noted that though Ireland at the end of the century was the acknowledged head and centre of a 'spiritual empire', no structures were set up to formalise the links.

Finally, there was the resumption in the middle of the nineteenth century of the practice of holding national synods. The first seems to have been called merely to score a point over a group of bishops, and an agenda thought up for it later. Though the Irish bishops took the step of calling a national synod in response to Rome's expressed wish, it is highly likely that in this matter also Rome was merely reacting to promptings from Ireland. Before 1891 no prior consent of Rome was required to convoke a national synod, but if Rome did not convoke it the individual bishops could exercise their right of staying away.

Acts of provincial synods had to be transmitted to Rome for approval, and once approved bound all within the province. We can reasonably assume that the same applied to national synods. In one of the decrees of the Synod of Thurles, the bishops declared their acceptance of all the rescripts on the Queen's Colleges *approved by Christ's Vicar*: this implies the possibility of appeal from a decree of Propaganda to the pope himself. The decrees of Thurles were in fact confirmed by Pius IX and so became binding (*367; 73*). Various matters dealing with ecclesiastical discipline formed the subject matter of the decrees (Thurles *Decreta*) and after confirmation were obligatory throughout the whole island. Decrees of a national synod tend to enact an agreed minimum, which can then be elaborated, if necessary, in provincial and diocesan synods.

The final decree, on the avoidance of disputes among ecclesiastics, was of particular importance for the future government of the Irish Church. No bishop was to be allowed pronounce on any matter of law which might affect other bishops until the other bishops had had an opportunity to examine it. In case of dispute the matter was to be referred to Rome. The point here was to prevent Dublin Castle getting the consent or *nihil obstat* from any one bishop to a course of action of which MacHale's party disapproved. This was directly contrary to a basic principle in canon law, *In dubiis libertas* (In matters of doubt there is freedom of action). In the cases of the Charitable Bequests Act and the establishment of the Queen's Colleges, the hand of the government was much strengthened and the force of MacHale's opposition weakened when it was known that some bishops approved of the proposed legislation. The decree of Thurles appears to have been aimed at promoting 'national solidarity' rather than at providing a remedy for a real abuse. Each bishop was subject directly to the pope with the right and duty of reporting directly to him. This right they would never surrender. The bishops preferred informal conferences rather than formal synods. The great disadvantage of the synod was that a bishop could be forced to sign decrees in which he did not believe. Each bishop jealously guarded the right to instruct his own subjects in faith and morals. After Cullen's failure, no further attempt was made to *enforce* uniformity on the bishops by canonical means. National synods were rare, apparently held reluctantly, and confined as far as possible to updating and harmonising canon law.

The Laws of the Irish Church

The question here is what laws, if any, were in force in Ireland in the nineteenth century. Dr Doyle had made it clear that papal bulls were not automatically applied to Ireland, but had to be accepted by the Irish bishops, and the same was true of the disciplinary decrees of general councils. While numerous appeals to canon law to be found in the diocesan archives show that the Irish clergy regarded themselves as bound by canon law, these dealt with disputes regarding the law, not with the existence of the law as such. It might very well be that the vast majority of the people had never heard of canon law, or cheerfully ignored it, but it still existed.

Ecclesiastical laws were not moral imperatives, or exhortations. They were defined as 'an ordering of the reason made for the common good of Christian society, by the competent ecclesiastical authority, and sufficiently promulgated'. Canon law dealt with the 'external forum' and was exercised through ecclesiastical courts, while moral theology dealt with moral matters and the 'internal forum' whose proper seat was the confessional. There was some overlap, as for example in the case of 'reserved sins' i.e. those sins the absolution from which was reserved to particular priests (*170; 139*).

Laws had therefore to be enacted by a competent authority, sufficiently promulgated, and according to the prevailing legal doctrine, received by the local Church.

Those who could make laws were the pope, a general council, the various branches of the Roman curia, cardinals, legates, bishops, abbots, superiors of religious orders and cathedral chapters *sede vacante* (when the see was vacant), each within his or its sphere of competence. The bishops could make laws for their own diocese, or acting with the other bishops in synod for the province.

There was no time limit put to laws, so in theory any laws made in Ireland or for Ireland since the coming of St Patrick could still be in force. In other words, all decrees of diocesan synods since the diocese was erected; all decrees of provincial, national or ecumenical councils relevant to a given diocese; as well as all relevant papal legislation, might be in force. There were some doubtful areas. It was not clear if the legislation of a bishop outside a synod but for his own diocese remained in force after his death. Also, verbal promulgation of laws seems to have been sufficient, in which case written proof of promulgation might not be easily found.

Legislation can be divided into that which originated outside and that which originated within the country. Legislation originating within the country was all the decrees of bishops or synods as mentioned above which applied to any given diocese. With regard to this latter kind of legislation, the only problem was to decide which parts were obsolete, or contradicted by later legislation or by approved contrary customs. External laws might be general laws of the Church, or they might be particular bulls or rescripts applied to Ireland or to particular persons in Ireland. It is doubtful if a complete list of this latter kind of legislation had ever been compiled. It is most likely to be of importance in matters concerning religious orders. Irish customs may indeed have arisen from the non-application of laws rather than the application of special laws. Rome wished that the relevant continental discipline be introduced, showing clearly that Irish practice diverged from the Roman at the end of the eighteenth century (73).

With regard to legislation originating outside the country, there were two problems. The first concerned the non-promulgation of laws because the statutes of *Praemunire* prohibited the exercise of any foreign jurisdiction. The second was the non-acceptance of papal or conciliar decrees in Ireland because of the 'conciliarist' theory that all legislation had to be 'accepted' by the local Church.

In what did the canon law (*jus commune* or common law, to distinguish it from particular laws, rescripts, rights, dispensations, constitutions etc.) consist? Before the codification of canon law in 1917 there was no definite body of laws, but merely collections of an official or unofficial nature of various enactments. The chief collection was to be found in the *Corpus Juris*. The laws in the Latin Church comprised the ancient law (*jus antiquum* i.e. earlier than the earliest part of the *Corpus*); the *jus novissimum* or most recent law, which was more recent than the compilation of the *Corpus*; and the *jus novum* which consisted of the various compilations in the *Corpus*.

The question then is, how much of Latin canon law was in force in Ireland? As far as I can see, the *Corpus Juris* in its entirety was accepted as canon law in Ireland, though I have not come across any reference made explicitly either to its acceptance or non-acceptance. But when the various clergymen were arguing their cases in Rome they were apparently doing so on the grounds of Church common law, not local statutes or even on grounds of equity. The Keenan case, in which the law and the canon law are referred to repeatedly, is a good example. The only real problem arises in connection with the *jus novissimum* or laws dating from approximately the time of the Council of Trent.

Was Trent promulgated in Ireland, and was later papal legislation promulgated? In the later nineteenth century the mere promulgation of a law widely in Rome without a further promulgation by each individual bishop in his diocese was regarded as sufficient. The extraordinary steps taken to promulgate the Brief *Dominus ac Redemptor* (1773) suppressing the Jesuits shows that at least for papal acts having a public or juridical effect it was highly unlikely that the procedure would often be used. Minor matters such as dispensations or privileges accorded to bishops or religious communities, for example, apparently entered Ireland, were received by the individuals concerned, and were thus sufficiently promulgated to any interested parties, simply in the words of Archbishop Murray as 'the communications of one gentleman to another'. It is reasonable to assume that no public papal decrees, other than that suppressing the Jesuits, were promulgated in Ireland. But on the other hand, if there was any piece of papal legislation directed specifically at the Irish Church, for example the bull

Quam in sublimi of Benedict XIV (1753) regulating Irish canonical elections, it could easily be promulgated by a circular letter to the individuals concerned.

This broad distinction between public decrees and private or semi-private papal decisions appears to account for the absence from Ireland or parts of Ireland of important elements of Church legislation and the undoubted acceptance of others. Whether any individual decree, canon, bull etc. actually was applied in Ireland must in each case be a matter for empirical investigation. By far the most important question was, however, that of the promulgation of the decrees of the Council of Trent, and perhaps a touchstone here was the presence or absence from any diocese of the decree *Tametsi* on clandestine marriages.

In accordance with the prevailing doctrine in Ireland, decrees of general councils did not apply immediately to each local Church, but were subject to acceptance or modification by the local Churches. Dr Doyle stated the case with regard to the promulgation of the decrees of Trent:

> The mode of receiving the council is this: the bishops of the province assemble and deliberate whether the discipline enacted at Trent would or would not be useful to their church. If they think it useful they immediately publish a declaration and cause it to be read by the parish priest in each chapel; and thus the decrees of discipline become published and have force (*170*, 571).

Doctrinal decrees of an ecumenical council were *ex se* infallible, and did not depend on being received by local churches. It is not clear if the unanimous opinions of the Irish bishops before the parliamentary enquiries reflected the juridical independence of the Irish Church, or was merely an agreed statement, somewhat gallican in tendency, to be made before a Protestant parliament. The unanimity of the bishops is somewhat suspect.

Dr Magaurin agreed under examination that all the important decrees of Trent were in force in Ireland. They could however have been accepted *in globo* with assent given to their proclamation, or they could have been re-enacted and adapted to Irish conditions. The most important one apparently was the decree *Tametsi* which was in force in Kilmore by 1690. At a provincial synod in Armagh in 1660 the conciliar decrees were declared published and received in the dioceses of Meath and Clonmacnoise and in Co. Louth, as they had been already received and published eighty years before in the other parts of the province. The decree *Tametsi* had not been promulgated in the province of Dublin up to the year 1828. J. MacLaughlin mentions in passing that the decrees of Trent were accepted at a national synod held in Waterford in 1643. This would have been during the Confederation of Kilkenny under the legate Rinuccini (*361; 393; 170*). But in view of the uneven promulgation of the decree it is perhaps best to assume that decrees were accepted in principle, subject to local re-enactment and promulgation. As late as 1870 two bishops, MacHale of Tuam and Keane of Cloyne, refused to promulgate a papal bull in their dioceses. The bull was that condemning the Fenians (*448*). It is reasonable to assume that the encyclical of Leo XII, *Quo graviora*, of 13 March 1826 condemning secret societies was not formally promulgated in Ireland, even if a Catholic like O'Connell knew about it. Any local bishop at any time in the century could of course promulgate it in his own diocese. Cardinal Cullen appears more than once to have assumed a particular decree of Rome to have been promulgated when it was not. Examples are the application of *Quo graviora* to the Fenians, or citing the clergy before lay courts in the O'Keeffe case.

With regard to local laws, it is necessary to examine each diocese in turn to see what diocesan or provincial statutes affected it. The only point to remember in this study is that such local legislation existed.

The Liturgical Books

A specialised part of the laws of the Church was that pertaining to the liturgical rites. In the nineteenth century the reformed post-Tridentine system of liturgical rites was in force throughout Ireland. As there is no mention of the change-over from the old books to the new, it is clear that the change had long been completed before the beginning of the nineteenth century. All liturgical books conformed to the Roman 'typical editions', except those used by some religious orders like the Carmelites and Dominicans whose rite varied slightly from the Roman one.

The Diocesan System

The Irish Catholic Church was organised formally into about twenty-eight dioceses in four provinces. In practice, each of these dioceses was independent and reported directly to the Congregation of Propaganda in Rome, not through the metropolitan or primate. The essential rungs in the hierarchical ladder in the post-Tridentine Church were pope, bishop, parish priest, layman. The office of archbishop or metropolitan was not completely abolished, but its function was extremely restricted.

This system, in its present form, dates from the twelfth century, and has remained virtually unchanged since that date. The boundaries of the dioceses have not been harmonised with more recent administrative boundaries. They appear to correspond to twelfth-century political boundaries. If, as Patrick Power surmises, the parishes correspond to the ancient Celtic *tuaths* or *triochacheds*, the actual boundary lines of the various dioceses may follow the lines of boundaries dating from early Christian times.

A peculiarity to be noted is the existence of 'islands' of one diocese within the bounds of another. The boundaries of Irish dioceses apparently were not rationalised, as happened to the Irish parishes, and to the dioceses in other European countries. The principal change since the twelfth century was the merging of some dioceses, but rarely did a diocese entirely lose its identity, although Annaghdown completely disappeared. When two dioceses were linked they sometimes retained formally distinct but linked diocesan structures.

There was one legal anomaly in the diocesan system at the beginning of the nineteenth century: the 'wardenship' of Galway. This was a group of parishes in the city of Galway under the jurisdiction of a priest, not a bishop, who was elected to the office of warden for a period of three years.

The wardenship of Galway seems to have been a prelacy *nullius*, i.e. under the rule of a priest who had episcopal authority but not bishop's orders. He could therefore rule the territory, but had to call on a neighbouring bishop to perform the rites reserved to bishops, such as ordaining or confirming. Catholic wardens existed from at least the year 1514 and were apparently elected under a bull of Pope Innocent VIII (1484-92).

According to Dr Doyle, the archbishop of Tuam had some rights of visitation, even though metropolitans did not normally have the right of visitation in the territories of their suffragans. There were other peculiarities about this little jurisdiction. Laymen as well as clergy had the right to vote in the election. According to Archbishop MacHale, even women had the right to vote in these ecclesiastical elections. One source of trouble was that the franchise was restricted to certain families known as 'the tribes', and the 'non-tribes' were excluded. Appointment to the various parishes was made simply by seniority. From at least 1782 there was trouble over the elections, and the matter was finally settled by Propaganda when in 1830 it raised the wardenship to the rank of bishopric subject to the new rules for the appointment of bishops (*Directory*, 1837; *170; 548; 399*).

The dioceses of Ireland were organised in the twelfth century into four provinces and this arrangement persisted, although it was of little practical value. The rights of metropolitans were limited to receiving appeals from the decisions of suffragan bishops. But in practice, an archbishop's scope of action was somewhat wider, even if he had few legal rights over a suffragan. He was to keep an eye on the activities (*invigilare*) of his suffragans. Possibly this meant that the archbishop could and ought judicially to collect evidence with a view to sending a report to Rome. He could convene a provincial synod. He could step in *sede vacante* and appoint a vicar capitular if the chapter failed to do so, and hear the appeals from the tribunals of their suffragans.

Archbishops could not interfere in the affairs of the diocese of one of their suffragans. MacHale was doubtless within his rights in keeping himself informed on affairs in the diocese of Killala but had reason for astonishment when Cullen started to pry into the affairs of another *province*.

The office was, however, more important than the formal

structure would seem to indicate. The archbishop presided at the election of suffragan bishops, and at the meeting of the provincial bishops to recommend a candidate. This made the office of metropolitan a strategic one. An archbishop could be consulted by Rome on a difficult problem, as when the four archbishops were consulted about finding a successor to Dr Crolly. Or an archbishop could be sent to make a visitation of another diocese as Archbishop Crolly was sent to Killala and Archbishop Dixon to Ardagh. The archbishop could also convene a provincial synod, when it suited himself.

The Council of Trent enacted that provincial councils or synods were to be held every three years. Synods were held irregularly in Ireland in the eighteenth and nineteenth centuries, though in the seventeenth century they had been held quite often.

Just a few points remain to be made about the dioceses of Ireland in general before dealing with the diocese as an individual unit.

The dioceses formed a complete ecclesiastical structure for the whole island, every part of which was under some bishop. The sees were regularly filled, so that there was a real structure, not merely a paper one. Bishops were in residence in their dioceses, at least for the greater part of the year: there were no absentees. Likewise, as the bishops had no parliamentary, legal or curial functions, they could and did administer the diocese directly and not through canons or vicars-general. In the early nineteenth century each parish priest had a bishop in residence to whom he was responsible.

On the continuing organisation of the Irish Church, even during persecution, and the need for such systematic organisation, the important point is made by de Freine:

> The popular idea of Ireland after the era of plantation is that of an utterly dispossessed people surviving religious opppression through their unswerving constancy to simple traditional pieties and the occasional ministrations of fugitive priests.
>
> The trouble about this picture is that while these details are undoubtedly true they do not constitute the

whole picture. There were other important relevant details.

The wandering priest, for example, is visualised as existing in a sort of ecclesiastical vacuum. The fact that he was part of an organisation (no matter how constricted), that he might be responsible to a bishop, and that he might have a permanent abode and Mass houses is too often overlooked (*184*, 141).

4
The Diocese

General Structure

This chapter deals with the formal organisation of the diocese. Activities within the diocese are concerned primarily with religious worship. There are two levels at which this worshipping activity is conducted. The first is the activity of the local community or parish, and the other is that of the bishop in the diocese, for different religious functions are allocated to the bishop and to the local priest.

A diocese is a tract of territory, normally continuous, ruled over by a bishop, who appoints several officials to assist him. It is divided into territorial parishes over each of which a parish priest presides. In episcopal churches the role of the bishop is more important than that of the priest.

The Role of the Bishop

The bishop combined in his person two distinct roles. One was the role of jurisdiction by which he governed the diocese by means of laws, norms, courts and sanctions. These were not sacred acts. Excommunication, for example, did not imply or effect moral guilt. On the other hand, the bishop was regarded as having sacred powers, the powers of orders such as the power to consecrate the bread of the Eucharist, thus changing it into the body and blood of Christ, the power to confer the Holy Spirit in confirmation, and the power to ordain other priests so that they in turn could exercise sacred orders.

Exercises of jurisdiction took up most of his time. Only occasionally was a bishop required to exercise his powers of orders. In the wardenship of Galway, the spiritual ruler had no episcopal orders, and managed by requesting a neighbouring bishop to perform those acts for him. When a bishop required assistance in the exercise of jurisdiction, he appointed one or more vicars-general. When he required assistance in the exercise of orders he asked Rome to appoint an auxiliary bishop.

The bishop governed in his own right, and not as delegate of the pope. He was the judge in the first instance on all matters dealing with faith, morals, discipline and all ecclesiastical affairs. He could make laws and impose canonical punishments like excommunication. He had a right to inquire into all matters pertaining to the Christian faith within his diocese. He could approve or prohibit preachers, censor and prohibit books. He was bound to supervise churches and sacred furnishings therein. He could give dispensations from the canon law. He could reserve to himself or named priests the right of giving absolution in the case of particular sins. He could create, unite and divide benefices and parishes, with due regard to the requirements of canon law in the matter. He alone could authorise the foundation of a church or chapel. (*139*; this list is taken from normal canon law: no discrepancy was noted in Irish practice. For an example of an Irish bishop's daily duties, see Appendix D.)

Besides the ordinary powers given by canon law to the bishop, he could be given extra powers or 'faculties' by the pope. These dealt chiefly with matrimonial dispensations.

The exercise of the bishop's powers were less constrained in Ireland than elsewhere as there were few diocesan dignitories, chapters, tribunals or lay patrons to oppose him, and the absence of a *concursus* for appointments meant that the priest was virtually dependent on his bishop for his career chances.

The Diocesan Officials

The organisation of an Irish diocese was simple in the extreme. In Derry, when the bishop went mad, in 1845, it was found that there was no dean, no chapter, no dignitary whatsoever, no vicar-general, no archdeacon. In Kildare and Leighlin there were two or three vicars-general (the number was not fixed), and that was typical of diocesan organisation in the early years of the century. Some few dioceses had complete chapters; others had retained a few dignitaries of the chapter like the titles of dean and archdeacon. All the dioceses had either a dean or a vicar-general (*573; Directory*, 1837, 1840). Gradually, a lower supervisory grade of priests was introduced, namely the vicars-forane, who had the duty to supervise a small group of priests. Unfortunately there is no way of knowing if the letters V.F. occurring in the directories give a complete picture.

Tackett remarks that in a French diocese the lower clergy dealt with the canons and vicars-general. Irish evidence shows the bishops taking a personal interest in all aspects of diocesan activity. In the ordinary work of the diocese the bishop was assisted by a vicar-general whom he appointed and removed, and to whom he personally gave whatever faculties he thought fit.

There do not seem to have been any permanent tribunals until the twentieth century. The bishop could act, *ex informata conscientia* without setting up a formal court, or set up a court *ad hoc* if need be. Nor was there a diocesan chancellery, an official, a promoter fiscal, a *defensor vinculi* (defender of the marriage bond), a chancellor, a notary, a secretary, or episcopal chaplains. More recent *Directories* show that in the twentieth century many of these offices had been recreated (*577; 124; 517*).

Likewise the officers of the chapter were for the most part absent, or when present were merely titular. Archpriests, archdeacons, deans, precentors, treasurers, theologians, penitentiaries, minor canons and vicars of the chapter were absent, though the titles survived partially in some dioceses (*Directories*, passim).

A cathedral chapter normally was established to sing the divine office in choir, to help the bishop in ruling the diocese and to take his place when he was absent. The diocese was, therefore, never without a head. The bishop was not a member of the chapter, of which the dean and archdeacon were the principal officers. Irish chapters did not, in fact, sing the office in choir. The functions of dean and archdeacon with regard to helping the bishop to administer the diocese were performed by the vicars-general. The bishop could and did ignore the wishes of the chapter. When there was no chapter the relevant parts of canon law could not be applied.

The real importance of chapters came when the bishop was removed by death, translation to another see, insanity, imprisonment etc. The chapter was then obliged to convene and elect a vicar capitular to govern the diocese. The eighteenth-century bull *Quam in sublimi* allowed parish priests to elect vicars capitular, and the 1829 rescript *Cum ad gravissimum* gave them the right to choose bishops, so the importance of the office of canon was diminished and became largely honorific. The lack of chapters, or their doubtful existence, combined with a lack of compensating legislation from Rome, was to cause some difficulties. If nobody elected a vicar capitular, the metropolitan could appoint one (573).

Dublin had a diocesan council to which the archbishop referred when dealing with promotions to parishes (563, 517).

The Parishes

The parochial system was remarkable for its rational uniformity. All Ireland was divided into organisationally identical parishes. Such variations as existed earlier in France, and still in the Established Church in Ireland, were not to be found. The contrast with the structure of the diocesan system with its irrational 'islands' is noteworthy. Whereas there were just over a thousand Catholic parishes in 1869, there were 2,428 Protestant parishes. Some of these Protestant parishes were tiny, being in fact suppressed monastic sites.

The whole territory of Ireland was shared out so that everyone in Ireland belonged to one parish and one parish only. According to Riepe, that rational and systematic organisation of parishes in rural areas really began with the Council of Trent. Though no formal study of the parochial system in medieval Ireland has been done, we can envisage a cathedral and chapter looking after the spiritual needs of the people in the cathedral city while the provision of spiritual assistance in rural areas was left to the initiative of individuals to provide benefices (see the *Corpus Juris*, 'De Officiis Ecclesiasticis', dist. xxv, C.I.; *487; 188*). Such medieval 'parishes' did not necessarily have definite boundaries. But the rationalising decree of Trent did not necessarily imply that the modern parochial boundary system began then. It may have been enacting into law what was the practice in many areas, and prescribing that the *bishop* had the obligation to provide for the spiritual welfare of those in any pockets of land not cared for by beneficed clergy or regulars.

Patrick Power gives two maps of the dioceses of Waterford and Lismore, the one showing the ancient parishes, and the other the modern parishes. Unfortunately he does not give the date for the map of the ancient parishes. When a strict parochial delimitation was being made, the probability was that the bounds would be made to conform to existing secular bounds which could be very ancient.

Modern Irish parishes are usually unions of pre-Reformation parishes. The Tridentine law of residence virtually enforced the unions of adjacent parishes in order to obtain a sufficient revenue for the parish priest. The present unions appear to have been effected during the seventeenth century (*421*).

Monastery and abbey lands disappeared. I know of only one reference to surviving separate monastic revenues even when the monastery lands were swallowed up in the diocese. This was the revenue of the monastery of St Fintan, which Dr Doyle held *in commendam* (*578*).

Dr Doyle stated that the bishop had the right to appoint parish priests. There are however several examples where they did not have this right. In Co. Louth, Sir Edward Bellew claimed a right of presentation in 1816. Some parishes in Meath were under lay patronage early in the nineteenth century. In the parish of Ballinasloe, Lady Moore and the Countess of Clanrickarde are mentioned as claiming rights of presentation. In a dispute between the Coppingers of Barryscourt and the bishop of Cork about presentation in 1820, Rome decided in favour of the former. The old abbacy of Cong, belonging to canons regular, managed to survive as a juridical unit till 1829 and appointed parish priests till that date. The Cistericans died out around 1750 (*303; 97; 164; 599; 367*).

Richard Shiel stated that the bishops normally appointed

to the parish the individual whom the parishioners wished to nominate, but only in Clogher, around 1817, have I noticed a claim of parishioners *as of right* to appoint parish priests. Wyse notes that three years' peacable possession gave a title to a parish, which would seem to indicate other ways of coming into a parish than episcopal appointment. The rescript of 1829 on the selection of bishops mentions parish priests who enjoy the actual and peaceful possession of a parish. The use of this phrase instead of for example 'lawfully appointed parish priests' seems to imply some doubt as to how possession of a parish was obtained.

In Kildare and Leighlin at least, up to the time of Dr Doyle, there was no ceremony of induction into a parish, the appointee simply being notified by letter. Doyle introduced the practice of getting the new parish priest to repeat the Profession of Faith, and take an oath of observance of the canons and statutes of the diocese. In France the new parish priest wearing a stole was brought to the tabernacle, the confessional, the pulpit and the baptismal font (*503*, 115).

There was no *concursus* for appointment to parishes in Ireland. The *concursus* was a theological dispute, and whoever won the debate, *ceteris paribus*, was appointed. Propaganda tried to have the *concursus* applied to Ireland at the end of the eighteenth century, but this was not done. At the Synod of Thurles it was still regarded as not feasible, and likewise at the Synod of Maynooth in 1875. In 1900 a qualifying examination by the diocesan theologians was imposed. Appointment to a parish was for life (*124; 170*).

With regard to revenue, parishes in Ireland were not 'benefices' for there was no property from which revenue for the support of the clergy might derive. Canon law on benefices therefore could not be applied. The clergy, however, were provided for by a twice-yearly collection.

The Parochial Clergy

The basic pastoral work in the Irish Church was done by the secular or diocesan clergy. Each secular priest belonged to some diocese. The Council of Trent finally made the adage *clerici vagi ne admittantur* effective (wandering clerics are not to be accepted).

A priest came to belong to a particular diocese on his ordination only. An individual could seek out any diocese which would receive him at the time of his ordination and was not bound to his native diocese. This was apparently the practice of the Irish students living on the continent. Even after ordination, a priest could seek leave to depart from the service of the diocese and seek to enter another diocese if he could find a bishop who would take him (*170*, 3 70; *549*).

According to Dr Doyle, a bishop could confer a parish on a priest from another diocese, but did not do so, for the clergy of the diocese felt they had first claim on the livings. Normally the senior curate in a parish was chosen but not always. Nobody was appointed parish priest until he had first served some years as a curate and given satisfaction. I have been unable to find corroboration that this rule was invariable (*170*, 339, 343).

The charge of a parish being for life, a parish priest could not be removed without adequate reason, or canonical cause. The authority of the parish priest was conferred by the canon law and not by the bishop and so could not be increased or lessened; it was, therefore, uniform all over Ireland.

There were two kinds of priest in the parishes, those in charge of the parishes, the parish priests, and their assistants who were called curates.

The parish priest was exclusively authorised to baptise solemnly, to hear confessions and to administer communion and extreme unction. For a marriage, the parish priest of one or other of the contracting parties had to be present. The parish priest had the right to control pious functions in his parish, such as the holding of processions, the ringing of bells etc. He alone was allowed to bury the dead and receive the appropriate emolument. His permission was required by other priests to say mass, to hear confessions and to preach within the limits of the parish (*139*, 253).

The parish priest might be assisted by one or more curates. Strictly speaking, from the canon law, a parish priest could appoint his own curate, give him the necessary faculties and for a just cause dismiss him. However from the Synod of

Thurles onwards it was reserved to a bishop to appoint curates. This may have been merely confirming existing practice, for Dr Doyle affirmed that he could freely move curates about (*170*, 341; *124*, 15). Fitzpatrick remarks that it was the curates who did the actual work. P. Kennedy too refers to the 'heavy parochial duty which is efficiently discharged by his young coadjutor'.

Unlike the position in some European countries, the diocesan clergy were fairly evenly spread over the whole country (*40*, II, 50). Before 1836 it is difficult to get exact figures for the number of priests serving in the parishes, because the *Directories* were either non-existent or incomplete. But the diocesan histories show that even around the year 1800, which was apparently a low point for clerical recruitment, all the parishes were filled, even if bishops had to call on the help of the regulars. So even around 1800 the number of parish priests probably did not fall below 960, not counting those parishes in which the bishop had administrators while he drew the revenue. In 1837 there were 974 parish priests (*Directory*, 1837) and in 1869 there were 989, reflecting the creation of parishes in the meantime. The number of curates *in parishes* rose from 1,184 in 1837 to 1,446 in 1869, which meant an extra curate for every four parishes.

In 1797 Dr Troy estimated that 400 places were necessary in the various seminaries to replace the annual loss of clergy in the Irish Church. A spot check on obituaries reveals that fifty-eight members of the secular clergy died in 1842 (*Directory*, 1843). The disruption of the courses of studies on the continent is probably of itself sufficient to account for a shortfall in the number of clergy around 1800. An annual mortality of sixty, and a six-year course of studies, indicate a need for 360 college places for secular priests alone, not counting the regulars.

The number of priests in Ireland probably reached an all-time low about the year 1800, partly because of the loss of the continental colleges and partly because of episcopal policies against the regulars. This would make the year 1800 a bad year to take as a base. Dr Doyle told the 1825 parliamentary enquiry that he had to restrict the number of clergy to what his diocese could afford. Paul Cullen, about 1840, told Propaganda that lack of money for education was restricting recruiting for the foreign missions. The friars, of course, educated their subjects free. Economics would seem to have been the limiting factor in recruiting the Irish clergy and the increase of the grant to Maynooth in 1845 just before the Famine probably averted another crisis of numbers (*12*).

5
The Clergy

Origins and Social Status

There is some evidence to suggest that at an earlier period than we are concerned with in this study the priesthood was passed down through families. Ó Dufaigh says of Dr Murphy that he was the last bishop of Clogher who promoted his relatives as a matter of course, and the Maginns were the last family in the diocese to form a clerical pressure group. 'Gaelic Ireland had always been ruled by the aristocracy of the *saor chlanna* (free clans), and it was to this class the clergy by and large belonged'. Of the parish of Ballinasloe Fr Egan says, 'Hitherto the parochial clergy of the diocese had been drawn from a limited number of families, the majority of whom were from the old Hy Many stock, and only towards the end of the eighteenth century was the virtual monopoly breaking down'.

The point was repeatedly made in the literature of the early nineteenth century that the Catholic clergy were drawn not from the lowest orders of the peasantry but from the superior class above that, 'from the humblest class of *farmers*'. Phrases such as 'born in the class immediately above the peasant', 'the state of life we call the Middle Class . . . either the agricultural order or the commercial order', and 'substantial farmers' occur with reference to the clergy in Kildare and Leighlin (*170*, 46, 366; *545*, I, 240; *385*, 452).

In *The Poor Scholar* Carleton mentions £200 as being what was required to put a boy through his studies. Doyle quotes the figure of £40 per annum or even £20 (presumably with a half burse) as being what was required in Carlow. With regard to Maynooth,

Dr Crotty estimated the *expense* of a student's education in Maynooth as 50 pounds for the first year and at least 12 pounds a year afterwards, that is when he enjoyed a burse or free place on the foundation. If a pensioner, it cost 70 pounds for the first year and about 33 pounds a year afterwards. Hence the poorer classes could not afford to educate their children for the Church and the students were generally the sons of substantial farmers or graziers, or shopkeepers and merchants in the towns (*225*, 219).

O'Connell mentioned the fact that some of the children of the gentry began to go to Maynooth, but Owen Madden later reported that this remained rare. In 1825, John Dunne stated that the bishops were then selecting only those from the better classes and this was regarded as desirable (*170*, 278, 46; *303*, 141).

Various writers mention the 'hedge priests'. The name has no connection with hedge school, and the first reference to it is in 1550, according to the *Oxford English Dictionary*. Apparently it meant non-university trained priests. So Carleton may not be quite correct when he says, 'This nickname was first bestowed upon them by the Continental priests who generally ridiculed them for their vulgarity. They were for the most part simple but worthy men.'

Doyle rejected a candidate for orders, alleging he was fit only to be a ploughman, apparently on the grounds of his manners, not his morals or piety. He also objected to certain priests from northern dioceses who were ordained without having done sufficient studies. The grounds on which Doyle rejected the men were uncouth personal appearance and obtuse intellect. Carleton noted the intense desire of the peasantry to have a son a priest, and the vicar-general of Armagh noted that there was an excess of unsuitable candidates (*175*, 359; *599*).

It is reasonable to assume that the 'hedge priests' were not well educated. But in the nineteenth century there seem to have been few if any of the secular clergy who had not passed some years at least in a seminary. One cannot estimate directly from the length of the seminary course how long students actually spent there, for the bishop could always give a dispensation from part of the course.

In the first decade of the century, Dr Murphy professed himself satisfied with the educational attainments of almost all of his parish priests, but of the fifteen curates he was satisfied with very few. It should be taken into account that some of the clergy in Clogher at the time were regulars, and the friars apparently kept up the custom of promoting their members to orders after they did arts, and before they began theology (*385; 175*).

From 1820 onwards, Laverty, for Down and Connor, shows that the clergy of those dioceses, almost without exception, had spent three or four years in Maynooth in addition to their classical studies. The Synod of Tuam required at least two years of theology in addition to the usual classical and philosophical studies. In the Report of the Commissioners of Irish Education Enquiry of 1826-7, it was reported that arts subjects were studied for four years in Maynooth followed by a three-year divinity course. Two-thirds of the students remained six years in the college, and the remainder seven years (*589*).

It would seem that in the early years of the century there were some ignorant priests in Ireland, hastily ordained for the needs of the mission, but this defect was quickly rectified and by 1825 a full classical, arts and divinity course was undertaken by the great majority of *ordinandi*. Doyle was not altogether enthusiastic about the seminaries in Ossory, Waterford and Tuam which could not provide the full course like Maynooth and Carlow. The minimum stay in Carlow was five years (*170, 365*).

The financial status of a curate beginning his ecclesiastical career was about £50 per annum, a salary equivalent to that of army ensigns, doctors and lawyers at the beginning of their careers. A parish priest could get £200 to £500 and a bishop from £500 to £1,000. The base line for comparison is the unskilled manual labourer in full employment who could get about £15 per annum. Noblemen, generals, admirals, great landowners and rich merchants might earn or receive about £10,000 a year. A very successful barrister like O'Connell earned several thousand. The income of the clergy corresponded to that of the lower middle class.

A question which concerned the status-conscious nine-teenth century was whether priests were gentlemen. By origin they were certainly not gentry. As O'Connell put it, they were 'the children of exceedingly vulgar people'. But O'Connell admitted that in Maynooth they acquired the 'manners almost the tone of genteel society'. The monastic seclusion of Maynooth did not prevent them from 'acquiring even the manners of gentlemen, and the courtesies of civilized life' (*170, 285*). O'Connell's snobbish remarks are significant. At mid century Forbes noted, 'Judging from what I myself saw, I would say they are gentlemen in the true sense of the word, and with as much polish as could be expected from men who for the most part, like the Scottish clergy, spring from the middle or lower classes.'

In political matters there was some disadvantage in the relatively low social status of the clergy. 'Of course you, and every man of your station, sneer at the notion of being dictated to by Father Luke, in the greasy leather small clothes, and dirty black boots — only himself a cottier once removed' (*285, 233*).

In the pages of Carleton we find the clergy mixing freely with the country people of their own class. But other novelists show priests moving in higher circles. We find a priest, an alumnus of St Omer, dining at the squire's house in the company of the doctor, the attorney and the son of an army major. Another of Lover's priests spoke with a rich brogue, the brogue of Irish gentlemen of the previous century. About him there was no hint of vulgarity, and Lover accepted his invitation to dine. The priest's house was a neat cottage with a clean yard, lacking a dunghill, a pig and a barking dog, features which distinguished the cottages of the peasantry. The floor of the priest's diningroom was boarded; there was a cloth on the table, and the priest had a neat housekeeper. The priest had been to St Omer. In the novels of Lever we find the priests mixing freely with the upper crust of Irish society. One priest was associated with Jack Hinton of the Guards. Fr Healy of Little Bray may have been the original of this type (*286; 12*).

The next question is that of the social status of the bishops.

With regard to origin, in the nineteenth century at least they seem to have had the same social background as the ordinary Maynooth clergy from which a large proportion of them were drawn. Some examples confirm this. Bishop Murphy of Clogher was born in a small farmhouse. MacHale and Doyle came from the lower middle class. Cullen's family were big farmers. (Exact details with regard to a sufficient number of the bishops is lacking, so we cannot come to firm conclusions.) The bishops in the eighteenth century may have been drawn from a superior class. The Butler archbishops of Cashel seem to have been distantly related to the earls of Ormond. Dr Murphy of Cork came from an exceedingly wealthy background, but the family were originally bootmakers. A bishop of Kildare and Leighlin early in the nineteenth century was on very familiar terms with Lord Cloncurry. In Armagh in the eighteenth century Primate Anthony Blake always kept a carriage, but Primate O'Reilly was 'the first bishop having an independent fortune to live up to his state' *(535; 385; 175; 399; 513; 599)*.

The archbishops of Dublin, and indeed it would seem all Catholic priests, like their Protestant counterparts, had entrée on invitation to the Castle. In 1849 Dr Murray was advised that he might be accompanied by a chaplain. The 'titular' bishops used only their surnames, and not that of the diocese. Dr Cullen, wishing to be provocative, refused to attend the Castle and used his territorial designation. The government was not provoked and ignored him. Catholic bishops were accorded the courtesy title of Doctor. Their precedence at official functions was immediately after the lowest grade of the nobility, the three hereditary knights. As a cardinal, Dr Cullen was accorded precedence over the Protestant archbishop of Dublin, who thereupon stayed away. Priests were addressed as 'Reverend Sir', bishops as 'Most Reverend Sir' so as not to imply any lay jurisdiction by the use of 'My Lord', which was the usual mode of address of the Catholic themselves. The correctness and courtesy of the Castle officials from 1820 on is noteworthy. Though Cullen and other bishops who consistently snubbed the Castle were probably guilty of intentional discourtesy, yet after 1850 suspicion of the alleged machinations of the Castle was so great among ordinary Catholics that it is hard to see how they could have ignored the feelings of their flocks.

Moral Status

Most of the comments on the moral state of the clergy at all periods are highly favourable. One can ignore, as Dr Doyle consistently ignored, unsupported complaints by interested parties. 'I wish I could furnish you with a list of all I disbelieve, of all the communications I commit to the flames without any notice, of all the prevarications I elicit' (*175*). Archbishop Walsh refused even to read anonymous denunciations of any of his priests. Bishop Murphy of Clogher, writing to Rome, was generally favourable. 'As to the moral character, zeal, and exertions of all the rest of the clergy, with three exceptions in so many pastors, I have every reason to be gratefully thankful' (*385*). The strict reforming bishop of Elphin reclaimed drunken and disorderly priests in his diocese, and only one, an Augustinian friar, remained recalcitrant. As for the rest of the clergy, 'They are a respectable, well-informed, and enlightened body, affording me all the assistance in their power' (*385*). Early in the century too comes the testimony of Dr Doyle:

> The ministers of this religion, however, are in general well stored with classical and scholastic knowledge, less refined perhaps than persons who are unacquainted with their vocations might desire, but not deficient in those qualifications which the parochial clergy of a young nation (for such Ireland might be deemed) should possess.
>
> They are energetic, active, laborious, shrewd, and intelligent; they are the most moral class of persons, not only in this country, but, I think, existing on earth; they are exact, or rather they are filled with zeal in the discharge of their duties. . . . They are always employed; there is nothing dull or quiescent about them (*175*, I, 281).

Testimony to the generally excellent character of the Irish priests of this period can also be found in the report of Dr Plunkett of Meath to Propaganda, dated 24 January 1790, and in the report of Archbishop Carroll of Baltimore with regard to the Irish priests in his diocese (*97*, 134; *209*, 758).

About mid century we have other excellent reports.

> I may here remark that all I have yet heard of the Roman Catholic priests in the districts through which I have passed is extremely creditable to their character and conduct. They seem to be most zealous in the discharge of their sacred duties and most blameless in their lives. . . . I was told by a man, who should be an unbiased witness, as he was both a stranger and a Protestant (an intelligent sergeant of the police) that during the fourteen years he had resided in the district, he never heard of any priests being accused of any personal immorality, and added that they were, to his own knowledge, a body of truly excellent men (*181*, I, 88).

On the other hand, a letter to Propaganda in 1823 tries to secure a bishopric for an individual by discrediting his rivals. Of one it is said '. . . we never told them that he was educated four years in a Protestant school, and that he haunted the brothels of Dublin for the four years – This is the way with all the students of Trinity College' (*264*, 295). As Larkin remarks, 'The appointment in the end went to Fr Laffan, and it might also be noted that there seems to be no basis in fact for the allegations made against either Fr Collins, or Fr Slattery.'

Allegations about immoral behaviour of priests in the confessional were made to Rome from time to time. Two such were made in the year 1847 in separate letters to Propaganda, one from Edward Murray of Killala, the other from an unnamed priest in Elphin. In 1819 the Catholics of the parish of Errigal Truagh described a parish priest they did not want as 'answering the character of Henry the Eighth, neither sparing women in his lust, nor men in his anger'. Similar denunciatory letters accusing the parish priest of perjury, incontinence, greed, dishonesty, irreligion and malevolence, hypocrisy and informing, avarice and simony are to be found in the Clogher archives (*601; 572*).

Not all the accusations were groundless. A female in Dundalk, by order of her confessor, denounced a clerical *student* for soliciting, and he was dismissed from the college. In 1868 Primate Kieran ordered a priest to get rid of his housekeeper. There is a case of a priest soliciting in Armagh in 1867, which may or may not be the same (*553; 266; 569*). But before going on to deal with other accusations, it is worth noting that if the woman allegedly involved stuck to her story the priest accused had no defence, and would have been removed from office. In Dublin the sin of soliciting in the confessional brought about an automatic suspension, and a similar provision was doubtless to be found in other dioceses. On the other hand there was a sin, reserved to the pope for absolution, of calumnious denunciation. Of the two sins, sexual immorality and calumny, the balance of probability is that the latter was the one the Irish were addicted to, for there is no confirmatory evidence whatsoever that the Irish priests were given to sexual immorality, while there is considerable evidence of ambition and calumny.

The real moral stain on the character of the Irish clergy seems, however, to have been drunkenness. There was a class of priests, commonly known as Fr Tackems or couple beggars, who were suspended from the exercise of their functions for their disorderly conduct, and who gained a livelihood, partly at least, by celebrating runaway marriages. They were not numerous. I am unable to obtain comparative figures as to whether drop-outs from the ministry were more numerous then than now. Some were still to be found even after 1850 in the archdiocese of Dublin (*580; 170*, 257; *24*, III, 234).

Even if priests did not go so far as to become alcoholic drop-outs, they were not all equally zealous. Doyle's biographer does not refer to immoral priests but to easygoing or lazy ones. Carleton too refers to the kind of priest who was 'regular, but loose and careless in the observances of his Church'. More solid facts come in a report of Primate Dixon on the priests of Ardagh in mid century. According to him, many of the priests drank more than was fitting, and many neglected preaching, there being he estimated only twelve parishes out of forty where the word of God was preached regularly (*535*, 26). There is no need to assume that the priests of Ardagh were in any way untypical of the priests of Ireland. Dr Murphy, in 1804, professed himself satisfied with most of the clergy in his diocese, all that is of the parish priests except three. Dr Plunkett of Elphin reported that he had some drunken and disorderly clergy formerly in his diocese, but all but one of these was now reclaimed (*535; 385*, 459ff, 479).

The real faults of the clergy were rather ambition and contentiousness, with the lack of Christian spirit that that implies. The archives recount many clerical disputes, usually between the leading priests of the diocese. They may have been connected with long-standing factions in the diocese. Armagh was divided into three parts, the clergy of Louth, Armagh and Tyrone; and the Tyrone priests did not like the Louth priests and vice versa. Canvassing was done by all, the prospective bishop, his backers and the local bishop. Curtis failed to get a vote for his vicar-general, Dr McCann, because the priest elector had already promised it to someone else. Later in the century Cullen dealt vigorously with public clerical disputes (*553; 560; 477; 517*).

With regard to the regular clergy, the following measured verdict on them was given by the vicar-general of Meath, afterwards second rector of the Irish College, Rome.

It cannot be dissembled that want of a regular system of education, the little care taken in the selection of novices, and the total absence of monastic discipline in the few convents that still exist in Ireland afford a very sufficient justification of the conduct of our prelates in withholding their support and protection from the foundations already in being, and resisting the introduction of new ones into their respective dioceses.

As for myself, I have not the least antipathy to any of the religious orders to be found here, but I am certainly of the number of those who would wish to see their houses suppressed if not conducted in the original spirit of their institution (*385*, Boylan to Ennis, 1820).

Even towards the middle of the century Dr Gentili, the Italian Rosminian, reported that the various generals of the religious orders had sent a long series of well-ordered requests to the good religious in Ireland, but it did not appear that they were disposed to do their duty and become religious once more. MacHale gave his opinion to Dr Higgins that an apostolic visitor was required and suggested Gentili (*280,* 325). It is difficult to get hard facts. In Clogher, there was no regular convent, but there were ten friars serving in the diocese. Two were employed as parish priests, and four as curates on a regular basis. There were three whom the bishop would not employ in any capacity 'on account of their irregular lives and morals' (*385,* 459ff.). The Dominican parish priest, it was noted by Carleton, the 'Reverend Father Finnerty, of the Order of St Dominic, and parochial priest of this excellent parish' was of regular, but loose and careless life. The *Life* of Fr Tom Burke gives an excellent picture of life in the reformed Dominicans later in the century.

In the early years of the century the practice of living together in a convent was not observed by the Capuchins, and they used money, apparently with legitimate dispensations. Doyle wanted to see that the whole Rule was observed by the friars (he was one himself) with the exception of the matter of dress; that they be obliged to live in communities of at least three persons; and that they be prevented from going around begging, because drink was freely offered in farmhouses (*23,* 58; *175,* II, 57ff.).

The archives recount various disputes among the religious. In 1848 a dispute among the Augustinians led to the appointment of Dr Murray as apostolic visitor. Writing to Archdeacon Hamilton in 1843, Murray referred to certain intractable spirits among the Franciscans. The second abbot of Mount Melleray was forced to resign because of drink, although the real problem in the monastery seems to have been a self-appointed reformer of excessive severity (*601; 580; 563*).

The Image or Stereotype of the Clergy

This image was an almost exclusively favourable one. The phrase 'soggarth aroon' (the dearly-loved priest) sums up a widespread attitude to the clergy. The usage seems to be Anglo-Irish rather than Gaelic, for the Gaelic form is a vocative, as in Banim's poem, correctly,

> Who in the winter's night, Soggarth Aroon,
> When the cold blast did bite, Soggarth Aroon,
> Came to my cabin door, and on my earthen floor

Knelt by me sick and poor, Soggarth Aroon?
                    (cited in *Directory*, 1837, p. 83).

The romantic image is clearly seen in Montalembert's *Sketches of Ireland.*

> You behold him there, with a virginal purity in his coun-
> tenance, and an unfailing tenderness in his heart, running
> from cabin to cabin, with consolation and remedies —
> passing his days in the confessional or at the parish school
> — taking long and painful journeys, and overcoming the
> most difficult obstacles. Again, you may see him in his
> white robe before the altar. . . . (cited in *Directory*, 1837).

O'Connell referred to a bishop as 'one who is of such austere
and ascetic piety, a man who is so much absorbed by the
other world' (*Tralee Mercury*, 7 February 1835). A commonplace in political speeches in the nineteenth century was the
remark that the priest was so engrossed in his sacred duties
that only the most pressing necessity could tear him away
from them into politics.

The vocabulary for referring to or describing priests was
stereotyped. The most usual epithets applied to them were
'venerable', 'respected', 'excellent', 'worthy'. They were
'zealous and active', possessed 'untiring zeal' and 'fervid
burning eloquence'; 'zealous exertions', 'zealous and learned',
'worthy and zealous' were used to describe them. If zeal was
the foremost accolade, piety was the second. 'Prelate of great
piety', 'accomplished and pious superioress', 'austere and
ascetic piety', 'the zeal, piety, and disinterestedness of the
clergy', 'pious but inactive prelate' are phrases which occur.
This ecclesiastical jargon does not occur in Carleton and its
origin is obscure. However its very existence should be noted.
It covered all forms of ecclesiastical activity and is found
typically in provincial newspapers reporting church events.
As it was a stereotyped jargon persisting over a century and
a half, it need not be interpreted literally.

There was another image of the priest, however, that of
the avaricious performer of sacred rites. This image was
rare in the nineteenth century but echoes of it occur in

complaints about priests cited above. 'Hold your tongue, stubborn priest, read your Litany and Confiteor, earn your half-crown and begone: I will keep my brother' (*116*, 181). The editor of Canon O'Leary's *Life* quotes a Gaelic verse associating the priest with demands for money for various spiritual services.

> One from the living, two from the dead,
> A pound marrying and a crown baptizing,
> Horses without coaches on long roads,
> Gave many a priest a life without ease.
>
> (*394*, 94, editor's translation)

This type of comment is, however, extremely rare in the nineteenth-century literature and may be nothing but a literary convention as mentioned above.

Rise in Social Status of Clergy

Over the same period the position of the priest in society changed significantly. From occupying a humble social position he began to move upwards in the social scale, and eventually, by the mid-nineteenth century, reached a level not far removed from that of the petty gentry, among whom he generally found acceptance (*340*, 103).

With regard to *relative increase in income*, there is some slight evidence (which I shall indicate later) which seems to show that the income of the clergy, though rising in the nineteenth century, was falling relative to other groups. With regard to *social* acceptance, it is doubtful that the priests trained on the continent in the eighteenth century were less acceptable to the gentry than the Maynooth-trained priests of the nineteenth century. The reverse in fact would seem to be the more correct.

If there was any change in status it probably came about through a more severe selection of candidates, those who were obviously 'peasants' being excluded, and also on a more rigorous enforcement of the regulations concerning clerical studies, so that the more ignorant 'hedge priests' tended to disappear.

On the change in social manners, the following can be quoted.

The rollicking, reckless, fighting, foxhunting squire or squireen, the half-pay captain of Dragoons, professional duellist, gambler, and scamp; the punch imbibing and humorous story-telling priest . . . how unreal and unrepresentative all these characters seem now. . . . We can scarcely imagine . . . a parish priest chanting 'An Cruiscín Lán', the love of my heart is my little jug, an cruiscín lán (full of whiskey of course) (*345*, 6).

More investigation would be needed to conclude that there was upward social mobility of the clergy.

The Work of the Clergy

In the year 1800 the Irish Secretary, Lord Castlereagh, established that there were 1,026 parishes and 1,824 priests. Of these priests, 400 were regulars, and of these 150 were in stable diocesan employment as either parish priests or curates. Of the rest, 187 were residing in monasteries while more than sixty were not attached to monasteries. There were between 500 and 600 curates of the secular clergy, the figure varying according to one's judgment as to exactly how many friars actually did parochial work. There were in fact fifty-three friaries scattered throughout rural Ireland. Their numbers fell to 200 about 1825 and they began to concentrate in towns.

Castlereagh attributed the shortage of curates to the destruction of the continental colleges. By 1837 the number of curates listed in the *Directory* was 1,184, and by 1869 this had increased to 1,446. Therefore in 1800 about 60 per cent of the parishes had a curate, by 1837 there were more curates than parishes, and by 1869 there was a further extra curate for nearly one parish in three. Between 1800 and 1869 the number of priests in the parishes thus rose from about 1,600 to about 2,400 or a rise of 50 per cent. Statistically, of course, 1800 is a bad base line because of the known but temporary shortage of priests. I have felt it advisable to separate the figures for curates from those of the parish priests, for this shows that all the parishes in Ireland were continually manned, so that a minimum of service was maintained throughout the country. The main problem would of course lie with sick or aged parish priests, for whom a curate, temporary or permanent, was essential. The increase in the number of curates was offset somewhat in rural areas by the movement of the friaries to the towns. Pastorally speaking, the number of priests in parishes is more important than the total number of priests.

It is worth noting that nearly all the priests in Ireland were available for parish work and were actually doing it. Ratios of clergy to people are meaningless until one establishes the nature of the structures within which they have to work and whether the clergy are available for certain kinds of work. What value was a ratio of one priest to 900 people in Naples if most of the priests were unobtainable for the parochial ministry? Or again, was it really efficient to have parishes in France with no more than sixty families?

An elderly or infirm priest in a large or mountainous parish might be sorely stretched on Sunday mornings or on the eves of feasts to which a special indulgence was attached, but generally there does not seem to have been too much work to do in any Irish rural parish for the rest of the time. (This point should be kept in mind when considering, for example, the activities of priests in politics: it does not follow that they were neglecting their spiritual duties.)

In 1831 there were 37,522 marriages in Ireland and this would work out at over thirty weddings per parish per year. A death rate of 16.8 per 1,000 would involve about forty sick calls, as the clergy did not make repeat visits except in cases of relapse. A birth rate of 33 per 1,000 might mean as many as ninety baptisms per priest per annum. A busy priest might therefore have possibly a baptism, a wedding, a sick call and a funeral each week, though it is not clear if the priest attended all or even most of these (*104*; see also Appendix B).

Confessions are another matter. We can make some estimate of the total number of confessions. In a population of eight million, we can reasonably assume that one-quarter of them were Protestants and another quarter under the canonical age required by canon law. This leaves about four million. As the men approached the sacrament of confession twice a year, this would work out at about eighty confessions a week per priest. We have no idea however how long was taken over each individual confession but the rough calculation seems to indicate that the burden on the clergy was not excessive. If the priest Carleton mentions was typical, the ceremony was quite perfunctory: '. . . he never axes questions; but whatever you like to tell him he hears you and forgives you at wanst.' This would in itself cause no difficulty but for the fact that confessions tended to come together at Christmas and Easter, or when there was an indulgence. In this latter case the clergy from the neighbouring parishes had to be called in to assist. Even at that, not all the people could be heard. Presumably the clergy on such occasions sharply reduced the amount of counselling, and indeed not all priests questioned overmuch. The Rev. Michael Collins also made the point that not all who applied for confession could be heard, doubtless for the above reasons.

This indicates only the bare minimum that a priest had to do. How much any priest actually did is another question. How long did he spend preparing a sermon? It is difficult to estimate how many hours on Sunday he felt it necessary to tramp round the parish looking for dances, or how much time he spent in seeking out errant members of the flock.

One piece of evidence shows that the burden on the priest decreased considerably in one respect. By 1880, it was the rule that religious instruction was given by the teachers in the schools and not by the clergy themselves. Statistical information about the greater relative frequency of religious services is difficult to come by. Godkin cites an Irish peer to the effect that 'The chapels are everywhere better attended on holidays, and the lower orders, at all events, are far more strict in their confessions, fasts, and other religious observances, than they used to be.' This does not tell us if the services were celebrated more often. Godkin also states that the reformation of morals by the Catholic priests had been almost completely successful by 1865, at least in rural areas.

The gatherings and the merrymakings which led to drunkenness and immorality were discouraged. The idleness, parent of vice, in which the holidays of the Church used to be passed has been changed into close attendance at chapel, and from this change visible advance in the orderly and decorous habits of the people has resulted.

6
Policy Making and Social Control

Social Policy Making

Examination of the initiation of major trends in the Catholic Church in Ireland in the nineteenth century could lead one to the conclusion that all or nearly all major changes in policy (excluding exclusively clerical affairs) were initiated by the laity or junior clergy. Let us look at some of the evidence. Voluntary Catholic charities were a feature of the period. Among the earliest instances we find a few lay people in Dublin starting a charity. Catholic education of girls was first championed by a laywoman, Teresa Mulally. Catholic education of boys is associated with the Waterford gentleman, Edmund Ignatius Rice. The Sisters of Charity seem to owe their origin to the zealous co-adjutor bishop of Dublin, Dr Murray, but the Sisters of Mercy were started on her own initiative by Catherine McAuley. The great temperance movement was begun by an ordinary friar from Cork. The political involvement of the clergy may be said to date from the storm of opposition to the Veto in 1808, and here the clergy of the second order and the laity opposed the policy of the bishops. The friars in Clarendon Street, Dublin appear among the earliest supporters of O'Connell's Emancipation campaign. A national Catholic book society was originated by a Catholic layman, even if he had to get the assistance of the hierarchy.

One of the major new trends in the nineteenth century was the building of large, expensive and ornamental churches, the prototype of which was the metropolitan church in Dublin. But when the project was first mooted in a practical manner in 1800, many people, including many of the laity, seemed to have been involved in the decision.

Many devotional practices seem to have originated through the efforts of individual priests or nuns. Dr Blake, parish priest of St Michael and John's, and afterwards bishop of Dromore, seems to have been the first to set up a bell to call the people to mass, and to sound the Angelus. The 'Holy Hour' is recorded in George's Hill Convent in 1809, apparently one of the first instances in Ireland. Devotion to the First Fridays was preached by Fr Henry Young, who apparently learned the devotion from the Vincentians in Rome. A group of Dublin priests formed themselves into the Irish Vincentians and organised both foreign and parochial missions (*443*).

Other initiatives in policy-making came apparently from bishops, the reform of the life style of the clergy being an example (see Chapter 9). Law-making conventions such as synods tended to be rare; national synods, even at their most frequent, did not meet more often than every twenty-five years. Synods, and more importantly bishops, had a more important *negative* role in policy making. No public policy could be initiated without the consent of the bishop, so that the office of bishop was a crucial one in preventing policy changes or developments. A national synod was a clumsy method for governing the Church in Ireland in a manner binding on all, and Dr Cullen tried to get another system introduced by means of which the decision of a majority of the bishops in conference would bind all (*73*, 150ff.).

Cannon notes — and this is an important point — that the Irish Church failed to adopt, as the American Church adopted at the Second Plenary Synod of Baltimore in 1866, any form of parliamentary rules for deliberation. In fact Cullen's rules for the holding of episcopal meetings were specifically designed to prevent free discussion, allowing only free expression of opinion once, when called on by the presiding prelate (*73; 326*). His role would then be crucial. Thus, as Miller observes, until the end of the century an independently-minded bishop could exercise a disproportionate influence over his colleagues.

This raises the question of the extent to which the Irish Church could be said to be democratic. The rulers of the Church were not of a different race, caste or class and so did

not rule as outsiders. There was a genuine election procedure for selecting bishops. There was *no democratic
choice* however for the most part in the process of
co-option to the clerical state. Anyone could offer himself
as a candidate for the priesthood, but could be arbitrarily
rejected. Thus there was no right of entry on the part of the
laity into the clergy. The laity too were excluded from
synods.

The structure of the Irish Church was autocratic. There
was little formal control over the actions of a bishop, even
on the part of priests. Promotion to parishes and dignities
was arbitrary.

> I ask you if the Court of Rome or any other Catholic
> country in the world was aware that in this country
> there is no law except the arbitrary will of an ignorant
> and perhaps corrupt bishop. . . . And yet such is the fact!
> No, but it is even worse, for the bishops in this country
> have formed themselves into a corporation whereby the
> clergy are even precluded from the benefit of an appeal,
> because it would not only be useless but even madness
> to prosecute an appeal at such a distance from the court
> of Rome, against such a phalanx (*572*, MacNally to Duffy,
> 12 November 1838).

Dr Keenan made the further point that the Roman 'agent'
was not an agent of the Irish clergy but only of the Irish
bishops. Later in the century Dr Walter MacDonald dwelt
on the point at length. It was true that an individual priest
had little chance against the united conference of the Irish
bishops, and such a priest got little support from his fellow
priests. As MacDonald admitted:

> . . . the great body of the clergy and laity were convinced
> that we were doing splendidly; and that if any reform was
> needed, it should take the direction of strengthening the
> hold of the bishops on the clergy and of both of these on
> the laity, especially in educational matters; while those
> who did not agree with this grumbled in private, but were
> afraid to take any public action (*353*, 225; *552*).

The conclusion is inescapable: if the Irish Church had an autocratic form of government, that was what the over-whelming body of clergy and laity wanted. Basically, one controlled the Church by controlling the election of bishops.

There is an interesting comment on this aspect of political control as practised by the Irish priests in Australia.

> The Irish clericalists who championed freedom and liberty against the Benedictine regime were not liberals, at least not in Church affairs. They rode the tide of liberal critic-ism in order to substitute for Benedictine authority another form of authoritarianism — their own. . . . Certainly the leaders of Irishism appealed to public opinion for support, but not in principle — for itself — but because public opinion was susceptible to appeals to Irish loyalty. They were on the move to destroy liberalism (*357*, 28).

If by liberalism was meant the freedom of the individual to dissent, perhaps the Irish were not in favour of it, at least in the second half of the century, but if it meant freedom of the tightly controlled *group* to take action with regard to other groups without constraint, then perhaps the Irish were liberal.

It was central to Cullen's policy that, firstly, individual bishops could not disagree with the majority of the bishops, and secondly that promotion to the order of bishops should be carefully controlled so that those liable to disagree should be excluded. There is no reason to believe that in this policy Cullen had not the support of the majority of clergy and laity in the Irish Church.

It would be a mistake to consider that these twin policies were peculiar to Cullen, except perhaps that he pursued them more single-mindedly and extensively than other bishops. What was special to Cullen was the fact that he was able to utilise in a manner not achieved before or since, a special relationship with the authorities in Propaganda. Yet once again, paradoxically, in an age of growing enthusiasm for papal affairs, this may have been a popular policy.

It would seem that the attempt of the bishops to gain and keep control of the Irish Church for the bench of bishops in fact reached its high point in the early years of the century, in the controversy over 'Domestic Nomination'. There are two points in this controversy, one that the Irish Church (not Rome) should have the right to elect bishops. This would automatically exclude the possibility of Rome conceding the right of Veto to the British government. The other point was the proposal to exclude all but bishops from the selection of bishops. This was settled in favour of the parish priests in 1829.

Throughout the century leadership was always more important than authority. The leaders were nearly always bishops with the rank and prestige of archbishops. Only Dr Doyle seems to have achieved national leadership with merely the rank of bishop. Archbishop Troy (Dublin), Primate Curtis (Armagh), Archbishop Murray (Dublin), Archbishop MacHale (Tuam), Archbishop Croke (Cashel) and Archbishop Walsh (Dublin) appear to have achieved national leadership, at least for a time. In other words they succeeded in giving direction to the Irish Church. Cardinal Cullen, through Rome, had some authority as well as leadership.

Dispute Solving

There were apparently no formal structures within the Irish Church for the settlement of disputes, either judicially or by arbitration. The strictures quoted from Dr MacNally, Dr Keenan and Dr MacDonald about the lack of institutions to control the bishops apply in this case as well. By 1904, when MacDonald was writing, some diocesan tribunals had been set up, but the position before that period was described thus by MacDonald:

> Now in Ireland, though priests were liable to be severely punished — of which no one could complain, and at which I should be the last, I think, to grumble — they had practically no protection against the abuse of power to which they were thus subjected.
>
> They could be deprived of a mission or parish without proof of guilt, and they had practically no appeal. For though the metropolitan could in theory hear their complaint he had practically no court in which to try it; nor

would an appellant have the ordinary means of presenting his case – an advocate, for instance, or witnesses.

He might of course get advice from some clerical friend, whose interference would be resented by the metropolitan and bishop alike, and, if witnesses refused to attend – as well they might, if their testimony was likely to be displeasing to the bishop from whose action the appeal was taken – there was no authority to compel them.

No wonder that appeals were almost unheard of; or that when they did occur metropolitans deemed them subversive of discipline, and gave them no attention. I remember hearing a certain archbishop tell me with pride how summarily he would deal with an appeal, which, it was said, was being made to him from the decision of one of his suffragans.

There are two points involved in this question: the absence of formal independent structures and processes by means of which a subject could with immunity engage in dispute with his superior, and the lack of support from his brother clergy. Early in the century, at least, there seems to have been no reluctance on the part of the clergy to dispute with the bishop, report him to Rome and get him deposed. At least two bishops were removed from office at this time, Dr Walsh of Waterford and Lismore, in 1821, and Dr O'Finan of Killala. Attempts to control Dr Murphy of Clogher failed, but he was reprimanded by Propaganda. Dr MacDonald was championing a minority movement within the Church, and one which had little to do with either religion or politics, for it was occasioned by the intemperate language used against the hierarchy by Dr Hickey of Maynooth in his attempts to get compulsory Irish established. We can note here in passing that though several priests, including Dr Hickey, were passionately involved in the language movement, it was essentially a secular affair. Individual bishops however might require some priests to learn Irish for pastoral reasons (*394*). Looking back one might conclude that Hickey was ill advised.

The lack of the proper legal tribunals and formal process of law was the major complaint. That the other judicial processes, apart from setting up a formal tribunal, were neglected was not alleged. A charge was made to the bishop, who investigated the matter, interrogated the witness etc., informally. There was always the possibility of appeal to the metropolitan, who might indeed be friendly and sympathetic. In a dispute, various other bishops might intervene to try to bring about an amicable settlement. In the O'Finan case the metropolitan was accused of excessive interference (Diocesan Archives, *passim*).

As the bishop was the arbiter for disputes within the diocese, a crucial question arose when there was a dispute between the bishop and one of the members of his diocese. If the case was lost before the bishop, one appealed to the metropolitan and to Rome. This latter was difficult and expensive. There was always the problem of language, it being virtually impossible to conduct a case effectively without knowing Latin *and* Italian. But the chief difficulty was likely to be raising cash. In 1814 a priest in Clogher raised £300 in mortgages to fight his case in Rome and he borrowed another £100 (*577*).

Disputes between the seculars and regulars had to be referred to Rome, because the rights and privileges of the regulars were approved by Rome (*175*, II, 150).

Social Control

By social control is meant not merely how the bishops controlled their priests, but how the priests controlled the bishops, how the clergy controlled the laity, and the laity the clergy.

A bishop could hold out the hope of reward in the shape of a parish, or a better parish, or of some honour or dignity. The ultimate hope of a priest was to become a bishop some day. Rebukes, temporary suspension from office, or permanent removal which could involve the loss of livelihood could also be used.

The priest might simply comply, or he might feel secure enough and satisfied enough to ignore the bishop. The office of parish priest, in canon law, was permanent, so the incumbent was relatively independent.

It is all my own fault. I was too free with my tongue. I said in a moment of bitterness: 'What can a bishop do with a parish priest? He's independent of him.' It was not grammatical, and it was not respectful. But the bad grammar and the impertinence were carried to his lordship, and he answered, 'What can I *do*? I can send him a curate who will break his heart in six weeks' (*463*, 1).

The parish priest and the bishop equally had a point. If the parish priest refused to obey, or to comply with the suspension, the bishop could not force or have recourse to the secular courts. In 1870, Fr Robert O'Keeffe adopted a strong line on this point (*517*). On the other hand the parish priest, if supported by his relatives or his faction, could nail up the door of the church and allow no other appointee of the bishop to minister. At least once a bishop himself took the step of nailing shut the door of a church built by friars.

A parish priest could take action against the bishop in the secular courts, as indeed could the bishops. The bishops appeared normally as defendants. A Dublin priest complained to Propaganda that he had been suspended by the archbishop (Murray) without cause or investigation, was now destitute and subsisting on charity, and was being pressurised by his relatives to assert his rights in the courts. Dr Doyle recommended extreme prudence to the Augustinian Provincial lest one of the friars who held the community property in his own name might be tempted to apply to Rome, or to take advantage of the law of the land. This refers to rights in civil law only. A cleric could not take a bishop to court in canon law, though a layman could take a priest to court (exposition of Dr W. Walsh in O'Keeffe case, *Moto proprio* of 1911; *517*).

A priest could normally go to another diocese. Dr Murphy of Clogher attempted to discipline a clerical student by refusing him further holy orders, and at the same time refusing him an *exeat* from the diocese. This apparently was regarded as excessively harsh, for the primate secured the student access to an American diocese.

Despite MacDonald's remarks there is no reason to believe that Propaganda did not give serious consideration to every case which reached it and in fact we know it took steps to discipline bishops or to remove them from office. And even a venerable archbishop like Dr Murray could receive a severe letter from Propaganda, as in 1851, if the Sacred Congregation felt that its decisions were not receiving the attention they deserved. The regular clergy were much better placed to fight the bishop in Rome both because they normally had revenues on the continent and had fluent Italian speakers in their ranks to argue the case.

A strong-minded priest could make life difficult for a bishop, and vice-versa. Real trouble started when two determined men faced each other, as seems to have happened in the Murphy versus Maginn controversy, in the Keenan-Blake controversy and in the O'Keeffe-Cullen dispute (*577; 522; 374*).

In such cases the length and complexity of the subsequent dispute had no necessary connection with the original cause, and no proportion to it: it just became a matter of principle for both parties. In Dr Maginn's case the original dispute seems to have arisen over an objection made, reasonably enough, to what seemed an excessive prohibition of the use of alcohol. In Dr Keenan's case, the parish priest was apparently guilty of some imprudence and an error of judgment in not immediately answering a sick call. O'Keeffe's case was that some curates called him a liar, and nowhere could he get redress. The *determination* of particular individuals to seek redress led to appeals to Rome, so their statistical frequency cannot be used as a measure of the morals of the Irish Church. A priest could also seek the support of the public, by writing to the newspapers for example.

In the early part of the century, some priests at least wanted the diocesan chapters restored to counter episcopal influence, but many of the bishops opposed this. In Clogher the bishop was accused of letting the chapter die out. Some of his priests reminded him that '. . . it is the natural council of the bishop – it represents the entire body of the clergy of the diocese, and is, of course, the guardian of the rights and privileges.' The bishop however believed that the chapter was at the root of all the disputes in the diocese for the previous forty years and apparently would do nothing without consulting the other bishops. Dr Doyle was scathing in his attacks on chapters and the abuses they caused. In that same year, 1829, the bishops pointedly omitted the chapters from those to be convoked to elect a bishop, and Rome inserted their right in the final draft. A neutral opinion was expressed by Dr McNally who did not think much of the bishop but did not approve of the chapter either (572).

The ultimate sanction a bishop could use was removal from office. This was done only for grave and notorious crimes.

> Among the causes for which a priest can be removed from his parish are these: if he be unable to discharge the duties of his state, if he becomes infamous, or if he became odious to the people.
>
> If a priest commit violence upon one of his parishioners, or if he get intoxicated publicly, a complaint is lodged with the bishop . . . (170, 390).

The reference to becoming 'odious to the people' is curious for it does not apparently involve a canonical fault, or any grounds in canon law for removal. However useful from a pastoral point of view it might be to remove a clergyman who was patently doing no good, it is hard to see what grounds in canon law the bishop could have for acting.

Any conclusion about the frequency of overt clerical disputes can only be impressionistic, at least in this study. It does seem however that overt or public disputes decreased as the century advanced.

The next point to consider is that of the control of the clergy over the laity and the laity over the clergy. Was it a case (as Trevelyan, speaking of the Scottish clergy in the eighteenth century, puts it) of a 'people-ridden clergy' or a 'clergy-ridden people'? With regard to the control of the clergy over the laity, the first line of control was that over the belief system. In theory, no works by heretics might be read, and only approved books, catechisms, sermons etc. might be printed and disseminated among the Catholics. Attendance, likewise, at sermons by the biblical preachers could be made a reserved sin. However in the towns at least, these were easily avoided. Cunningham notes that the Church legislation on censorship and the prohibition of books was not formally enforced till 1897. It became a notable feature of the Irish Church. *Imprimaturs* existed all through the century.

The teaching of Christian doctrine, preaching and rebuking publicly or in private could also be used as means of exercising moral influence. The obligation to go to confession once a year meant that everyone was expected to give an account of his deeds to a priest at least once in the year. People could be made to stand during mass, admission to the sacraments could be deferred, or in certain cases the bishop could reserve the granting of absolution to himself. In cases of theft, the thief was obliged to make restitution. If a man joined a secret society, absolution could be refused. A man was held responsible for the acts of his fellow conspirators, with consequent obligation to make restitution for any acts of injustice in full, if he participated in the unjust act in any of the following ways: *jussio, consilium, consensus, palpo, recursus, mutus, non obstans, non manifestans* (by giving command, advice, consent, by flattery, accepting an appeal, remaining silent, not preventing the injury, or giving warning in time). Restitution was of course confined to the possible. In extreme cases the bishop could excommunicate. Forbes at mid century noted that the authority accorded to the clergy in the fields of religion and morality was quite extraordinary.

There were also informal social controls, exercised by the 'clergy and the better class of both communions'. Ordinary parishioners could enforce the religious obligations rather more forcefully, however. As Carleton recounts, some delinquents were nearly chastised for planting cabbage on a Sunday. But it is difficult, if not impossible, to find any set of attitudes or values in which the clergy differed notably from the laity, either in the religious or in the secular sphere.

The laity had their own means of resistance and control. If they wanted to join a secret society they avoided approaching the sacraments. And though there might be a censure or excommunication for not coming to the sacraments, the effectiveness, as the Rev. Collins testified, depended on 'the influence of public opinion, and when they are more under the influence of their bad feelings, they set at naught our menaces'.

More direct pressure could be put on the clergy. As Thomas Wyse said with regard to the participation of priests in the agitation for Emancipation, they had to choose between going along with the crowd or being ignored. There was always the possibility that the friars might take the popular side if the secular clergy did not, and this possibility could not be ignored. The clergy were directly supported financially by the laity, and while there is no need to assume that the priests were so venal as to refuse to insist on the moral law if their livelihood was threatened, yet in neutral matters it did not behove the priest to antagonise his parishioners unnecessarily. State provision for the clergy would weaken this source of lay power, so it is not surprising to find it constantly resisted (in 1848, *549*; in 1869, *374*).

Not only could the laity stop the priest's revenue, they could burn his corn and threaten his life. A letter threatening to murder a priest is in the Clogher archives. In Limerick a zealous young priest was actually murdered. In another case a band of robbers entered the priest's house and demanded that he hand over the Christmas dues. He refused, so they roasted him over his fire to make him talk, but he refused nonetheless (*170; 35; 268*).

Anticlericalism of the continental type was almost non-existent. It was organised briefly by the Fenian leaders but quickly disappeared. On intimidation of clergy and people during the land war and boycott, see Sheehan (*465*).

It goes without saying that whenever the bishops, the clergy and the laity were unanimous on a point, their combined influence would be immense. McCarthy however seems to exaggerate this influence (*349*). For the most part the absence of national unified structures of social policy making and social control prevented the adoption of unified policy. Rome had no policy as such to impose, and Cardinal Cullen failed in his attempt to establish a central directorate. When the clergy was united, it was for reasons of belief and sentiment.

7
Parish Life

Official Religious Practice

Everyone belonged to a parish and was subject to a parish priest for the ordinary functions of the ministry, and belonged to a diocese and was under the general supervision and control of the bishop. Formal religious observance was based on the parish, even if it contained more than one church. As set out in the catechism, there were certain matters to be believed, certain moral acts to be performed, certain rites and prayers to be attended to. So religious instruction had to be given, religious rites performed and moral support provided to maintain the exercises of prayer and moral rectitude. Predictably, the belief and organisation systems were standardised, as was religious practice.

We will deal first with the effectiveness of religious instruction. Carleton speaks of the 'strong but vague undirected sense of devotional feeling and reverence' of the Irish peasantry. Also, at the very beginning of the century formal institutions for catechetical instruction were only being developed: the Confraternities of Christian Doctrine were beginning to spread, the clergy were beginning to take an interest in the schools which were run by lay masters for personal gain. Thirdly, the bishops regarded the people as being rather ignorant of their faith, and made improvement in catechetical instruction one of their main objectives in the 1820s.

With regard to the hedge schools it does not seem that the catechism was always necessarily taught in them. Fr Egan, in his history of the parish of Ballinasloe, stated that religion was taught in them. Kennedy notes one school at least where catechism was taught to both Catholics and Protestants,

the Catholics from *Devereux's Manual*, while a Protestant
boy *heard* the whole of the short *Church Catechism*.

Carleton is emphatic that the hedge schoolmasters, whatever their other qualifications (and they were considerable)
were not instructors in morals. 'Schoolmasters were a class
of men from whom morality was not expected by the
peasantry' — immorality in the Irish context meant drunkenness. Dr Doyle too had a very low opinion of the hedge
schools: 'their masters are in many instances extremely
ignorant, their schoolhouses are mere huts'.

Not all the evidence is equally black. A report on the
schools in Wicklow parish shows that they were privately
run for profit, yet the teachers were regarded as sober and
upright, and some religious instruction was given. Yet in
1824, 7,600 out of about 8,000 schools run by Catholics
were under lay management. And as Thomas Wyse notes,
it was not until the threat of proselytism became serious
that the Catholic clergy took a serious interest in education
(*582; 21*, 48; *545*, I, 236).

There is plenty of evidence on the other hand to show
that the people were reasonably well instructed in their
religion. In 1804, Dr Murphy reported to Rome that the
people in his diocese had made outstanding progress in a
few years in the study of Christine doctrine. Dr Doyle, on
a visitation, challenged a curate who presented a large
number of people for confirmation, saying that they could
not be properly instructed. The curate replied that they were,
and so it proved. Carleton too gives an example of a man
being interrogated by the parish priest in his knowledge of
the catechism, and from the example we can see that the
man had a reasonably accurate knowledge of Catholic belief.

In Carleton's *Traits and Stories*, many points of Catholic
belief are referred to as common knowledge. There are
references to God, to Christ, to the Virgin, the Twelve
Apostles, the saints, St Michael the Archangel and the other
angels. The people knew of the devil, hell, afterlife, purgatory,
heaven, salvation and damnation. They knew of the Church,
no salvation outside the Church, that hell was supposed to
be under the earth, the real authority of the *Catholic* clergy
and of the pope, the power of holy orders, the sacraments,

penance, eucharist and the last anointing. They knew of prayer, fasting and almsgiving, they prayed for the living and the dead, they invoked the intercession of the Blessed Virgin. They believed in the efficacy of holy water and the scapular. They knew the Ten Commandments and the Precepts of the Church. There is no reason to regard Carleton as unreliable on this point (*217*). (It may not be superfluous to add that we would not expect an entire population to be equally well instructed. We would expect a normal distribution or bell curve if statistically examined. Individual cases of great learning or great ignorance would be included in the normal distribution.)

Whitty, referring to North Connaught in 1824, remarks that the biblicals did not find the Catholic peasantry an ignorant benighted people just awaiting the message of the gospel. The evangelicals 'found the Catholics sturdy defenders of their faith, and those who suppose they are deficient in theological knowledge should converse with them to be convinced how erroneous that opinion is' (*531*). Furthermore, when faced with the biblical preachers, and finding they could not get sufficient instruction from the parish priest, they began to read books. 'The *Catholic Christian Instructor* was now read by all; De Feller's *Philosophical Catechism* translated into English, was in every man's hand in the village.' Later in the century a bishop mentions that less than twenty children out of 2,400 failed their examination before confirmation (*270*).

Where, and by whom, was religious instruction given? Bishop Murphy in 1804 reported that the peoples' progress in the catechism was due to the zeal of the parish priests who held Sunday schools in the chapels on Sunday mornings and Sunday afternoons, and also to the assistance of well-disposed lay people. Dr Plunkett of Meath made it clear to his priests that it was their duty to teach the catechism personally, even though they might allow a clerk or schoolmaster, who could sometimes be the same person, to teach some of it.

Kennedy mentions a definite catechism hour in his school during which both Catholic and Protestant catechisms were taught to their respective adherents. While one cannot state as a general rule that catechism was taught in all the pay-schools, it was an age in which lay persons took their religion seriously and regarded moral or religious instruction as a normal part of schooling (*254*).

Bibles and religious works were used as texts in schools but were supplied by the parents. Griffin remarks that the parents, often themselves illiterate, bought the books from a pedlar, satisfied to know that it was a 'reading book, and complete from cover to cover'. Croker remarks that many of the schoolmasters in the south and west were endowed with republican principles and were involved in acts of terrorism.

Private religious reading was also done, but rarely from the Bible. Religious books were available to those who could read (or be read to) and who could afford them. P. Kennedy recounts the habit of reading aloud in the chapel from a religious book before mass.

Preaching was part of the function of the parish priest, and sermons were of considerable length. Whitty mentions an hour as being the duration of the Sunday sermon. Dr Murray thought thirty-five minutes adequate during a high mass as the service was already very long. Gallagher's sermons, if preached, would take from seventy-five to ninety minutes.

How often did the clergy preach? A basic difficulty in deciding this point is to know what exactly counted as a sermon. The omission of an hour-long sermon does not imply that briefer homiletic remarks were also omitted. In fact we know that some priests did give short practical addresses to their parishioners. This semi-conversational instruction disappeared by mid century. Carleton mentions a man who only attended mass whenever a sermon was to be preached, so clearly a full sermon was not preached every Sunday. In his early visitations (c. 1780) Dr Plunkett of Meath stressed the need for the pastor personally to give at least a short instruction every Sunday, which would seem to imply that at that period either the pastor personally did not give instruction or the instruction was omitted altogether. The examples given by Carleton and Lover indicate that there was a very familiar relationship between the priest and the people, the priest even making personal remarks, and the person addressed being permitted to reply. It was possible, and indeed very likely, that instruction and rebuke was given in this form. When Dixon reported that in many parishes of Ardagh the word of God was not preached regularly, he may be referring to formal hour-long sermons. In 1890, rebutting charges that the clergy in Drogheda did not preach, it was stated that they preached every Sunday and feastday, while the friars gave mid-week instructions.

Finally there was religious instruction imparted in the home. F. C. Hoey reports that Carleton's parents did not instruct him very well in religion but Carleton knew the catechism at least (*383*). Dr Doyle was instructed by his mother, as was Fr Tom Burke, assisted in his learning by his mother's strong right arm! Kennedy recalls that they spent Sunday mornings, when young, copying engravings from prayerbooks.

This parental instruction was sometimes limited. In a visitation in 1811, Dr Plunkett commented on the fact that some parents corrected their children with curses and imprecations. Carleton mentions a case. '"God forgive you, Denis", the wife would reply, "it's long before you would think of larning him his prayers, or his catechism, or anything that is good."' Or according to the Banims, '. . . as it is suspected, he had never burthened his mind with more than any one prayer than by mere force his mother compelled him to learn in infancy.'

Thus examples indicate that the amount of instruction given in the home could vary. Carelton's verdict of a 'strong but vague undirected sense of devotional feeling and reverence' may not have been too far wrong. In fact improvement in the quality of catechetical instruction was a great aim in the early nineteenth century. But on the essentials of Catholicism, and the differences from Protestantism, instruction seems to have been universally effective.

The next point to be considered is religious or devotional practice or observance. The exposition here follows the order usually found in the catechisms.

It would seem that baptism was universally received. Direct evidence that baptism was administered in all cases is hard to come by but indirect evidence points in that direction. Whether baptised into the Catholic or Protestant Church, it would seem that all children of Catholic parents received the sacrament. Failure to baptise was never an issue. During a visitation in 1780, Dr Plunkett pointed out that it was the duty of pastors to ensure that midwives were capable of administering the sacrament of baptism.

With regard to extreme unction, it is well attested that the Irish Catholics made a special point of getting the priest before dying. The clergy were under the strictest obligation to attend the dying at whatever hour of the day or night they were called on. The bishops made a special point of investigating complaints on this score. The Catholic priest called but once in order to administer the last sacraments to the sick person. These were not repeated, nor did the priest apparently make a pastoral visitation of the sick, but if the sick person partially recovered and had a relapse, then they were repeated. Forbes mentions a belief of the common people that if the person remained in bed there could be no fresh commission of sin and so no need for fresh absolution.

No great emphasis appears to have been placed on marriage as a sacrament conferring spiritual grace, even though it seems to have been celebrated always in front of a priest. Marriages were celebrated freely in front of couple beggars, validly ordained priests who were no longer employed in the official ministry. In those areas where the decree *Tametsi* was published, such marriages would have been invalid and would have had to be properly celebrated again. But I have come across no reference to this validation of invalid marriages. It is possible that the exception clause provided in the decree, namely 'the common and continued impossibility of getting a priest', was applied instead. In the province of Dublin as late as 1770 it was felt that it was still impossible to apply the full laws of Trent. There is no reference to anyone from the other provinces going to Dublin province where the decree *Tametsi* was not in force, but they did go to Dublin to find couple beggars. In fact, at least in the earliest years of the century, a fairly easygoing attitude was apparently taken by clergy and laity alike.

The marriage rite was very informal. In Kennedy's account,

there were no banns, no confession, no communion, no mass, if the priest was satisfied that the couple had been to the sacraments recently, and there was no search for hidden impediments. The priest put on his stole, lighted the candles and proceeded with the ceremony. The couple beggar merely satisfied himself that the people involved could pay, and Kennedy notes that the legitimate priest also refused to give credit for performing the ceremony. There was no Marriage Act, nor any restriction legally on the whereabouts of marriages. In writing to Dr Hamilton in 1844, Dr Murray expressed a wish to see a wedding ceremony carried out before the altar, as was done lately in Leamington, and described in *The Tablet*. Marriages, with the proper dispensation, were frequent between second cousins and, on occasion, occurred between first cousins (*254; 293; 367*).

Mixed marriages were a somewhat different problem and seem to have been dealt with very severely by Dr Blake of Dromore at least. The bishop had no faculties to dispense when the marriage was already contracted before a Protestant clergyman (*Contractum inter haereticos*) (*367*). The parish priest refused to allow them to attend mass or to go to the bishop to have the censure removed. Ordinary mixed marriages seemed to have presented few problems. Archbishop Murray personally performed the Catholic ceremony in the viceregal lodge for the lord lieutenant, the Marquis Wellesley, when he married a Catholic. Cullen prohibited them altogether.

The priest strictly speaking had to take care that couples within the forbidden degrees did not marry. Bishops had special faculties allowing them to dispense from certain degrees. Dr Logan, writing to Dr Blake in Rome, stated that lack of authority to dispense in certain specified cases 'has been attended with considerable inconvenience', so this seems to have been fairly common. The bishop also forced parties to separate where ignorance or fraud were involved — ignorance or fraud, of course, nullify a contract and make a marriage invalid (*552; 553*).

With regard to confirmation, once again it is difficult to get exact figures. There is no reason to believe that every Catholic did not receive confirmation at some time in his life.

Deferral of confirmation for many years was not necessarily due to negligence. Berthe notes that in Naples in the early eighteenth century there was a habit of deferring confirmation until maturity or even old age. Some bishops may have postponed confirmations for several years, but all this meant was that the age of receiving confirmation would rise (*175*).

Holy orders were generally held in high esteem. A positive anticlerical spirit only existed among members of those illegal organisations whose activities were denounced by the clergy. With the exception of the disruption caused by an outbreak of fever in Clogher, it is reasonable to conclude that the shortage of priests early in the century can be linked directly with the loss of the Irish colleges on the continent. But there is also the possibility that principles of free thought and deism had the effect of turning young men away from a clerical life. There is some evidence that young men were losing their faith, even if not necessarily permanently. Carleton mentions that some priests dissuaded him from becoming a priest, but this may have been connected with the disturbed state of the diocese under Bishop Murphy (*25; 97; 207; 386*).

With regard to the sacrament of penance or going to confession, and eucharist, or the Lord's Supper, these seem to have gone in pairs. According to Carleton, men were expected to approach these sacraments twice a year, at Christmas and at Easter. Once a year was the ultimate canonical limit since the Fourth Council of the Lateran, 1215, below which one might not fall and still be accounted a member of the Church, but Carleton mentions one man who had not 'gone to his duty' for several years. In Meath, Dr Plunkett noted that 'a few continue obstinate and hardened these thirty years and approach not the sacraments ... the great bulk of the people approach the sacraments, but do not always shew the fruits of these means of salvation'. Edward Hay, writing to Propaganda after 1815, stated that travellers to the continent reported that the Irish attended the sacraments more frequently than was customary on the continent in Catholic countries at the time. (Hay to Litta, *Dublin Evening Post*, 1822). Very early in the century a Dublin priest, Fr Murray, afterwards archbishop, surprisingly for the period, allowed a penitent to go to daily communion (*14*).

Infrequency in approaching the sacraments was not necessarily a sign of lack of either religion or devotion. Communion but once a year was a sign of Jansenistic austerity. Kennedy refers to a priest who deferred absolution from week to week. Fitzpatrick refers to traces of a Jansenistic rigorism in Ireland. In a French diocese at the same time, the curé of Ars tried to get the men of his parish to go to communion four times a year (*503*).

The Rev. Michael Collins expressed himself satisfied with the attendance of his parishioners at the sacraments and on some occasions at least he was not able to hear all who presented themselves. Excessive numbers on feast days were reported from Meath in 1827. Attendance at the sacraments seems therefore to have been infrequent by later standards, but not below what was expected at the time. In periods of disturbance, attendance might fall off for a while but was usually speedily restored (*553; 170*).

With regard to attendance at mass on Sundays, it is very difficult to get any precise idea of how many attended, as no records were kept. Estimates in Ireland were vague. In the period before Emancipation, the *Evening Post* estimated that there was an attendance of 1,000 simultaneously at 1,500 chapels, which would give a total of 1.5 million people attending mass. However there could have been more than one mass in many of the chapels, while the *Directory* of 1837 lists over 2,000 chapels or mass places. The figure of 1,000 for average attendance is obviously a very rough and general one and perhaps rather suspiciously high, considering the small size of the chapels. But on the other hand the congregation could stand outside.

The *Directory* in 1837 estimates the mass attendance as being three million (out of a Catholic population of six to seven million). Granting a rapidly-growing population with a very large proportion of the population under the age of seven years — and so not obliged to attend mass — the proportion of those obliged to attend mass who did actually do so would be very high. The mass attendance was at a satisfactory level can be inferred indirectly from the fact that there was no concerted campaign to increase attendance at mass, nor does absence from mass appear as a subject of reproof in strictures during visitations or elsewhere. On the other hand, Wellington noted that Irish soldiers in the Peninsula did not bother to go to mass (*208*).

An attempt was made by David Miller to establish the figures for mass attendance more accurately from the figures collected by the Commissioners of Public Instruction in 1834. By his own admission there were limitations in the data. Round numbers were used, there were gaps, it was sometimes impossible to tell whether the figure given referred to several services combined or only to the principal service. He decides not to exclude those under the canonical age, a decision that is likely to make comparisons with subsequent periods invalid. Is one to count attendances as a proportion of the total Catholic population, or is one to exclude those excused by reason of youth, age, ill health, distance, nursing or minding invalids or young children, absence from home, being detained for reasons of occupation – for example minding a sick cow – or even due to lack of suitable attire? To get anything like a 100 per cent attendance, the principle of excluding those *not obliged* to attend must be followed.

Though clearly modern statistical standards cannot be applied, Miller computes as follows. In Gaelic-speaking districts, attendance rates were between 20 per cent and 40 per cent; in English-speaking rural districts attendance rates were between 30 per cent and 60 per cent, reaching even 72 per cent in parts of Wexford, while in certain towns it ranged apparently from 70 per cent to 100 per cent. But this 100 per cent of the Catholic population would mean every babe in arms, every invalid etc., i.e. more than 100 per cent of those obliged to attend. (Recourse to the original figures in the Sessional Papers does not throw any further light on the subject.) O'Leary incidentally noted the intense extrovert devotion of Gaelic speakers when receiving communion.

What other evidence is there to support Miller's conclusions that there was a wide regional variation in the numbers attending mass on Sundays, or that mass attendance was significantly lower in pre-Famine Ireland than afterwards, and that Ireland's well-known devotion did not come from a Gaelic milieu?

Firstly, attendance at mass does not seem ever to have been a target for reformers. Dr Plunkett of Meath leaves what seems to be a fairly comprehensive list of the titles of the sermons he preached around the parishes of his diocese during his long episcopate, but failure to *attend mass* on Sundays was not one of the abuses he had tried to root out. On the other hand there is testimony that attendance at mass was regarded as satisfactory. According to Dr Kelly, Catholics 'regularly resorted' to mass even from a distance of four or five miles (*170*). According to Lover, '... so strict is the attendance at public worship on the part of the Irish peasantry, that the man must be very far gone in crime who disregards it'. There are two possible explanations for both the absence of strictures and the positive testimony. One is that, numerically, attendance at Sunday mass was actually very high. The other is that attendance at Sunday mass was in fact numerically rather low by present day standards but was regarded as satisfactory at the time. Or to put it another way, the poor state of the chapels, the poor roads and perhaps chronic ill health in winter may have been regarded as providing a sufficiently *grave incommodum* (grave difficulty or inconvenience, especially in combination) to excuse from attendance, especially if one attended a 'station' during the week. Evidence is so far insufficient to decide exact percentages. (See Appendix A for problems of interpretation; this is unfortunately the only case where anything like statistical figures are available.)

This particular case illustrates the extreme difficulty in establishing *rates* of practice, or *indices* of observance or non-observance in the Catholic Church in Ireland in the nineteenth century. There is some evidence of a numerical variation of attendance at mass from region to region and from period to period, even though the evidence is not conclusive. Still, these variations do not necessarily indicate variations in religious zeal or observance because of the possibilities of varying interpretations of the law, and of actual conditions.

What has been said with regard to mass attendance applies equally to those other religious practices for which there was an obligation, to go to confession and communion at least once a year, to be confirmed etc. Besides the attendance at mass on Sunday, there was an extra-legal custom which afforded people an opportunity to hear mass and go as well to confession and communion. This was the custom of holding 'stations'. By a station was meant the practice of saying mass in the houses of various farmers on week days (75).

The mass itself was celebrated rapidly and in Latin, without choir or singing. Various observers commented on the devotion of those attending. They do not note any carelessness, talking or laughing, but on the contrary speak of rapt devotion. W. Griffin states that walking about or talking during a service would not have been tolerated. McCarthy, as usual, is a severe critic of the conduct of the clergy. The salutation of the host after the consecration, now re-introduced into the Roman rite, apparently survived at least in Gaelic-speaking congregations until 1900 (75; 254; 293; 207; 349; 290).

Direct evidence or even comment on how the minor religious obligations were observed are hard to come by. Servile work was apparently universally abstained from on the Sabbath. Carleton mentions the indignation of the people at certain breaches of this obligation. Kennedy's description of Sunday afternoon clearly implies that the young people were not working and had to find something to do. So haymaking or harvesting on the Sabbath, unlike in the parish of Ars, was not apparently the custom in Ireland. There was no clerical campaign against servile work on Sundays.

But there were other problems with regard to Sunday observance. Kennedy notes the habit of people congregating on the edge of a parish for unsupervised drinking and dancing. At mid century, a Protestant clergyman complained that in the diocese of Clogher there was much 'business' behind shutters and closed doors on the Sabbath, with much drunkenness and rioting. Dr Plunkett noted breaches of the Sabbath by unnecessary servile work, amusements, and dancing at improper hours. He often preached on the due observance of Sunday, but the above shows the kind of abuses he had in mind.

With regard to the observance of holy days, it would seem that abstention from manual labour was common. Cloncurry

objected to the number of holy days because they contributed to an increase in drunkenness, which implies that
the men were not working. Observance was uneven, however, so that tenants on one of his estates were working,
while those on another were not. Not merely the abuse
of drunkenness but also economic reasons persuaded the
Irish bishops to seek to have holidays reduced in number.
Writing to Propaganda, Doyle estimated the cash loss to
Catholics hired by non-Catholics was £150,000 sterling (*175;
170; 548*).

On the observance of Lenten fast and Friday abstinence we are once again reduced to inference from the fact
that violations were not denounced, nor an active campaign
to promote these observances staged. At the end of the
eighteenth century de Latocnaye noted that Lent was
strictly observed. Fitzpatrick notes that the Lenten regulations in Kildare and Leighlin were more severe under
Dr Doyle than they were later in the century, but Doyle
apparently had no difficulty in enforcing them. Some
instances of eating flesh meat on forbidden days were
noted by Dr Plunkett in 1810. The great relaxation of the
Lenten fast did not come till after independence.

With regard to other public religious exercises, Carleton
refers to the 'Sunday of the Purcession', doubtless the
Sunday nearest to the feast of Corpus Christi as it still is
today, but Dr Doyle was opposed to having religious processions in mixed areas. One of Doyle's predecessors, Dr
Delaney, introduced a procession of the Blessed Sacrament
and adoration into his diocese (*75; 170; 101*).

In the archdiocese of Dublin there were extra indulgences,
and these were extended to the rest of Ireland in 1832.
Indulgences were popular and of considerable pastoral
importance. Dr Logan, writing to Dr Blake, said that the
priests of the parish, even with the help of the neighbouring clergy, were unable to cope with all who came to confession with a view to gaining the indulgence.

Kohl comments on the general public character of the
Catholic Church in Ireland early in the century. There was
little external sign of Catholicism, no processions, no monks,
no clerical dress in the streets. Later in the century Canon

Sheehan noticed an unwillingness to manifest devotion, especially when Protestants were around. There were, however, some typically Catholic religious exercises in the churches. By 1820, Benediction of the Blessed Sacrament was given in all the parochial churches in Dublin once a month. Benediction, vespers, sermon and procession were given in winter, the procession presumably within the confines of the church. In at least three Dublin chapels belonging to the regulars there was public recitation of the rosary, and three others had public celebration of the Stations of the Cross. A writer in a Dublin paper mentions weekday services in the friars' churches in Drogheda also. Kennedy mentions a brief informal religious service for children to conclude their Sunday School. Lover mentions vespers in a country chapel but does not give any date. Without a study of eighteenth-century religious practice it is impossible to say if these elements were traditional or if they were part of the new crop of 'devotions' then being introduced into Dublin (see Ronan). It is unclear to what extent 'spiritual direction' in the interior life was practised. Archbishop Murray personally directed Mary Aikenhead and Teresa Ball, and Fr L'Estrange was O'Connell's director (*443*).

Morals of the Laity

The next major point to be investigated is the *moral conduct* of the laity. More precisely, was there an improvement, a revolution, in the morals of Irish Catholics in the nineteenth century? Carleton refers to the Irish as 'honest, thoughtless, jovial, swearing, drinking, fighting, murdering Hibernians'. This is doubtless what they were: some drinkers, some swearers, some even murderers, but these faults must be put into perspective, and indeed a reading of Carleton himself shows a quiet, ordered rural community.

Doyle's comments on his return from his first visitation of his diocese were in general favourable both to the clergy and the laity, though he did occasionally hear of public scandals. When Dr Murphy was reporting to Rome in 1804, he commented chiefly on their progress in learning Christian doctrine: he did not mention lack of morals. According to a pastoral letter of Dr Oliver Kelly in 1820:

Drunkeness, so incompatible with your temporal and eternal welfare, is not now so prevalent amongst you. Morning and evening prayer, that most essential duty of Christian piety, is universally enforced and very generally observed. The Sabbath is no longer profaned by servile work, or by vain, unprofitable, or criminal amusements. Perjury, into which the ignorant in many districts have been too successfully seduced by the machinations of wicked and interested men is now, and I trust forever, at an end (*Leinster Journal*, 12 January 1820).

Perjury was still being deplored in 1825 by the Rev. Michael Collins. (It was still regarded as prevalent in lawsuits even in this century.) Slightly earlier, in 1780, Dr Patrick Plunkett of Meath, in his report to Propaganda, speaks of the good morals of nearly all of his flock, except a few who adopted the loose morals of the heretics. The bishop of Elphin reported to Propaganda in 1826 that when he took possession of the see he found it in a disorderly state owing to the activities of the secret societies, but this matter was rectified. A similarly short-lived disturbance was reported by Oliver Kelly in Tuam but the moral conduct of the people he considered 'tolerably good'. Mentions of agrarian crime will be treated separately.

Dr George Plunkett reports on the condition of the town of Athlone when he first became bishop. The parish priest, a timid man lacking the capacity for the job, never officiated in the parish church.

Hundreds of persons had not been to confession for twenty years. Hundreds of couples had been married who had not made their first communion. The flock was ignorant of what was necessary to be known *necessitate medii*; attendance at mass on Sundays, not to talk of festivals, was disregarded, and innumerable couples had lived as man and wife who had never been married, and many others in flagrant and notorious adultery (*264*).

Most of these complaints are not about morals but about the non-observance of the Church's laws, with one exception. The non-observance of Church laws is perhaps not surprising in view of the apparently total neglect by the parish priest of his duties at a time when anarchy and 'French principles' were widespread in the diocese. But the charge of adultery is surprising. Mason, in his parochial survey, notes the numbers of common prostitutes in Athlone, the amount of mendicity, the presence of widows and soldiers' wives and the fact that Athlone was a garrison town. This latter fact may account for much of the immorality in Athlone. Crime statistics are not really any help as they do not make the distinctions necessary. Crimes connected with agrarian and related violence should be kept separate for these require special treatment. But the published figures do not distinguish between them.

Illegitimacy figures were very low in Ireland. Fitzpatrick, citing the alleged fact that the majority of the English poor were mothers before they were married, stated that the morals of Irish women were infinitely higher. When we get definite illegitimacy figures by mid century we find Irish figures far below those of the rest of the United Kingdom. The figures given of the proportion of illegitimate to legitimate births are: England 1 to 1.49; Wales 1 to 0.87; Ireland 1 to 16.47; Connaught 1 to 23.53. The figures given by Fr O'Riordan for the end of the century are much lower still (*181; 401*). The Report of the Royal Commission on the Condition of the Poorer Classes shows an abnormally low level for Connaught, though the rates were higher in parts of Munster. In Macroom, Co. Cork there were thirty bastards baptised in three years. In Schull, Co. Cork there were twenty-eight or thirty from among 1,400 births (about 2 per cent). In Kinsale, Co. Cork there were about twelve every year, in Cahir, Co. Tipperary four out of 360, in Kenmare, Co. Kerry twenty out of 300, in Killarney twelve out of 400. Most parishes in any given year had no bastards, or only one or two.

In the visitations of Dr Plunkett we get evidence of the kinds of abuses with which the bishop had to cope. As the listed heads of his sermons show, he preached on various occasions against cursing and swearing; detraction; on the necessity of an annual confession and communion; on profane meetings on Sundays and holidays; on swearing;

on drunkenness; on slander and calumny; on the neglect
of the paschal communion; on rioting and quarelling;
on scandal and drunkenness. Most of his sermons, however,
dealt with some positive aspect of religion like salvation
or prayer.

It can easily be assumed that many of these bad habits
were in fact related, that on Sundays and holidays men met
and drank too much, and indulged in quarrelling, swearing
and rioting, which, in fact is the picture painted by Kennedy.

Clearly, there were two problems of excessive drinking
in Ireland. The first was that of the habitual drunkard who
spent all his money on drink to the neglect of his family. The
other was the problem of the occasional drinker who drank
excessively at a fair or a wedding and got involved in riotous
behaviour. It is this latter which I think we must keep in
mind when considering the sermons against drunkenness.
Daniel O'Connell made the point that consumption of
spirits in Ireland *before* the Temperance Movement was
only a half or a third that of Scotland. In 1796 de
Latocnaye commented on how little in general the Irish
drank. We would expect those in receipt of a regular cash
income to be more regular drinkers than those who had no
such regular income. And indeed Townsend notes that
tradesmen were fond of drink and careless of their families,
clothes and appearance. When denouncing drunkenness
among the well-paid boatmen on the Slaney, Fr James Cullen
also accused their wives of tippling and neglect of their
children. The peasant on the other hand drank only on
occasion: 'their debauches are for the most part occasional,
at fairs and public meetings.' He notes also their habit of
thrift, spending only on their daughters' dowries.

Kennedy refers to a matter which is worth keeping in
mind — the sale of bad drink, doctored beer and whiskey.
The following recipe for making an 'improved' beverage
needs no comment: a gallon of whiskey, a pint of rum, a pint
of methylated spirits, two ounces of corrosive sublimate
(mercuric chloride) and three gallons of water! Hussey also
gives it as his opinion that drunkenness was less prevalent
earlier in the century than later, an observation which is
consistent with the suggestion made above about the

correlation between drinking and cash wages (*241*).

Another point made by Hussey was that prostitutes were always found in Dublin and the big towns. William Meagher in his funeral oration on archbishop Murray refers to 'vices, too gross to be more than alluded to, stalking through the streets'. Prostitutes were also found in Athlone, a garrison town, and presumably some at least of these were Catholics. But the kept woman or 'gentleman's miss' was subjected to severe moral reprobation, and had little chance of getting a husband unless she married the father of her child. Servant girls, other witnesses testified, were particularly at risk, and some farmers got their female servants pregnant. (*592*).

This leads on to the question of infanticide. Mr St George believed that infanticide was more common than was usually imagined but offers no evidence (*592*). Some cases of infanticide were reported from Erris, and six cases of desertion of infants, all believed to be illegitimate, reported from Boyle (*592*). But as Lecky observed, 'Infanticide, desertion, wife-murder, and other crimes indicating a low state of domestic morality, have been much rarer among the Irish poor than among the corresponding classes in England.' He also comments:

> Under the influence of the religious spirit which was now [in the eighteenth century] pervading the nation a great moral reformation was silently effected. A standard of domestic virtue, a delicacy of female honour, was gradually formed among the Irish poor, higher than in any other part of the Empire, and unsurpassed, if not unequalled in Europe.

When there was a case of a runaway marriage, and these were frequent, there was no hint of illicit intercourse. Referring to incest, O'Connell stated that an Irish peasant, though living crowded together with his family in a tiny hut, would destroy himself if such a charge were seriously made about him. Incest was not in fact heard of, he said (*170*). (For these reasons I am inclined to interpret the adultery in Athlone strictly in the context of the social conditions in a garrison town.)

The abuses which the clergy complained about were

not serious. Doyle complained of the lack of 'respectful distance' between boys and girls when referring to over-crowding, while in a similar vein Kennedy refers to couples sitting in 'unedifying proximity'. Doyle too, referring to certain hedge schools, stated that the children 'were piled on each other, and the sexes promiscuously jumbled together (*170; 254; 175*).

The impression of a generally high level of morality is confirmed by the reports of the various parish priests which they had to make to the bishops on the state of morals in their parishes. I have not been able to get many of these from the various archives, but those I found confirm the impression of a high moral standard in the various parishes.

In Donabate, Co. Dublin (25 August 1857) six people had not complied with their Easter duty, and one man had lived in a state of concubinage for eighteen years. The principal abuses in the parish were public dances on holidays, card playing and clandestine marriages. In Damastown (19 August 1851) one man was living in incest, having been married by the couple beggar's housekeeper when the couple beggar was drunk. There were no public dances or wakes in the parish and cases of drunkenness were rare. In Skerries, Co. Dublin it was reported that four or five were seriously addicted to drink. In one report from the diocese of Dromore the parish priest reported no abuses such as illegal combin-ations, faction fights, violation of the Lord's Day or scandalous wakes or dances (*580; 552*).

According to Ronald Knox, disapproval of dancing was one of the marks of Jansenism long after Jansenism had ceased to be a genuinely religious inspiration. But Kennedy stresses that the clergy did not disapprove of dancing as such, but only of the unsupervised dances in remote parts of the parish, where doctored drink was dispensed. The clergy even danced themselves at properly conducted private dances in private houses.

Some Irish Catholics were of course sinners, but so far, positive evidence seems to indicate consistently high moral standards throughout the century. To what extent this was the result of intense social control is an open question. We do know that some Catholics at least allowed their children to go to proselytising schools, and that some lost their faith on leaving Ireland. It would seem that a proportion of the Irish Catholic population was ready to embrace Protestantism, either in prison, or at the persuasion of the proselytisers, or in a Protestant milieu abroad (*425*).

Were certain crimes more common in Ireland than the literature would seem to indicate? Was an excess of attention devoted to crimes like drunkenness, or sexual sins, and too little to fraud? Consider the following reference. 'He knew of a *large number* of young women who had been defrauded by trustees, or who had lost all through bank failures.' The only records of fraud I have come across were all concerned with the affairs of convents, which were of course more likely to be recorded (*556; 421*).

Hatred too, especially of Englishmen, landlords and Protestants seem to have been widespread but rarely commented on. The Christian theory that one should hate the sin but love the sinner does not seem to have been widely preached. But hatred of England was a complex phenomenon, varying from individual to individual and from time to time. With it must be associated feuds and revenge, especially in the context of the agrarian problem. Was there a failure in Catholic religious instruction here? Canon Sheehan's picture is horrifying (*467*).

On usury too we lack information. What proportion of the hated moneylenders or gombeen men were Catholics, and how many were extortioners? Drug taking, in the nineteenth century forms of opium eating and ether drinking, was largely confined to Protestants in the North. Though prostitutes existed in the towns, it is impossible to say if their cutomers were numerous or whether they were Irish or Catholic. Duelling, common early in the century among the Catholic gentry, died out.

Agarian Crime and Terrorism

I have kept this question separate from that of morals in general because of the doubt as to whether those involved regarded their actions as being morally reprehensible or morally justifiable. However much the people involved may have been condemned by the Churches, the law enforcers or the voices of public opinion as recorded in the newspapers or in parliament, those involved may have considered themselves in the right and have been supported by local opinion.

Under the heading of agrarian crime, the most widely publicised include the violence of miners and trade unionists. The peculiar character of this kind of crime was noted by Carleton among others:

> It is not in Ireland with criminals as in other countries where the character of a murderer or incendiary is notoriously bad, as resulting from a life of gradual profligacy and villainy. Far from it.
>
> In Ireland you will find these crimes perpetrated by men who are good fathers, good husbands, good sons, and good neighbours, by men who would share their last morsel or their last shilling with a fellow creature in distress — who would generously lose their lives for a man who had obliged them.

In 'Wild Goose Lodge' (see also *Newry Magazine*, 1817), Carleton gives a description of the activities of the agrarian terrorists based on an actual incident.

Violence was not restricted to the agrarian scene. It was also used for industrial aims, by miners, by trade unionists, in the craft industries, with regard to tithes and tenant right. Intimidation in politics was probably only effective when the interests of those who usually resorted to terrorism were involved. (Agrarian violence and terror were by no means unique to Ireland at this period.)

Agrarian terrorism was not the same thing as faction fighting though they are sometimes confused. In a study of faction fighting, P. O'Donnell shows that it was nothing more than a rough sport, with some risk of serious injury or even loss of life. On fair days the men got drunk and then fought a highly ritual combat from which injured men just dropped out. O'Connell and the priests felt that the sport gave a bad image to Ireland about the time of Emancipation and tried to suppress it. The general good nature of the faction fight is stressed by Carleton, who contrasts it with the viciousness and ill-feeling in a fight between Catholics and Protestants.

Agrarian violence is usually associated with membership of secret societies like the Whiteboys or the Ribbonmen or the Molly Maguires, but some of the violence may have been the work of individuals. No really satisfactory study has been done of the secret societies; it is difficult to say what the various societies were or whether their membership remained constant, or what were their methods of organisation, their beliefs, or their aims. Their methods remain constant. It was stated before the parliamentary enquiry in 1825: 'They generally complained of tithes, taxes, grand jury cesses, the payment of the Catholic clergy, the high price of land, all those things together.'

Trench was of the opinion that the group he was dealing with was merely a local protection racket aimed at paying no rent at all. He may have been right. Their attacks were aimed less against the landlord and agent as in the later 'land war' as against Catholic tenants who would dare take a piece of land they regarded as their own. In the 'land war', terrorist tactics and severe social pressure were aimed indiscriminately at the landlord and anyone who sided with him for any reason whatever (*254; 500; 400; 270*).

Some groups at some time may have had millenarian and nationalist views. Trench also at a later date refers to millenarian views associated with the 'Prophecies of Pastorini' (see Appendix C). About 1838 an attempt was made to organise Ribbonism into a large-scale national movement with political objectives, so causing a fusion with the physical-force party in the national movement (*383; 479*).

Dr Doyle and other bishops were unsparing in their denunciations of agrarian and other violence. But by 1848 a note of sympathy not with the methods but with the grievances of those who engaged in murder had crept into the correspondence. Crolly attributed agrarian violence to the harshness of the landlords (*duritia*), while Murray refers to the 'excessive cruelty of the landlords'. This became the common view (*601; 268*).

Personal Religion

This section is concerned with those religious practices in which the individual engaged in addition to the public exercises. Bible reading was not common, for it was precisely to rectify this state of affairs that the Second Reformation was launched, but there was some spiritual reading done (*513; 254*). Tynan noted much later in the century that Catholics did not read the Bible. Archbishop Kelly noted that morning and evening prayer was generally performed in his diocese, and there is no need to assume that Tuam was unique. But prayers were said also for the souls of the dead, for the sick, or for protection on a journey. Carleton notes people praying or reciting the rosary for the sick and at the graves of deceased relatives and prior to going on a journey. But there were also briefer and more spontaneous acts and religious exclamations, the sprinkling of holy water and the wearing of scapulars or making signs of the cross. These are very widely attested. In one country chapel at least people 'made the Stations', i.e. meditated on the Passion of Christ before fourteen images of scenes from the Passion (*75*, 166). In one cottage Mrs Hall noted pictures of the saints on the wall, but there is lack of evidence to indicate how common this practice was early in the century. By the end of the century holy pictures were very common. In another house the presence of an ivory crucifix was noted. Night prayers were said in the kitchen with the people kneeling with their backs to the fire. Evidence on the frequency or distribution of pious inter-jections like 'God rest him' is hard to come by, but it was noted by Forbes who also mentions, surprisingly, in view of later practice, an absence of cursing and swearing.

At mass, it was observed, some people were able to follow the service in devout abstraction, but others had to use beads and manuals as props and try not to look around too much. Some individuals were extremely devoted to prayer and led lives of extraordinary asceticism and prayer. An example of one of these early in the century was Carleton's father. Matt Talbot is the best-known example later in the century. There was also a class of very devout or observant persons whose religion was somewhat suspect. Those who went beyond the ordinary Christian norms were called the 'devout' or 'voteens', the same who in Scotland were called the 'unco guid'. (Voteen is apparently a diminutive with contemptuous connotations.) Voteens could also have been 'bogcachs' (or 'boccochs') of which more in a moment.

Annually, people went to the pattern, pilgrimage or station (which seem in general to have been the same thing). The 'pattern' was the celebration of the feast of the patron, and it was held at a particular 'station' (not the same as the mass or confession stations) and people went on pilgrimage to the station and there performed pious exercises. A constant complaint was that these patterns usually degenerated into bouts of drinking, dancing and rioting. From these complaints it is difficult to ascertain how much real abuse, actual drunkenness and rioting or moral danger to young girls was present, or how much the complaints arose from the general dislike of the authorities for drinking and dancing, or a feeling that religious devotion and amusements were ill assorted.

The devotions at the pattern consisted of saying *Paters* and *Aves*, some of the people with both hands and voices uplifted and with considerable gesticulation. Others, in a less noisy fashion, counted their prayers on their beads with much apparent fervour, or counted them on pebbles. (The usual practice was to say seven or ten *Paters* or *Aves* at various points.)

> Near these wells, little altars or shrines are frequently constructed, often in the rudest manner, and kneeling before them the Irish peasant is seen offering up his prayers with that wordly abstraction which proceeds only from the strength of religious faith, undisturbed by the casual visitor and seemingly unconscious of the presence of an intrusive spectator (*116*).

Bishop Murphy of Cork forbade the pattern at Gougane Barra in 1818 because of faction fights, but faction fights were phenomena with no necessary connection with patterns. It is likely that the objection to stations lay in the admixture of the sacred and the profane, especially when inordinate amounts of whiskey were drunk.

Those who describe the patterns note the presence at them of the 'boccochs'. The Gaelic word itself means a lame man, and by extension a beggarman. These went from pattern to pattern but it is not clear in individual cases if devotion or gain was the primary motive. At the patterns they sold beads, gospels and such like. Carleton's picture seems to indicate that they were a fairly religious class of person, at least in external appearances, but Croker regards them as secular persons. Sir Walter Scott in *The Antiquary* describes a similar class of king's bedesmen or bluegowns in Scotland. They existed elsewhere in Europe, the most famous being a Frenchman who joined a Trappist monastery and left to spend his days going from one shrine to another on the Continent, St Benedict Joseph Labré. So some at least of the boccochs may have been genuine (*503*).

There was certainly some superstition woven into orthodox religious practice, putting holy water into the whiskey; charms; banishing the devil by addressing it in Latin, the sacred language; the priest's cure of a blast from the fairies; charms and spells and cures against diseases; a special or peculiar blessing of holy water by the boccoch; the liberty accorded to ascetics not accorded to other men on account of their fasting. The pattern was believed, among other things, to keep the murrain from the cattle. Why rags were tied to bushes at holy places is unclear. These superstitions seem rather variations of Christian rites than survivals of pre-Christian ones. Charms were regarded officially as being an invocation of the devil, in accordance with the sturdy text of the Vulgate, 'All the gods of the Gentiles are demons', *Omnes dii gentium daemonia* (Revised Standard Version Ps. 96.5: 'All the gods of the peoples are idols'). It is unclear to what source the ordinary people attributed the efficacy of charms or pishogues.

The question as to what amount of real holiness was to be found in Ireland poses insurmountable conceptual and empirical problems, for true holiness is known only to God. Did the Catholic Church in Ireland in the nineteenth century aim at producing a well-drilled people or at true sanctific-ation of the heart? It is clear that the ordinary people had nothing but contempt for those 'voteens' who practised many external observances. So we may say that the dis-tinction between true holiness, and the abundance of external observances, the righteousness of the Scribes and Pharisees, was understood.

8
Changes in Parish Life

General Nature of the Changes

The kind of changes which came over the Irish Catholic Church in the first half of the nineteenth century (and I say *change* in preference to either *reform* or *development*) is aptly summarised in the following quotation.

Catholicity pure and undefiled is everyday advancing in Ireland. Although the people are still persecuted and impoverished by men who give them nothing in return, yet *new churches* are erecting in every diocese. Those *convents* and *monasteries* are again adorning the face of the country. The *religious ladies* of various orders . . . are increasing their nunneries. . . . Our venerable prelates have taken the lead in promulgating admirable ecclesiastical statutes. . . . In every diocese the clergy of the respective districts have *conferences* at stated periods. An *annual retreat* of the clergy headed by their respective superiors is held for one week. . . .

Thus a spirit of *enlightened piety* is promoted amongst the laity. The *divine mysteries are more frequently administered* than in past days of proscription. *Sermons and exhortations* are more common:— abuses at wakes, fairs, and funerals are diminished: *parochial libraries* are on the increase: *confraternities* and *religious sodalities* in almost every parish unite and combine in many pious exercises.

Education is on the increase: Catholic *colleges, seminaries, academies,* and *schools* . . . are multiplied. The *Sabbath* is in general well *observed* . . . suppressing the horrid crime of *drunkenness*.

Through the medium of the *Catholic Society of Ireland*

and the *Catholic Book Society . . . periodical Catholic* literature, at present so shamefully deficient, can be placed in a flourishing condition (*Directory*, 1837, 79-81; I have added the emphases in order to indicate better the various areas of change.)

This list of changes and developments is nearly complete. Almost all these changes originated before 1850. Missing from the list is the development of *orphanages* and other *charitable institutions*. On the other hand it can scarcely be said that periodical Catholic literature, despite the hope expressed, was in a flourishing condition.

The list easily sorts itself into those changes which took place in the parish, and those which were primarily in matters under the direct control of the bishops. So one chapter will be devoted to changes in the parish, and another to changes in episcopal affairs.

Church Building

The nineteenth century was a great period for church building in Ireland. Almost all the churches in Ireland were built or re-built. We should not imagine however that few churches or chapels existed in Ireland before 1800. Where we are able to check the dates of buildings we find that the new chapels were in nearly every case a replacement of one that had existed on or near the same spot. And indeed, in quite a few cases, the churches built early in the century were themselves replaced later in the century by bigger and better ones. In fact, we should look on the process of church building rather as one of continuous upgrading of churches rather than a once-for-all commencement or renewal.

Not every mass place in a parish had a chapel on the spot. Some places had little more than a shelter over the altar. But generally there was a rather small plain building.

A barn church is usually built of coarse rubble masonry, lime rendered, with plain round-headed windows (usually eighteenth century) or pointed windows (usually nineteenth century), with simple glazing and clear glass, and a roof of moderate or low pitch (*481*).

It presents the appearance of a T, like our famous old rural chapels (*Directory*, 1837).

The chapels were usually thatched. L. M. Cullen (*119*, 95) gives an illustration of a chapel which best matches the literary descriptions. He shows a picture of a long, low, thatched building, with the thatch in bad repair. As vestments too were in bad repair, one suspects carelessness.

Such a long, low, thatched chapel in a state of indifferent repair may perhaps have been the most typical church in Ireland, but in fact there was a very wide range in the quality of the chapels. There were some notable chapels like those in Waterford or the Carmelite Church, Clarendon Street in Dublin, and on the other hand rude shelters over the altar, and presumably almost everything in between. In Tuam, for example, in 1825, there were about 106 places of worship, fifteen to eighteen of which were solid, slated chapels. All the others were thatched, some were wretched, none sufficiently spacious to contain the congregation, and some were mere sites in the open air. This evidence must be treated with a certain amount of caution, as the ·bishops may have been looking for financial assistance from the Board of First Fruits, and so exaggerated somewhat the wretched condition of the chapels. Dr Plunkett of Meath in 1790 reported to Rome that there were 135 chapels in his diocese, of which, since 1779, thirty were re-built and forty-two enlarged and repaired.

In 1800 Dr Plunkett of Meath complimented the people of Ardbraccan on their handsome new church. The people of Oristown were complimented on the decent condition of the chapel, as also were the people of Rathmullan. At Loughan the improved state of the chapel was noticed. The poor state of the chapels at Ardcath, Nobber and Fore was noted (*97*).

From other sources we get descriptions of various chapels. A chapel in Ballymoney was described as a very small brick house with a thatched roof, built in 1794 at a cost of £200, accommodating only 200 people. The church in Armagh was described as a plain rectangular stone building, built in 1771, the interior plain, with a small gallery and not 'ceiled'.

There were no seats, only a few forms. The windows were gothic. Carleton noted about another chapel that it was unfinished and the pigeons had built nests among the rafters in the 'unceiled' roof (*585; 75*).

The chapel in Kells, Co. Meath was designed by the architect Francis Johnston and built in 1798, the Marquis of Headfort contributing towards the cost. Good churches were built in Waterford between 1792 and 1797. St Teresa's, Clarendon Street was described as the only 'respectable' church in Dublin before the Union.

The rapidly growing population of Ireland forced the clergy to take steps to accommodate it in the churches. This could be done either by building larger churches or by increasing the number of the clergy. Either course would have meant an increased financial burden. In fact almost every parish rebuilt its chapels. Speaking of Waterford and Lismore, Power says:

> A wave of church building passed over the diocese during the first twelve years of the century, and succeeding waves about Emancipation and in the early forties respectively. All the churches erected during the first half of the century were plain unambitious structures, cheap but solid, suited to the climate, and to the circumstances of the congregations, and roomy enough to accommodate the then dense rural population.
>
> About the early sixties a revival of building set in, under the influence of which churches of greater architectural pretensions arose. Gothic — generally the early variety — was the then prevailing fashion. . . .
>
> The churches of the second half of the century, if artistically more beautiful than their predecessors of the first half and otherwise more ambitious, are perhaps no better suited to the need of a country congregation.

We can note in passing the opinion expressed by Power that the chapels were adequate to accommodate the dense rural population of pre-famine Ireland. This is contrary to the opinion expressed by Larkin who held that the pre-famine Irish chapels could not physically have accommodated the population. Power's opinion is much more plausible. When it is shown that most of the chapels were rebuilt between 1800 and 1850, it is reasonable to assume that the clergy built them precisely to accommodate all those obliged to attend mass, *at least standing*.

Power notes that the churches which were built or rebuilt in the second half of the century were more splendid by contrast with those which went before, which were plain compared with the later ones. But it would be a mistake to believe that the earlier churches were built in a plain unpretentious manner intentionally. On the contrary it would seem from contemporary sources that they were built as large splendid structures in comparison with *their* predecessors.

Power gives most of the dates on which the various chapels of the diocese were either built or rebuilt. The first decade of the nineteenth century saw *seven* new churches, the second decade saw *nine*, the third decade *twenty-three*, the fourth decade *twelve*, the fifth decade *three*. After 1850, church building was renewed on a smaller scale. 1850-59 saw *nine* new churches, 1860-68 saw *two*, the next decade *three* and the 1880s *eight*. It is clear that the great era of church building in Waterford and Lismore was from 1820 to 1840. In this period the great plain slated parish churches in Ireland were largely built. Later in the nineteenth and also in the twentieth centuries some of these were replaced by more architecturally pretentious buildings.

Waterford and Lismore was not unique. By 1840 all but two of the thatched chapels were replaced in Ardagh by slated chapels. In Clogher, for a sample of dates given, twenty-six are before 1850, and ten after 1850, the decade 1810-19 with ten new churches being the modal decade. In Kilmacduagh new churches were recorded in 1817, 1819, 1820, 1828, 1833, 1839, 1840, 1841 and 1845, even though many of them by 1837 were still poor. In Kilfenora in 1810, a new thatched chapel was built which was described at the time as being 'handsome and comfortable'. It remained until 1856. 'At that period the opinion had become general that the Lahane chapel was neither "handsome" nor indeed suitable for divine worship. . . .' A new church in the gothic style was accordingly built (*171*).

The *Directories* show that the building of chapels was occurring all over Ireland in the pre-famine years. There were many new churches in Armagh, in Derry several new churches, as also in Down and Connor, and Kilmore. By 1848 MacHale and Higgins estimated that about 2,000 chapels had been built in thirty years. But in 1868 the *Freeman's Journal* Commission regarded the figure as being 1,842 churches built after 1800. Clearly there is room for differences of opinion. The round figure 2,000 clearly corresponds to the 1,999 parish churches and chapels-of-ease listed in the *Directory* of 1840. It is not probable that all of these were *rebuilt* in their entirety before 1848, but it is likely that they were repaired and upgraded. And in 1845 a witness remarked that the worst evils of poor chapels were 'almost now entirely remedied' (*204; Directories* and diocesan histories *passim*).

It is clear that the motive in building or rebuilding chapels was not merely to provide more accommodation for an expanding population. The kind of church built when finance allowed, as well as the remarks of contemporaries, show us that the new churches were intended to have an expressive or symbolic function as well.

When Dr MacHale was appointed to Killala, there were, as he informed Propaganda, no proper churches in his diocese but 'mere cabins covered with thatch'.

> In this absolute indigence of all helps towards religion I have asked myself what I should do when I was, though unworthy, raised to the co-adjutorship. . . . I applied myself, first of all, to rear a cathedral that might contribute to the majesty and splendour of religion in the town in which I reside, and that should also serve as a model and incite the clergy to undertake the building of like edifices in their respective parishes (*399*, I, 113).

The rich archdiocese of Dublin provided the best examples, but other examples were to be found in the larger provincial towns. The churches built in Dublin, in the opinion of one authority on architecture, were among the finest architectural buildings anywhere in the British Isles in the 1820s. The gem of the lot was the Church of the Conception in Marlborough

Street, Dublin. It was designed as the most expensive church to be built in the British Isles since the completion of St Paul's Cathedral, and with the exception of this latter was the greatest church built in these islands for three centuries. Many people had wished to have it built on Sackville Street but it was felt that this might be just too provocative and so it was built a block away from the contemporary GPO.

A good site was regarded as important. 'A good site is of much importance (*Directory*, 1837, 151). Among the reasons for building a new church was given the 'obscurity' of the old site. Fr Meagher, the chronicler of the events in the episcopate of Archbishop Murray, sums up the attitude as follows.

> Upon the dawn of their better fortunes the faithful of Dublin resolved to erect a church harmonising somewhat in style and dimensions with the dignity of the archiepiscopal residence, and with the superior wealth and respectability of the inhabitants (*324*, 95).

Though only a personal visit and inspection can do justice to the quality of the building, yet the following description of the interior of one of the Dublin churches can give some indication of the richness and complexity of ornament.

> The interior of the cruciform church is 40 feet high, terminated by a horizontal ceiling, disposed in quadrangular and octangular coffers with enriched mouldings and rafled rosettes in each, all highly relieved.
>
> The ceiling rests on a continuous entablature with enrichments, and surmounting a series of pilasters in the modern Ionic Order, 30 feet high, arranged at proportionate intervals on the surrounding walls, with capitals after the Roman College, having *alto-relievo* cherubim on the abaci.
>
> In the inter-pilasters are dressed arcades, 20 feet high, opening the nave to the minor chapels, with clerial [*sic*] storey windows surmounting the arches, which light the centre church (*Catholic Penny Magazine*, 15 February 1834, 17).

Dr Blake, when appointed pastor of St Andrew's Church, though several thousand pounds had already been spent on patching up the old church, decided to build an entirely new one, and 'undertook to build the present church of St Andrew's, the most capacious, and with its commodious presbyteries, perhaps the largest and most costly edifice in the Kingdom' (556).

We have some idea of the cost of these cathedrals and great city and town churches. In pre-famine times the costs can be regarded as comparable with each other: or in other words we can assume that all those churches were completed to a comparable degree of furnishing and applied ornamentation. For later in the century it is not wise to make direct comparisons of costs.

When Dr MacHale and Dr Higgins were attempting to prove that the Irish Church could support a Catholic university, they submitted to Propaganda a list of expenditures actually paid by the Irish Church in the previous thirty years. Special figures were included for many churches. The Church of the Conception, or pro-cathedral, cost £50,000 by 1844; St Paul's, Dublin, £16,000; St Andrew's, £20,000; St Nicholas', £18,000; St Francis', £12,000; St Audeon's, £14,000; and St Lawrence's, £12,000.

The cathedral in Armagh had cost £15,000 by 1846; the parochial church in Dundalk, £15,000; the cathedral in Tuam, £20,000; in Newry, £20,000; in Kilkenny, £20,000; Killarney, £20,000; Ardagh had already cost £30,000, Carlow £16,000 and Killala £12,000. Ronan notes that when the building fund for the pro-cathedral was closed in 1845 it showed receipts of £45,000, though it is not clear if this is the total cost of the church. As Ronan noted, this meant the collection of one thousand pounds a year for this purpose alone.

The rural churches did not approach this level of cost. At times the parish priest had to act as his own architect in order to achieve a sufficiently pretentious chapel at the least expense, and this could mean travelling to Dublin to look at, and copy, city chapels. O'Shea estimates the cost of a pre-famine church at about £400. Archbishop Kelly estimated the cost of a rural slated chapel to be in the region of £600 to £800. In Galway, Fr Peter Daly built and equipped one church at a cost of £373 and another at a cost of £343, the sacristy, the painting, the churchyard wall and the tower being later additions. A chapel with accommodation for 1,800 people in Clogher cost £1,400 in 1833, while another in the same diocese in the same year cost £1,000. The church in Gort built in 1828 cost £1,000 (Ordnance Survey Memoirs and diocesan histories, *passim*).

The figures quoted for the post-famine churches are considerably higher. Power cities £2,662 in 1862 as being one of the cheapest gothic churches. A church in Clonmel cost £7,000 in 1883 and one in Kill in 1874, £6,000. Another in 1879 was 'practically rebuilt' for a mere £1,500. Another gothic church in 1860 cost £6,000. In Tramore, between 1856 and 1871, £18,000 was spent on a chapel, which is not out of the way when compared with the earlier expenditure of £15,000 on a parish church in Dundalk. (The cost of St Patrick's, Dundalk is totally out of line with costs of the provincial parish churches of the period which were not cathedrals. One wonders if the people of Dundalk wished to have the seat of the bishopric transferred from Drogheda to Dundalk instead of to Armagh.) More money was being spent on fewer churches in the second·half of the century.

Construction of the walls and the roofing with slates, the glazing of the windows and the insertion of doors, together with the construction of an altar, can be regarded as the 'prime cost' of a chapel. But that by no means meant that work on the chapel was finished. The following list shows what remained to be added. St Mary's Church, Carrickmacross was completed in 1786. In 1796 the high altar was added; in 1797 the chapel yard; in 1802 the altar piece was painted; in 1810 a small house for the priest; in 1813, repairs to chapel school; in 1814, a road up to the church was made; in 1815 candlesticks and a cover for the altar were provided; in 1817, paintings were procured for the church, crimson curtains were put in front of the galleries (?) and the interior walls limewashed and the interior woodwork repainted. In 1819 a rope was required for the bell; in 1821 a chalice and paten were donated; in 1821 the church was flagged; while in 1827 a new gate was provided, walks made in the chapel grounds, and a new parochial house built, as well as stabling for horses during mass-time. In 1842 the exterior of the church was pebble-dashed (*362*).

In the *Directory* of 1842, certain allegations were recounted regarding the state of the chapels and also the results of a survey carried out to find the true facts. Both the allegations and the survey are tendentious, for the one party wished for state aid for the clergy and the other party wished to disprove the need for it.

The allegations were as follows: that the interiors of the churches were in general unfurnished, the inside of the roof unplastered and the glass in the windows often left unrepaired for years; the sanctuary, though in general 'boarded' (floored?) was usually filthy, with even the altar covered in cobwebs; the altar utensils and vestments were poor; priests were seen saying mass 'booted and spurred'; lists of payers and non-payers were read from the altar.

In Kildare and Leighlin the vicar-general noted that all the chapels were 'plastered and ceiled'. In Ferns, the vicar-general reported that the chapels were in general well and decently furnished, the roofs 'plastered', and windows promptly repaired. In Cashel, the churches even in the country districts had galleries, altars of a superior description and windows well repaired. In Cork, chapels in general lacked pews or pictures, the inside of the roof was plastered and the windows were kept in a good state of repair. In Killaloe, only about three unslated chapels now remained. They were not, it is true, 'cove ceiled' but the interior of the slates was 'rendered' or plastered. Italian paintings were lacking. Similar conditions were reported for other dioceses.

It should be noted that there was sometimes a slight qualification in the testimony, with words such as 'in general' or 'generally' being used. But the picture given is clear. By 1842 the fabric of slated chapels had been completed, and the interior walls plastered, with the interior of the slates plastered or rendered. The windows were glazed, and usually kept in good and prompt repair. Interior furnishings such as seating or pews were lacking, though there were some paintings. Refinements such as cushions and carpets were of course lacking in most chapels.

It was noted in Kerry that the floor of the altar (or

predella) was rarely carpeted. Waterford and Lismore reported the presence of many confession boxes and well-finished altars with tabernacles, and many chapels with paintings.

By 1843, a new note was creeping into Catholic thought on church design. The business of providing adequate accomodation and decent buildings, which had preoccupied Archbishop Kelly in 1825, was now largely completed. But a new interest in church architecture as such was being manifested. The views of Augustus Welby Pugin (it would seem) on the subject were given in the *Directory* of 1843, together with notes on 'Catholic architecture' from the *Dublin Review*. The author of the latter article reproached earlier Catholics for having abandoned 'Catholic architecture' for 'Genevan', the accusation – probably justified – being that the plainness of Irish church architecture was caused by a conscious imitation of Calvinist models.

The chapels built in the post-famine period were more consciously Gothic, Puginesque and expensive. It may be true that there was a hiatus in building during and immediately after the famine, but the ideas which underlay the post-famine style of church architecture are already found clearly expressed in 1843. Some examination of this is required, for one feels the last thing a priest would do would be to lay off workers, at a time when work-making schemes were being widely established. There was no shortage of actual cash in the country as a whole. Again, though the synodal fathers at Thurles in 1850, and especially Cullen, insisted on the provision everywhere of such church furnishings as confessionals and baptismal fonts, the time was in fact ripe for their provision in the ordinary course of events.

Finally, it should be noted that around the 1880s some chapels built about the 1820s were demolished and replaced by more up-to-date structures. The fact that two or three chapels were built on the same site successively indicates that permanence was not one of the qualities church builders in Ireland necessarily intended.

The nineteenth century was, therefore, marked by two phases of church building. From about 1800 to about 1840, almost all the old thatched structures were either swept away or extensively remodelled. Though compared with later standards, the chapels in this first phase were relatively plain, except in the case of the great Dublin churches, at the time they were regarded as marking a distinct improvement over their predecessors. After the famine, building was resumed on a smaller scale and coincided with the gothic revival. The ideas of Pugin led to more expensive and more ornamented churches. Thomas Kennedy however notes the outstanding quality of the pre-famine churches.

The New Charitable Institutions

During the period of persecution and dispossession, organised charities such as hospitals, orphanages etc. virtually ceased to exist in the Catholic Church in Ireland. In 1825, Dr Doyle testified to the fact that there were few mendicity institutes, and no parochial establishment. By 1790 the bishop of Meath had organised an annual collection in his diocese and the funds thus collected were judiciously distributed to supply for the lack of hospitals, orphanages and the like. Towards the end of the eighteenth century, certain small charities were established in Dublin (*102*).

The Irish peasantry were very generous in helping the unfortunate, but this was left to individual charity and was in no way a community, still less a parochial, effort. When an Irishman had to beg, he left his native community and went elsewhere.

Specifically Catholic charities can be traced back as far as 1750, though in a very small way. (Protestant charities abounded and it is reasonable to assume that Catholics contributed to their support.) In 1750, certain gentlemen agreed to subscribe a certain sum each week to be paid to the Franciscans in Adam and Eve church, Dublin, for charitable purposes. The Teresian Orphan Society attached to the Carmelite Convent, Clarendon Street claimed to date from 1790. Other penny-a-week subscription charities were in existence around 1800 but they appear to be very few in number and very small in scale.

By 1840, the following institutions were in existence. A date is accorded to each, as given in the sources, but there may be some inaccuracy in the case of some of them as conflicting dates are sometimes given. The error is likely to be slight.

1804 Orphan Institute, Harold's Cross
1806 Orphan Asylum, Cork
1810 Christian Doctrine and Orphan Society
1812 St Andrew's Orphan Society, Sisters of Charity
1813 Convents and monasteries of St Brigid, in Kildare and Leighlin
1814 Clongowes Wood College founded by Jesuits; a 'refuge' founded by Mrs O'Brien, later transferred to the Sisters of Charity, Stanhope Street
1815 Sisters of Charity take over orphanages from Trinitarian Orphan Society, and establish a convent devoted to charitable works in North William Street
1817 Purgatorian Society devoted to spiritual and corporal works of mercy; St Peter's Orphan Society; St Francis' Orphan Society
1819 Society of St Joseph for spiritual and corporal works of mercy
1820 Institute of St Bonaventure; Purgatorian Society of St John the Evangelist; official chaplaincies in the penal colonies in Australia
1821 Loretto Sisters; St Patrick's Society, Kingstown; Harold's Cross Academy; St Patrick's Juvenile Society
1822 Metropolitan Orphan Society; Malachean Orphan Society; St Nicholas of Myra Orphan Society
1823 St Patrick's Asylum for Old Men
1824 Catholic Book Society
1825 St John of the Cross Orphan Society; Female Penitents' Asylum, Marlborough Street
1826 St Vincent de Paul Orphan Society
1827 Sisters of Mercy; St Michael's Orphan Society; St Patrick's Orphan Society
1828 Society for Destitute Orphans; St Stephen's Orphan Society
1829 Catholic Cemetery, Goldenbridge (this was a voluntary charity)

1830 Orphan Society, St James's Gate
1832 Orphan Friends Society; County and City of Dublin
     Orphan Society; House of Aged Females, Paradise
     Row
1833 Female Penitent Retreat, Mecklenburgh Street;
     St Mary's Asylum for Penitents, Drumcondra Road
1834 Catholic hospital, St Vincent's

Omitted from this list are those institutes for which I could find no date of foundation, the foundation of individual convents, the building of free or charity schools or collections for the support of teachers in Catholic free schools. I terminated the list somewhat arbitrarily at 1834 because to continue it further would have been misleading. The Poor Law, the manifold foundation of convents, and the spread of the Society of St Vincent de Paul, meant that there was less room for small institutes based on a local church or parish. The list does however give a clear picture of the *kind* of institute that was being founded.

In the first three decades of the century, nearly all these institutes were in Dublin, but they marked the beginning of a nationwide trend as consultation of any of the *Directories* from later in the century will show, especially under the headings of the various convents and religious orders. Outside Dublin evidence taken in 1835 gave the following picture. In the parish of Headford, Co. Galway, orphans were supported by means of small collections at the chapel gate and by house-to-house collections. In Tuam archdiocese the support of orphans fell on the relatives and no Poor Law provision was contemplated except for deserted children. Dr MacHale testified that no legitimate children were ever deserted and the others were cared for by religious orders. Newry, Co. Down had a mixed population. Of twenty-two deserted bastards, ten were supported on the parish rates and twelve by Protestant societies, while twenty or thirty others remained with their mothers (*592*).

The institutes in Dublin were small. Between 1826 and 1840 the Society of St Vincent a Paulo (not St Vincent de Paul) rescued fifty orphans. Between 1817 and 1840, St Peter's Orphan Society rescued 150. St Bonaventure's

Institute, between 1820 and 1840, rescued 140. St Nicholas of Myra's Orphan Society rescued seventy orphans in nineteen years. The intake therefore seems to have varied from about three to seven per annum.

These orphanages were often connected with some church. The Metropolitan was connected with the cathedral parish, St James and St Joseph, under the clergy of St James' church. The Orphans' Friend Society was connected with St Andrew's, Westland Row; St Michael's with St Michael and John's; St Bonaventure's with the Franciscans, Merchant's Quay, and so on (*Directories, passim*).

But though the clergy were connected in some way with these institutes, they were in fact lay institutes staffed and run by lay committees. Even convents had lay management committees to supervise the finances. The committee usually met once a week and was responsible for monies received and disbursed, for appointments of personnel and general supervision of the running of the institutes. There was a strong tendency to recruit a lady or a gentleman to sit on the committee or to associate his or her name with it. Lord Cloncurry agreed to act as 'president' of the monastery and collegiate school of Mount St Joseph, Clondalkin. The Metropolitan Male and Female Orphan Society was 'patronised' by Dr Murray, and had Sir Thomas Esmonde, Bart. as its president, and so on.

The Royal College of Maynooth had the Earls of Fingall and Kildare, Viscount Gormanston, Lord French and Sir P. Bellew among its trustees. On the committee of the Female Penitents' Asylum were the Countesses of Clanricard and Howth, the Baroness de Roebeck, the Hon. Mrs G. French, Lady Bellew and Lady Murray.

The Orphan Society of St Francis of Assisium had governors, consisting of a president, a vice-president and a committee of nine, together with twelve guardians. They met together on Sundays in John's Lane to receive subscriptions and donations. The committee met on the first Thursday of every month to discuss relief petitions and to transact the affairs of the institution. Some committees met on Sundays, others on weekdays. In one case a full account is given of the annual general meeting with the election of the officers and committee, showing that these groups were not haphazard or informal ones but were governed by a strict, formal procedure.

By 1870 many of the above-mentioned institutes were still in being, some but not all under the direction of religious orders. Convents had increased enormously in number, and many more specialised institutes such as asylums for the blind, for deaf mutes, or night refuges and reformatories were in existence. Notable too was the effort made by the nuns in various convents to stimulate industry and provide jobs for women making lace, socks etc. Foxford Woollen Mills is the most famous example (*401*).

Religious and Charity Schools

In this section I deal with those schools which were not state schools or pay schools (i.e. those run for personal profit or gain). But the section includes those schools which imparted a basically secular education, i.e. teaching reading and writing plus some religious instruction gratis to the poorest children, and those which taught the sons and daughters of gentlemen at considerable expense (the schools of the Jesuits and the Ursulines).

Compared with the totals of the pay schools and the later National Schools, they were comparatively few in number, though they probably totalled several hundred. A parochial school system, or one staffed entirely by Christian Brothers (as they came to be called) and teaching Sisters, never became feasible despite the dreams and efforts of Archbishop MacHale.

For a charity or free school, two things were required: a building or room in which to teach and a means of support for the teacher. Up to about 1830 the chapel was normally available, but apparently after that date chapels ceased to be used. Endowments were technically illegal within the kingdom, though doubtless there were ways of avoiding this as we can see from the way the teaching orders managed to hold on to money given to them.

The Rev. Michael Collins paid a master £20 per annum by means of a tax of 'two ten pennies' on the sponsors at each baptism. As that did not come to the full amount, he paid the balance himself. Dr Doyle, sometimes on the death of a parish priest, kept the parish vacant for a time and took into his own hands such revenues as were left over after paying the curate, and applied them to the building of schools. Some Dublin parishes apparently managed to run free schools, totally free of charge. At Goldenbridge there were male and female, day, evening and Sunday schools, supported by subscriptions and some donations which enabled the committee to procure desks, forms and other school requisites, and to pay the rent and the salaries of the master and mistress free of all charge. This is the only case I came across where this claim was made.

But it was always possible to get additional support by charging some of the children and admitting others free. A charity school could be attached to a fee-paying boarding school. Thus the Ursulines had such schools attached to their boarding schools. Likewise the Loreto Sisters had free schools attached to their boarding schools, and also the monastery of Mount St Joseph, Clondalkin.

Archbishop MacHale tried to establish a diocesan system. The *Directory* of 1869 comments, 'The parochial schools under lay teachers are, considering the circumstances of the country, fair in number and tolerably efficient (*Directory*, 1869).

The financing of these schools in Tuam is a matter on which the sources I consulted were silent. It is not even clear if they were genuine charity schools, or penny-a-week schools, or some mixture. They could have been financed by a system of licensing by which only one master was allowed to set up school in the parish, or by a tax on the parish such as was levied by Fr Collins.

In the rest of Ireland some of the schools apparently followed a mixed system, those whose parents could afford it paying something, while the others were educated free. The Christian Brothers, Hanover Street accepted a penny-a-week subscription to cover the costs of the school, and in no way to support the Brothers, or to cover the cost of the school building, which incidentally in 1813 cost £2,244. 18. 9, the entire amount of which was advanced by individuals. A penny-a-week subscription was of course more than it sounds and would be equivalent to a sum of some shillings in recent money.

The story of the development of the charity schools is really the story of the development of the teaching religious orders which comes in a later section. With regard to the vast number of parishes in Ireland, all the bishops except MacHale saw no hope of financing a decent or respectable system of education without state help. So the policy adopted in Ireland was not to set up a voluntary parish system but to get a state system over which the clergy had adequate control.

The basic motivation for having Catholic schools at all and teaching secular subjects like reading and writing is obscure, and educators did not philosophise about what they were doing. One reason may have been that if the Catholics did not educate them, the Protestants might. Another reason may have been a close association made by people between ignorance, idleness and vice:

> Is it better that children should grow up in ignorance, idleness and vice than run the chance of being Christians without believing some disputed points or than merely associate with Protestants, or be indebted to the charity of Protestants for a Christian education in your own principles?

The programme of instruction in the Christian Brothers' schools was such that religion and morals were inculcated as well as secular instruction. Practice of religious exercises was carried out throughout the day. Prayers and litanies were recited from time to time during the day. Religious books were used as textbooks. The masters made appropriate moral and religious comments from time to time. A half hour was devoted to formal religious instruction, in which prayers and the catechism were taught. A school library was provided, from which boys could borrow pious books, and it was hoped that the boys would read aloud from these books to their parents on Sundays and holy days and at night. The attendance of the boys at church and at the sacraments was carefully supervised. It is reasonable to assume that a similar regime characterised the other schools run by the religious orders.

But the Irish bishops as a whole were prepared to back a system in which the emphasis on Catholic religious practice was much less pronounced, provided that time was allowed for instruction in Catholic doctrine, all danger of proselytism was avoided and the religious books used were neutral as between Catholics and Protestants. Fr Collins stated that though Catholics would prefer a full religious form of education if they could afford it, yet they had no objection to instruction in purely secular subjects if they could get no other.

In 1826 the Irish hierarchy agreed on the following principles as a basis for negotiation: (1) Catholic and Protestant children could share the same school for purposes of 'literary instruction', provided the religion of the Catholics was safeguarded and adequate time allowed for Catholic religious instruction; (2) the master or assistant master must be a Catholic, depending on the proportion of Catholic children in the school, the appointment and dismissal of such a Catholic master being subject to the approval of the *Catholic* bishop of the diocese; (3) four Catholic model schools for the purpose of training masters (and separately mistresses) to be set up, one in each province, at government expense; (4) books used should be approved by the Catholic bishop for use by Catholic children, and no book be used for *common* instruction in literature which was disapproved of by the Catholic bishop. The dispute among the bishops over national education turned on the point as to whether these principles were being observed or not.

The Irish Christian Brothers decided not to put themselves under the national system, and in this they were followed by the anti-proselytising Sisters of the Holy Faith. According to Edmund Rice's biographer, the Christian Brothers objected to the principle of total separation of religious and secular instruction, the suppression of all religious teaching and devotional practices and the hiding away of religious emblems except on specified days. A suspicious anti-government and anti-Protestant feeling can be clearly seen in the following passage from the Vincentian, Fr Gowan, with regard to the Sisters of the Holy Faith, who were deliberately and consciously following the lead of the Irish Christian Brothers.

What compensation would money be for the degradation, and we might add sin, of carrying out such orders of the Inspectors as 'Prohibit these children from making the sign of the Cross. Take away that crucifix — you must not permit the image of the Virgin to be seen during the hours of secular instruction: this catechism must be locked up. If I find it lying on the desk again during school hours I'll report you to the Board. Why do you allow these children to pray at forbidden times' (*189*, 246).

The dispute in fact was over minor externals of religion. Dr Murray, who had brought the Irish Christian Brothers to Dublin, wished to see them participating in the scheme of national education and had several interviews with Edmund Rice to persuade him. As Rice's biographer put it:

> For the previous thirty-three years Br Rice had taught his pupils that they should be neither ashamed nor afraid to proclaim their Catholicism. He would continue to proclaim it openly and suffer for proclaiming it. He would not hide or put under cover the emblems of religion even though to do so would bring financial reward.

I have dealt at some length with the attitude of the Irish Christian Brothers and the Sisters of the Holy Faith because it underlines the question of the role of Catholic voluntary schools and especially those of religious orders in the field of education after Stanley's Education Act of 1831. Unless the religious orders were going to provide a full Catholic education totally independent financially of the government, what reason was there for having primary schools staffed by religious? The answer would appear to be none. In primary schools at least, religious sisters and brothers do not appear to have been doing anything that the Catholic lay teachers could not do, and did do, equally well. It was of course perfectly legitimate for any Catholic teacher to take vows and live in community. But the continued presence of religious in primary schools under the Board would appear to owe more to sentiment than to logic.

Possibly more important from the point of view of the Catholic Church was the question of secondary education and seminary education. With regard to the education of future priests, it was necessary to have three grades of school or schooling. The first taught the elements of literacy and might be received in a hedge school, a charity school or at home. The next grade was that of the grammar schools which taught Latin. Then there was the stage of studies proper to the priesthood which were carried out in the seminary. For the sons of gentlemen, the third stage involved going to university. This latter could be done at a Protestant university in Ireland or Scotland, or at a Catholic university on the continent. For daughters of gentlemen, education seems to have been confined to the first two stages. As far as we can see, secondary education within Ireland was always better provided for in the case of girls than in the case of boys. Some convents which took in the daughters of gentlemen survived in Ireland all through the penal times.

But a new era in Catholic education began in Ireland with the coming of the Ursulines. In 1767 the future bishop of Cork, Dr Moylan, made his first approach to the Ursulines in Paris, but they did not found a convent in Ireland until 1771 when they came to Cork. It was not until the Catholic Relief Act of 1782 that a similar school for boys could be attempted. An Augustinian named Fr Edmund Keating started a classical and commercial school in Dublin in 1783, but it came to an end in 1787. In fact any priest or layman could start an academy, but unless some collegiate form or organisation was adopted or it got episcopal backing, it depended on its founder. This fact makes it difficult to get statistics on the number of Catholic grammar schools at any given time.

In their report in 1848, MacHale and Higgins estimated that a total of twenty colleges or schools had been *built* at a cost of £200,000. Fr O'Riordan estimated that forty-seven 'colleges' were built between 1793 and 1872, and several more between 1872 and 1905. Between 1850 and 1872, twenty-seven colleges were built, showing that the greatest expansion in the provision of secondary education for boys was in the third quarter of the century.

In 1825 Dr Doyle stated that there were major seminaries in Waterford, Kilkenny and Tuam, besides in Maynooth and

Carlow. In 1843 there was still a course of theological studies in Tuam, as well as in St John's, Waterford and St Kieran's, Kilkenny. St Mary's, Youghal apparently had a theological course for the students for the foreign missions (*Directory*, 1843, 412ff.). Dr Murphy attempted to establish a theological seminary in Clogher, but failed, so he transferred the burses to Maynooth. Cardinal Cullen established a diocesan seminary for Dublin, but the majority of the bishops were satisfied with the national seminary. Irish priests were therefore trained not in the universities or directly by the bishop, but in large semi-monastic seminaries on the Sulpician model. Within ten years after Waterloo, Irish colleges were restored in Rome, Paris and Salamanca.

Beyond noting that in the course of the nineteenth century boarding schools for young ladies increased in numbers, the nature of these establishments makes the direct use of statistics, even if they could be collected, misleading. If one looks, for example, at the advertisements in the *Directories*, one finds references to 'Miss Taylor's Seminary for Young Ladies', or the 'Roman Catholic Boarding and Day School for Young Ladies under the Direction of the Misses Fitzgerald'. Without further information as to the numbers attending, or how long they survived, it is impossible to estimate their numbers or their importance at any given time. The Census of 1861 shows that there were fifty-two 'superior schools' attached to convents, besides private schools, and as these had 2,486 pupils, the average number was forty-eight (Census, 1861). A superior school was defined as one in which a foreign language was taught. Convent schools educated 2,430 Catholic girls, while 2,074 were educated in other schools, giving a total of 4,504. The total number of pupils in 'superior schools' was 20,162, many of whom of course were Protestants.

The quality of the education is a factor which is hard to measure. According to Dr Doyle, the youth of Ireland above the level of the peasantry had merely an acquaintance with the 'preliminaries of knowledge'. 'They acquire just as much of classics and of science as is sufficient to deceive them into the notion that they are educated, and to precipitate them unprepared into the labyrinth of public life' (*149*, 21).

There may be much of the subjective in this judgment, but even half a century later when Walter MacDonald entered St Kieran's College the standard of teaching seems to have been extremely low, and looking back he was scathing in his references to the way he was taught. Standards of education in a seminary like Maynooth were of course higher, but as the *Eighth Report of the Commissioners of Irish Education Enquiry* observed in 1826, the fact that the students at Maynooth had little or no experience of the subjects taught before coming to Maynooth meant that they could not be expected to gain more than a smattering of the vast range of subjects taught in their first year. Until standards were raised in primary schools, and in secondary schools, there was little that could be done to raise the standard of education in seminaries. In the 1830s, Archbishop Murray made a start by directing that all clerical students from the archdiocese should first have passed through the new diocesan minor seminary (secondary school) at Castleknock. In order to achieve and maintain academic standards, the colleges of Carlow, Kilkenny and Thurles were affiliated to London University, and many other colleges were affiliated in some way to the Catholic University when it came to be founded. Some such relationship was essential but it came only later in the century. Matriculation implies academic standards.

After long resistance, the government allowed grants for denominational 'model schools' and male and female Catholic training colleges were built.

Though not all of the clergy and laity were equally enthusiastic, many churchmen pressed on with the establishment of a Catholic university (*Catholic Bulletin*, 1911). The university did not prosper but as the Queen's Colleges did not prosper either it is difficult to draw firm conclusions. In England, where the opposition by the laity to Cardinal Manning's Catholic university in Kensington was intense, the opposition was based on the fact that young Catholic gentlemen would not meet and mix with their peers socially. This may also have been the case in Ireland. In the Royal University, the Catholic lords Emly and O'Hagan strongly opposed Cardinal MacCabe in the university senate. The moribund Catholic University was reorganised more than once and was altered into a recognised college of the Royal University, as its own degrees were not recognised. Finally it was absorbed into a constituent college of the National University in 1908. University College Dublin, though in theory a lay university, in practice was always a denominational one. The Queen's Colleges in Cork and Galway were similarly 'baptised' when they also became constituent colleges (*358; 517*).

In the ecclesiastical seminaries, the standard continental authors were used. No particular tendency is discernible. There was some rigorism in moral theology up until the canonisation of St Alphonsus Ligouri (1839) when his opinions were universally adopted. It is unclear if the still milder opinions of the Jesuit theologians were widely accepted in the nineteenth century, but it is unlikely. Some little attempt was made in Maynooth to produce native textbooks (*367; 517; 110*). But there was nothing corresponding to the great English efforts at publishing Catholic literature of all sorts. Books by English converts especially formed the staple in religious reading, as a visit to any old religious library will instantly confirm.

Confraternities

Confraternities were associations of laymen under the direction of a priest for some pious purpose. Such purpose could be personal sanctification, good works or the cultivation of some devotion or pious practice. By the end of the eighteenth century there seem to have been few confraternities surviving in Ireland. It is possible, as Egan notes, that the system of confraternities may have been more widely spread than surviving records would seem to indicate, but against this is the silence of other witnesses especially P. Kennedy and Carleton. Some friaries had lay 'third order' groups attached to them (*446*).

In the course of the nineteenth century, those priests and bishops who were anxious to improve the spiritual state of their charges instituted confraternities in their parishes and dioceses. Myles Ronan attributes the impetus for the spread of confraternities to the zeal of Dr Michael Blake. In 1817 he founded the Purgatorian Society of St John the Evangelist in the Dublin parish of SS Michael and John and this was used as a model for many other societies. The rules for the society were modelled, apparently, by a zealous Dublin priest, Fr Henry Young, on those of the Sodality of the Blessed Virgin which the Jesuits had introduced into Ireland after the Reformation.

The aims of the society were to instruct the ignorant, to administer comfort to dying persons, to relieve the suffering souls in Purgatory and to extirpate drunkenness at wakes. The members of the society ran a Sunday School in which not only religion but also reading, writing and the casting of accounts were taught. The members of the society attended wakes where they read pious books aloud and recited the office of the dead. They also attended the sick and the dying and prepared them to receive the last sacraments, as well as contributing a small sum each week which was expended on material relief for the unfortunate (*443*).

In Kildare and Leighlin, Dr Doyle everywhere introduced Confraternities of the Christian Doctrine. As the name implies, the chief function of this society was to teach Christian doctrine. In 1825 he had formed a branch in nearly every parish. Young men and women used to assemble at an early hour on Sundays to teach the catechism to the children before mass, and in some cases after the mass as well. Immediately after Doyle became a bishop, he laid down a plan for the development of these societies and promptly set about implementing it. Those who wished to join must have lived a sober, pious life for some time previously, they must have made a general confession and gone to communion at least once a month for an entire year. (This may possibly imply that *some* laymen went to communion once a month even if the majority went only twice a year.) When they joined, the members were to assist the parish priest at all times in instructing the ignorant, teaching the catechism, reading pious books aloud, preparing children for their first holy communion and assisting sick persons to die in the Lord (*175*).

Other societies like the Holy Family Confraternity were intended chiefly for the spiritual benefit of the members themselves. They met once a week for prayers and went to confession and communion once a month. Conditions of membership were the same as for the Christian Doctrine Confraternity. Members of the confraternities were expected to live sober, Christian lives; if any member was found to frequent wakes, ale-houses or idle company, he was forthwith expelled. In the Purgatorian society formed by Dr Blake, a member who was seen drunk was fined 2/6 for the first offence, 5/- for the second and was expelled for the third. He was fined 10d if he sat down in a public house in the parish, on a Sunday or pay-day. Fitzpatrick recounts that when Fr Tom Burke's mother, who had been a Franciscan tertiary, married, all the confraternities looked grave. This would seem to imply that it was felt that for girls at least celibacy was considered normal. Fitzpatrick seems to think that the people confused cloistered tertiaries with lay tertiaries, but this seems highly improbable. It is on the other hand probable that becoming a member of a confraternity was often a first step on the way to becoming a nun.

By the last quarter of the century there was an extraordinary variety of sodalities and confraternities to choose from. The *Directory* of 1869 lists those of Our Lady of Mount Carmel, Red Scapular of the Passion, Blue Scapular of the Immaculate Conception, Cord of St Francis, Archconfraternity of St Monica and St Augustine, Sodality of the Living Rosary, Christian Doctrine Society, Society of the Evening Office, Sodality of the Sacred Heart etc. The visitations of Dr Murray show that in the rural parishes of Dublin there was often more than one confraternity in each parish. Lusk had four, Donabate, one; Balbriggan, two; Clondalkin, four; Damastown, one; Baldoyle, where the parish priest was Fr William Young, Fr Henry's brother, there were no less than eleven, six of Christian Doctrine and five of the Blessed Sacrament; Skerries had two. In the parish of Lurgan in 1845 there were four religious societies, two of which were thriving and two of which were not. It would seem that it was the custom to establish more than one sodality or confraternity in each parish and one of them was normally a branch of the Confraternity of Christian Doctrine.

Libraries and Book Societies

Dr Doyle established religious libraries in every parish in his diocese, well stocked with books of moral and religious instruction. Books were given out from these to heads of families upon their paying a penny a week or fort-night for the use of the books. To the poor the books were given out gratis. The books were given out and returned on a Sunday.

In Kilmore in 1837, there were libraries established in several parishes. By 1840 they were in almost every parish in Ardagh. But at the same date Raphoe does not seem to have had many, or indeed any, libraries or confraternities. Parochial libraries were very general in Clogher. In the same year it was regretted that libraries were but few in Kilmacduagh and Kilfenora. In Kerry in 1843, there were circulating libraries in all the towns and in many of the country parishes. Evidence with regard to the spread of parish libraries comes almost entirely from the *Directories*, and in these the references are not systematic, depending in all likelihood on the information given to the editor.

In some dioceses at least a central theological library was set up for the benefit of those priests whose means would not allow them to purchase theological books. There was a need for such libraries. Some institutions like Maynooth obviously had to have libraries, but Maynooth regarded its own theolog-ical library as inadequate in 1825. In 1834 the *Catholic Penny Magazine* deplored the absence of an adequate refer-ence library and noted that in the course of a recent con-troversy it had been necessary to travel as far as Manchester to verify a quotation. This magazine considered that each priest should be conversant with the writings of the Holy Fathers, the history of the Church and the liturgies of the nation, besides the Holy Scriptures and the standard works on dogmatic and moral theology. The writer noted that these latter were 'generally the first, and we may add the last, books in the hands of Catholic ecclesiastics'.

Individual bishops had their own collections of books and some of these collections were quite large. Dr Murphy of Cork had 40,000 volumes. Dr Troy made considerable purchases of theological and juridical works. Dr Blake sold his collection of 1,300 books to raise money for the Irish College. Dr Murphy's collection was dispersed.

Clearly there was need of theological reference libraries and *some* were established in Ireland (*Directory*, 1840, 229). To maintain a supply of cheap books, two national book societies were set up. These were established apparently to try to counteract the campaign through the written word carried on by the 'Bible Societies, Tract Societies, and Reformation Societies'. Several attempts were made to print and publish cheap Catholic books, but without success until a scheme was proposed by a Catholic publisher and controversialist, W. J. Battersby, who also later put the publication of the *Irish Catholic Directory* on a firm footing. In 1821 Battersby, after having written several letters on the need to form a national book society, summoned a meeting of leading Catholic laymen and members of the secular and regular clergy, and at this a society was formed. The new society received backing from Dr Doyle and was formally proposed to the hierarchy. Dr Curtis agreed to act as president of the new society, and Dr Murray in whose diocese the society operated agreed to supervise its work. W. J. Battersby was made 'agent'.

The operation was conceived on a large scale from the very start and even in its first year of operation the society had disseminated half a million 'Books, Tracts, and Catechisms'. They also acted as suppliers at a cheap rate to poor schools of spelling books, tablets, copy books, slates, pencils, quills and reams of paper, an extremely important factor in Catholic education. By 1837 the society had printed or published *five million books* that would not perhaps have been otherwise published, and sold them at a half or even a third of the normal price (*Directory*, 1837; *443*).

The other book society was the Catholic Society of Ireland. Its object was to supply books *gratuitously* to the poorer classes and to assist in forming parochial lending libraries. Between 1836 and 1840, 40,000 moral and religious books were sent to 117 parishes in Ireland and even to the remotest parts of the Empire. Among the particular aims of this society, which also had the blessing of the hierarchy, were the following, 'to supply Catholic soldiers, sailors, convicts, inmates of institutions with prayer books and other works, and to circulate tracts against Drunkenness'.

The Catholic Truth Society dates from the end of the century. Several attempts were made from 1840 onwards to set up Catholic periodicals, with indifferent success. Cheap devotional periodicals had more success than serious ones (*363*).

Convents and Monasteries

Some convents and monasteries of men and women survived in Ireland from medieval times. In the 1820s, the religious orders of men were represented almost exclusively by the orders of friars, the Augustinians, the Dominicans, the Carmelites and the Franciscans. These assisted the diocesan clergy by preaching, saying mass and hearing confessions. They were not very numerous, numbering about 200 in 1825.

Besides the friars there were the newly re-established and returned Jesuits. They had a school at Clongowes, and had a curious reluctance to inform even their bishop that they were Jesuits, though this was in fact commonly known. Very early in the century there was little to distinguish the activities of the secular from the regular clergy, even if in theory they were quite distinct. On the one hand the regulars could do parish work, and on the other the seculars could run schools etc.

Besides these active orders, it is only fair to include the contemplative order of the Trappists or Cistercians. Though no house of this order existed in Ireland from midway through the eighteenth century until 1831, there was a very strong Irish group in the monastery of Melleray in France. From the figures given to us it is not possible to fix the precise number of Irishmen in that community. Sixty-four came in a body to Ireland on their expulsion from France in 1831. But there may have been Irishmen among the sick who were not expelled immediately, and among the novices. Most of these Trappists were lay brothers, or perhaps lay choir monks; only three Irish monks were priests. Even before the 1830 revolution, Archbishop Murray had wished to have a Cistercian monastery in his diocese, and the Irish prior of Melleray, the future first abbot of Mount Melleray, had made various attempts to have an Irish foundation made. The contemplative life was therefore known and valued, and recruitment to it among Irish Catholics seem to have been proportionately very high (*514*).

When the monks settled on a site in the diocese of Waterford and Lismore, the local people led by the priests gave them a tumultuous welcome and thousands of men assembled with spades to dig the land. The enthusiasm of the ordinary Catholics to support this rather specialised form of the Christian life is not easy to explain. Mount Melleray became the pride and joy of the Irish Church and was the subject of many enthusiastic eulogies. It has been claimed with some plausibility that the return to regular observance by the friars owes much to the example of these austere religious. The chronology fits in any case.

Early in the century, the regulars comprised the four orders of friars, the Jesuits (who technically, in canon law, were clerks regular) and the Cistercians who were monks. The *essential* mark or note of a regular was the solemn public profession of the 'evangelic counsels' of poverty, chastity and obedience. The practical life style of the regulars and seculars in the conditions in Ireland in the early nineteenth century did not differ very much, just as their pastoral activity did not differ very much.

Organisationally, however, the two bodies were very distinct. The regulars, in theory at least, were organised into provinces. This meant that all the members of a given religious order were subjected to a superior of a region called a provincial. In Ireland the province almost invariably coincided with the national boundaries of Ireland. The province, or country, was to the regular in most ways what the diocese was to the secular priest. In theory, any money which was received by the regular was received by the province, which then had the obligation to feed, clothe and support the regular all his life. But the fact that the regulars could not legally own property apparently made this part of the rule a dead letter, and each friar or small group of friars in a monastery or convent supported themselves as best they could, the property being held by individual friars (*175*).

Convents of nuns could be organised into provinces but this was not essential. They could be subjected ecclesiastically to the male branch of the order if such existed, or directly to the bishop. Which authority they were under depended on their respective constitutions or individual rescripts from Rome. (Despite the simple theory, the actual organisation of religious, especially nuns, in the Western Church is a bureaucratic nightmare.)

The regular clergy in these provinces were not subject to the bishop but to the pope. The bishop of Limerick did not wish the regular clergy to have more liberty than the secular clergy and tried to make them submit to the diocesan statutes. Dr Doyle assured the bishop of Limerick that his statute on the conduct of regulars was *nil defectu juris* (i.e. the bishop lacked the requisite legal authority). Doyle himself tried to restrict the activities of the Jesuits in his own diocese from absolving people whom the bishop did not wish readily to absolve, but the Jesuits were able to quote papal authority. This authority to absolve *in their own churches* was to become very important.

The activities of the regulars were in theory also controlled by the provincial. But any dissatisfied friar could apparently request to be allowed to work in a parish and to live outside the convents of the order. The provincial of the Augustinians found it necessary to make a rule that any friar who thus went out should not be allowed to return to any convent of the province as long as he remained provincial. He had already allowed three friars to leave conventual life, and would allow no more.

There was considerable dissatisfaction expressed at the non-observance of the rule by the regulars. Change took two forms, the one quantitative, the other qualitative. The quantitative improvement is difficult to measure with any exactitude, though a cursory glance at the successive *Directories* shows a clear increase in numbers, because we have no idea what proportion of the members of a given province were abroad at any given time.

Qualitative improvement is also difficult to measure, but we know that a reform was undertaken in the ranks of the Irish Dominicans which led to a strict observance of the rule.

Apparently the reform of the Irish Dominicans antedated that of the French Dominicans under Lacordaire and Jandel. The Dominicans abandoned their country posts and re-established themselves in the towns. This meant the abandoning of the custom, deplored by Dr Doyle, of the friars living in ones and twos. The revival of Dominican regular life may be said to date from the erection of their new church in Cork in 1832. One of the Dominicans who brought about the return to regular life, Fr Bartholomew Russell, wrote, 'God did for some of us what our novitiate and college did not do or pretend to do.' Gradually, in the course of the century, a stricter and stricter interpretation of the rule was introduced (*334; 178*).

Reforms among the Franciscans also began around 1830 but there was much resistance to the proposals to wear the habit, sing the office in choir, hold theological conferences, make annual retreats, meditate in church etc. An attempt of one provincial to enforce discipline by calling in Cardinal Cullen may have provoked a reaction. As many of the above points were not part of the Rule of St Francis, but were merely practices commonly but not necessarily wisely adopted by religious in the nineteenth century, a more tactful approach might have been advisable. In 1888 the superior-general in Rome, dissatisfied with the progress being made towards the restoration of regular observance, suspended the novitiate and enforced a drastic reform. The Franciscans were not one of the success stories and their numbers declined throughout the century. They became very successful and popular later. The discalced Carmelites, concentrated in only two houses till 1785 when a third was added, seem to have had a tranquil transition from penal conditions to full restoration of the province in 1895 (*103; 348; 446*). A point to be studied is whether the various orders went through a period of excessive reform which had subsequently to be rectified. Excessive reformers at times cause more trouble in a monastery than those they are attempting to reform. Fitzpatrick, in his life of Fr Tom Burke, notes excessive zeal in the house in England to which Fr Burke was sent, but does not say if this was characteristic of Ireland. Much trouble in Mount Melleray was clearly caused by overzealous reformers (*601*, vol. 29).

The changes in the manner of life of the Irish regulars cannot really be called a reform, for a reform implies that the friars were leading irregular lives. There is no implication that this was the case in Ireland, apart from complaints about individuals: rather the cause of complaint against them was that they were like secular priests without being subjected to the discipline of secular priests. This matter seems to have been remedied by a movement within the orders and not by external compulsion to observe, in Dr Doyle's words, 'regular discipline, as far as is consistent with the laws of the country — that is in everything except dress'. When the Dominicans went so far as to restore the wearing of the tonsure, one prelate, the bishop of Galway in 1860, protested that this was carrying the observance of the rule too far.

The nineteenth century also saw the growth of several new orders of teaching brothers whose presence in Ireland was to become such a feature of the Irish Church. The most famous of these were the Brothers of the Christian Schools of Ireland, commonly called the 'Christian Brothers'. They were founded in 1801 by Edmund Ignatius Rice. Differences with the bishop of Cork caused a split, so that alongside the Christian Brothers, the congregation of Presentation Brothers arose. The Patrician Brothers were started by Dr Delaney of Kildare and Leighlin about 1808 and grew into a widespread order. There was also the Third Order Regular Franciscan Brothers founded by Franciscan lay tertiaries in 1818, the jurisdiction over whom was transferred in 1830 from the provincial of the Franciscans to the archbishop of Tuam, and they remained in that diocese. The Carmelite Brothers of Clondalkin who began as a lay confraternity in 1795 were still in separate existence in 1915, and still under the jurisdiction of the Carmelite Provincial (*140; 446*).

The growth in the orders of women was even more remarkable. The Poor Clare and Dominican orders which had survived the Reformation in Ireland in a few convents got a new lease of life in the nineteenth century and both developed their active sides, and eventually their contemplative sides, as also did the Carmelite nuns. However in 1809, besides the

Presentation Convent at George's Hill, there were in Dublin but two or three ancient convents, with few nuns languishing and barely alive (*324*).

Of the new orders, the first to arrive were the Ursulines who came to Cork in 1771. They were followed almost immediately by a native Irish foundation, the first of the various congregations and societies founded by Irish men and women in Ireland, the Presentation Sisters. Presentation convents were founded in 1775, 1793, 1794, 1798, 1799, 1800, 1807, 1809 (2), 1811, 1813 (3), 1815, 1817 (2) and 1818 (2). About 1812, Archbishop Murray took steps towards founding the Irish Sisters of Charity by sending Mother Mary Aikenhead to the Bar Convent, York to do her novitiate, and then made her the superior of the newly founded convent. Unlike the Presentation Sisters, the Sisters of Charity worked outside the convent enclosure. In 1835 the Irish Sisters of Charity started the first Catholic hospital in Ireland since the Reformation. Murray admired the religious spirit in the Bar Convent and sent two foundresses there for their formation. The result was that there was nothing amateurish about the Irish foundresses, a fault not always avoided elsewhere.

Numerically the greatest growth was recorded by the Irish Sisters of Mercy, founded in Dublin by Catherine McAuley in the late 1820s. In 1841 there were 100 Sisters of Mercy; in 1856 there were about 3,000; by the end of the century there were 8,000; and at the centenary there were 23,000 in many countries of the world. Until her death in 1841, Catherine McAuley founded several of the Mercy convents. A convent schoolgirl herself, Katharine Tynan discusses the extraordinary attraction convent life had for girls. Nuns, she concludes, were not only holy: they were ladylike. On the other hand, James Cullen was put off by the all-too-human face of the Jesuits at Clongowes, though he later joined them. Tynan notes too the capacity for business and the high achievements in practical matters like cookery or needlework to be found in the convents.

The census of 1851 recorded 1,160 nuns; that of 1861, 2,609 nuns; that of 1891, 6,642 nuns; that of 1901, 8,031 nuns. A figure of 14,941 nuns was given for 1971, and

13,938 for 1976 (*Irish Times*, Religious Affairs Corres-
pondent, 3 December 1976). Interestingly, if these figures
are plotted they give almost a straight line, showing a steady
expansion except for the last figure. Even by 1870 the
number of nuns was only about a quarter of their present
strength and consequently in the preceding period were even
less important numerically.

Religious always played a secondary role. The Christian
Brothers lacked the rank and prestige of priests. So too did
the women religious who in addition had the social disadvantage of being female. But even the religious orders of
priests had a secondary position. The diocesan clergy were
accorded a higher rank by canon law (rules of precedence)
and they kept it. The bishops, the canons and the parish
priests dominated the entire scene. The regulars filled out
niches in the Irish Church but did not challenge the seculars.
It may be that the chief aim of the regulars was to maintain a
base in Ireland with a view to working abroad. Their achievements in Ireland did not reach their full potential. They
never matched Maynooth, for example, as leaders of theological thought.

The Devotional Revolution

Official religion followed closely the dry, formal catechism
exposition of duties and prohibitions. According to David
Croly, the secular clergy especially agreed for the most part
with Protestant sentiment in attaching little value to habits,
cords, scapularies etc.

But the nineteenth century saw a great development in
the emotional side of religion. Services were introduced
with a large emotional content and private prayers, popularly
called devotions, increased. A devotion is a set of religious
prayers or acts which is practised not because it is necessary
for salvation or is prescribed by canon law, but because it
expresses the religious feeling of the devout. An example of
a public devotion is the benediction of the Blessed Sacrament.
In this rather short service there are hymns, lights,
ceremonies, prayers and the use of incense, built up into an
emotional exercise. Private devotions usually consisted of
prayers centred emotionally on some aspect of religion.
Examples are given below.

One of the earliest devotions we notice was to the mystery of the Presentation of the Child Jesus in the Temple. Two major religious congregations were founded under this title: Nano Nagle's Presentation Sisters, and Edmund Ignatius Rice's Christian Brothers. Devotion to the Sacred Heart could have been found in Ireland at any time from the seventeenth century onwards when it received its characteristic forms in the revelations to St Margaret Mary Alacoque. But its popularity seems to date from the time of the preaching of Fr Mulcaile S.J. who first publicly preached the devotion in Ireland in the last decades of the eighteenth century. In 1809 a Confraternity of the Sacred Heart was founded in George's Hill Convent and the members undertook to make a 'holy hour' of devotions in honour of the Sacred Heart. This was one of the earliest examples of the practice of the Holy Hour recorded in Ireland. The modern form of the Holy Hour was not established until 1829 by the superior of the Jesuit house in Paray-le-Monial (where St Margaret Mary Alacoque lived). Perpetual adoration of the Blessed Sacrament was begun by the Loreto Sisters at Rathfarnham in 1844.

Dr Murray introduced the devotion to the Sacred Heart to his new congregation of Sisters of Charity, had them affiliated to the Confraternity of the Sacred Heart and obtained for them the right to have a proper mass of the Sacred Heart celebrated on the Feast of the Sacred Heart. He formed a confraternity in Maynooth in 1812 along with Fr Peter Kenny S.J. The archbishop obtained the proper office and mass of the Sacred Heart for the archdiocese of Dublin in 1821. Fr Henry Young probably learned of the devotion to the Sacred Heart in the Vicentian house where he stayed in Rome and he zealously propagated it. He promoted the devotion of the nine 'first Fridays' in honour of the Sacred Heart, with special prayers and benediction after mass on those days. He never said mass in any church without placing in it an image or picture of the Sacred Heart. By 1835, the devotion of the First Fridays was in full bloom in the Franciscan church in Dublin where they were celebrated with solemn high mass, litanies, benediction and indulgences (*443*).

Devotion to Mary appeared in various forms. When Fr Henry Young began his priestly ministry in 1814, besides devotion to the Sacred Heart of Jesus he promoted devotion to the Heart of Mary. This devotion was associated with the first Saturday of each month and Fr Young was a pioneer of its spread in the diocese. This devotion owes its origin in its modern form to the French priest St John Eudes (d. 1680). A public devotion to the Sacred Heart of Mary was begun in St Audeon's in 1840 and a sodality of the Sacred Heart of Mary, which became very popular, was begun in the parish. The archdiocese of Dublin was aggregated by Archbishop Murray to the Arch-confraternity of the Immaculate Heart of Mary in Paris in 1840.

In 1823 Archbishop Murray got the pope to extend the feast and office of the Seven Dolours of Our Lady to Ireland, and obtained the right for the priests in his diocese to say votive offices of devotion to the Blessed Virgin under the titles of Sacred Heart of Mary, Purity of Mary, Maternity of Mary, and Mary, Help of Christians. He also promoted the devotion of the Living Rosary, i.e. a circle of fifteen persons who agreed to form a unit for saying the rosary; in a pastoral letter in 1841 the archbishop noted the rapid spread of the devotion. About 1840 also, Archbishop Murray wished to see the devotions of the month of May in honour of Mary introduced into Ireland, and this was done with great solemnity by the Loreto Sisters in Rathfarnham. Fr Henry Young was then apparently requested by the archbishop to preach and spread the devotion. During his preaching missions, Fr Young also spread devotion to the rosary, to the souls in Purgatory, to the Sacred Heart of Jesus, to the Heart of Mary and to the Passion (*443*).

Not all requests for extra public devotions were necessarily granted by the bishop. One Dublin priest wished to have benediction of the Blessed Sacrament every day in August, but Archbishop Murray allowed it only during the octave of the Assumption, or during a novena prior to that feast. On another occasion the archbishop told Dr Hamilton not to bother his head 'with those pious ladies who have made a holy hobby out of statues':

Depend upon it that with all their 'holy indifference' they are a sturdy race, and that when the interests of piety appear to them to be concerned it is not very safe to come into collision with them.

Someone, I forget who, had the audacity to compare ladies to pigs. It is hard matter to turn either race of animals out of its way.

By 1850, Sion Hill Convent had *exposition* of the Blessed Sacrament on Maundy Thursday, Corpus Christi, the Feast of the Sacred Heart and the Feast of the Immaculate Conception. They had *benediction* of the Blessed Sacrament on all Sundays and holy days, every day during March in honour of St Joseph, and during August in honour of the Immaculate Heart of Mary, on every feast of the order, on the feasts of the Apostles, the Evangelists, St Stephen, St Mary Magdalen, the angel guardians, the archangels, the patronal feast of each sister and the first Friday and Saturday of each month. The 'devotional revolution' had arrived in full bloom in at least one convent.

Kohl, in 1844, noted the subdued character of Irish Catholicism, with little external sign of the Catholic religion. Dr Blake (about 1815) introduced the ringing of a church bell and the ringing of the Angelus, for the first time in public for three hundred years. Dr Blake was also apparently the first priest to ornament divine services with a permanently installed organ (*443*).

The Jubilee of 1825-6, the first for fifty years, was celebrated with great enthusiasm in Ireland. As a Roman-trained priest, Fr Henry Young was called on to advise on the proper manner to celebrate a Jubilee in the various parishes, and was consulted by parish priests and leaders of confraternities alike. One of the items he introduced was a procession with the banners of the confraternities, the first in Dublin since the Reformation. A reference in Ronan's book seems to indicate that the devotion of the Forty Hours was introduced at the time of the Jubilee, but whether it did not catch on at the time or was not favoured by the bishops because of its excessive display, is a point which would have to be more fully researched.

Even by the last quarter of the century, the public display of devotions was not up to the standards to which we have become used in the twentieth century. A careful scrutiny of the periodical literature of the period between 1865 and 1875 shows comparatively few references to devotions, public or private. The Apostleship of Prayer dates from 1863 and the *Sacred Heart Messenger* from 1888. Popular devotion to the Sacred Heart on a wide scale probably dates from Fr James Cullen's (no relation of the Cardinal) crusades at this period. Fr Cullen instituted the Pioneer Total Abstinence Association, thus joining temperance with reparation to the Sacred Heart. Only women were allowed to join at first. By the end of the century, however, it is interesting to note a sales-resistance growing among reverend mothers to the hawking of new devotions by preachers (*363*).

The consecration of Ireland to the Sacred Heart in 1873 shows how far the idea of a *Catholic* Ireland had progressed and how completely the desire of not offending Protestant sentiments had been abandoned. One might say that from then on the partition of Ireland was inevitable. In this year too the periodical *Catholic Ireland* was started, specifically to promote devotion to the Sacred Heart.

The Temperance Movement

The Temperance Movement is in some ways an anomaly in the Irish Church in the early nineteenth century. In the first place it did not flow from traditional Catholic theology which stressed the *moderate* use of alcohol. Secondly, the organisation, or lack of organisation, of the movement was not tied into the diocesan-parochial structure or into any supra-diocesan structure such as that of a religious order. Thirdly, the manner of joining the movement differed in many ways from the manner of joining the other organisations then springing up. There was no careful selection of candidates, no period of probation, no definite standards of moral conduct required, as in admission to the confraternities and the priesthood or religious orders.

The 'Temperance Movement' or 'Total Abstinence Movement' in Ireland means in effect the movement launched by Fr Theobald Mathew and revived by Fr James Cullen.

It was entirely distinct from the regular campaigns waged by the bishops and the clergy against excessive drinking, especially on the Sabbath.

Fr Mathew himself in the Capuchin friary in Cork devoted himself to converting the excessive drinker to more moral standards. The chief problem, especially with those drinkers in receipt of a regular wage, was that they got drunk on a Saturday night. Fr Mathew was urged by three Protestants to lend his name and authority to their work for total abstinence and in 1838 he finally did so. The inspiration for the temperance societies came from America where they had been in existence since the end of the previous century. Fr Mathew was apparently not the first priest in Ireland to form a temperance society. The Temperance Society of St Nicholas's, Dublin, under the direction of the Rev. M. Flanagan, Francis Street, was apparently the first, followed closely by the 'National Total Abstinence Society' of Dr Spratt, O. Carm., both founded in 1838. The Metropolitan Total Abstinence Society of SS Michael and John's, and St Paul's Temperance Society founded by Dr Yore followed in Dublin the same year. St Audeon's also had a parochial temperance society, and there were three more in rural parishes. Though Ronan does not say so, it can be supposed that these *parochial* societies were strictly controlled with regard to admission etc.

These were largely eclipsed by the phenomenal spread of the 'movement' initiated by Fr Mathew. He preached temperance, people took the pledge in thousands and formed themselves into local groups. Mathew was opposed to any kind of organisation, being convinced that he was living through a miracle of divine grace which human activity could only ruin.

> The intention of that holy, apostolic prelate, Rt. Rev. Dr. Kenrick to form the poor Irish teetotallers into a confraternity with rules etc. . . . has overwhelmed me with anguish. The results of the great temperance movement are allowed by all to be miraculous and to be the work of God, and so no one ought to interfere (*23*, 233).

All Fr Mathew required was a 'resolution' to abstain for life from all intoxicating drinks. (The precise obligation of the 'pledge' was a stormy point for the next half century.) He did not require an oath or a vow. Fr Mathew took the pledge in 1838. Within three months, 25,000 people signed; within five months, 131,000; within nine months, 150,000. In Limerick in 1839, 150,000 took the pledge in three days. Soon there was a quarter of a million pledges in Munster. Temperance rooms were hired where people could meet socially without drinking alcohol. Temperance bands became a rage. 'The rage for getting up bands soon became a music mania' (*309*).

> *The Luminary*, continues, 'There were several beautiful banners, on which were inscribed a number of admirable devices — in praise of Temperance, Union, and Industry. Tea and coffee were served whilst the excellent Teetotal band played a number of delightful airs as "Patrick's Day", "Garryowen", "God Save the Queen". . . . The Queen and Prince Albert were toasted with great cheering.' (*443*, 191)

Dr Murray welcomed Fr Mathew to Dublin and supported his movement, but not all the bishops were equally enthusiastic. MacHale opposed him, using violent language, calling Fr Mathew a 'vagabond friar' and even dispensing all the members of his archdiocese from the pledge. According to Rogers, the archbishop preferred a more limited commitment and felt that the pledge should not ever exceed five years. Later Dr Leahy, archbishop of Cashel, said he rarely administered the pledge for life, preferring shorter terms. Rogers also notes that MacHale objected to Mathew's habit of passing from diocese to diocese to address meetings, but the appointment by Rome of Fr Mathew as Commissary Apostolic of his order to some extent removed the grounds for that objection. Fr Augustine discusses at length the cause of the acrimonious dispute between MacHale and the members of the temperance movement and concludes that there was considerable hastiness and misunderstanding on both sides. He does not mention however that Fr Mathew was resolutely neutral in politics, a supporter of Archbishop Murray, and that temperance bands were distinctly pro-union and loyal.

Fr Mathew refused to take a part in politics, refused to allow temperance medals to be worn at political meetings, refused to allow temperance bands to attend political meetings and refused to vote personally in case his personal preference for a candidate might become known. O'Connell wished to harness the temperance movement to the repeal movement, and as lord mayor of Dublin he took part in temperance parades. The very fact that O'Connell was taking part so alarmed Fr Mathew that he would have cancelled the parade in Cork in 1842 if he were given the slightest excuse.

The organisation of the movement was sketchy. However Fr Mathew had to maintain a sufficient staff to print and disseminate handbills, tracts etc., to help in setting up temperance rooms and temperance bands, to shore up local societies in danger of collapse, to defray expenses connected with the big parades and demonstrations and to organise the journeys for himself and his companions and see that their travelling expenses were paid.

One of the ways Fr Mathew tried to meet expenses was through the sale of medals but this was inadequate and he was soon heavily in debt. A group of gentlemen including the Duke of Leinster wished to form a committee to deal with his personal affairs but this he absolutely refused to allow. A collection was made which paid off the creditors for the moment, but Fr Mathew was totally unable to control the expense either of himself or of his followers. Bands ran up bills with tailors and instrument makers and then had recourse to Fr Mathew for settlement.

Perhaps rather predictably, the great majority of the people did not adhere to the pledge taken in Fr Mathew's movement. Forbes carefully enquired about the state of temperance in his tour around Ireland, and noted that by that time most people had abandoned their total abstinence pledges. Among the reasons cited for this by Fr Augustine are: the famine and consequent social disturbance; the political events of 1848, with their disturbances; Fr Mathew's prolonged ill health; his long absence in America; and the despair in Ireland over the Sadleir and Keogh betrayal. But perhaps more importantly, the clergy had come round to

MacHale's way of thinking. Most of the Maynooth students asked for dispensation. Forbes noted that temperance leaders no longer relied on mere enthusiasm, but rather on the safer ground of reason and experience. Rogers notes that the non-denominational character of Fr Mathew's movement led to its being ignored by the hierarchy, and it was not mentioned at the Synod of Thurles.

I have been unable to get any figures or statistics with regard to the parish temperance societies set up under the regular supervision of parish priests. It is likely, however, that the majority of the hundreds of thousands whom Forbes noted as still keeping the pledge belonged to one or other of the Catholic parish societies or Church-related Protestant organisations.

Though later work for temperance is usually associated with Fr James Cullen and his Pioneer Total Abstinence Society (1898), this society did not attain in the nineteenth century the numbers and influence it was to attain in the following century. More important perhaps was the normal pastoral campaign of the bishops and clergy against what was becoming a national evil. Eventually this bias towards temperance education and training was to become a noted characteristic of the Irish Church. But it came about through the ordinary pastoral ministry at all levels, not through a revivalist-style movement. Matt Talbot rather than Theobald Mathew is the characteristic figure. Total abstinence, though voluntary, was, and still is, a feature of Irish Catholicity which is regarded as an oddity by foreign Catholics. The history of the temperance movement after Fr Mathew is given in the Life of Fr James Cullen. The 'confirmation pledge' dates from the 1890s, though it was applied in some dioceses earlier (*424; 363*).

Retreats and Parish Missions

Retreats differ from parish missions largely in the fact that retreats are preached to smaller groups who usually assemble within a given building for the purpose, while a mission is directed at all the people of a parish, even though a series of religious exercises similar to those held during retreats are preached in the parish church.

The first missions to the country parishes in Ireland seem to have been those given by Fr Henry Young at the direction of Archbishop Murray in 1827. Fr Young had stayed with the Vincentians in Rome when studying and was familiar with their methods. The missions conducted by Fr Young lasted for weeks or even months in a given parish and during it he visited personally every single family. He attacked abuses at wakes and fairs. He preached devotion to the Sacred Heart, to the Immaculate Heart of Mary, to the Passion and to the Souls in Purgatory. He instilled the idea of temperance into the people, set up the Stations of the Cross, the Purgatorian Society, and enrolled members in the Brown Scapular of our Lady of Mount Carmel. Between 1836 and 1838, Fr Young seems to have been switched to giving retreats all over Ireland to communities of religious and to students (*443*).

This was really a one-man effort. In 1832 four Dublin priests, with the blessing of the archbishop, banded themselves together for mission work. It was not until well on in the 1840s however that the regular practice of giving parish missions got under way. Their first mission was preached in the parish of Athy in the archdiocese of Dublin in 1842. Just before this, in 1840, in the Jesuit Church in Gardiner Street on the occasion of the tercentenary of the foundation of the Society of Jesus, the Jesuits preached a nine-day public retreat after the manner of the Exercises of St Ignatius. This public retreat, really indistinguishable from the parish mission as it was to become, caused a spiritual sensation in Dublin. The first enclosed retreat for lay people was organised in 1846 by the Loreto Sisters. The real excitement came with the arrival of the Italian missionaries later in the decade. The ensuing enthusiasm for hearing the preachers can only be described as a craze. Fr Tom Burke, the famous Dominican preacher, used to poke fun at the Italian preachers during clerical gatherings ('without face you cannot be shaved'), although Leetham attributed the popularity of the missions to the great faith of the Irish.

Dr Gentili, the Italian Rosminian, spoke English perfectly. In 1848 he introduced the devotion of the Forty Hours, and the Blue Scapular of the Immaculate Conception. Frederick

Lucas, however, in *The Tablet* noted that his accent was difficult to follow. The first Passionist mission was preached in 1849 by Fr Dominic Barberi. The Belgian Redemptorists, and the ever-famous sermons on hellfire, came to Limerick in 1853. It is difficult to get any kind of statistics about the spread of these parochial missions, but in 1852 MacHale, writing to Propaganda, says that he exhorted his clergy to make use of this means of spiritual assistance. This letter is dated earlier than that of Pius IX to MacHale exhorting him to use retreats and missions. Apparently parochial missions were regarded at the time as a great panacea, and a safe one. Pius IX's exhortations overlooked the fact that there was at that date a great shortage of qualified missioners in Ireland, and MacHale had no difficulty in pointing this out to Propaganda. It was estimated that there were about twenty missioners in Ireland in 1862.

Retreats for *working men* were adopted from France and Belgium early in the twentieth century (*398*).

The Foreign Missions and the Propagation of the Faith

Irish priests worked abroad for centuries but few of these were missionary priests. When Irish students completed their studies in continental colleges they had to seek employment in some diocese. Such dioceses might be in North America and these could be genuinely described as missionaries. Unlike the regulars, Irish secular priests did not arrive in America in any great numbers till the Revolution. A few Irish priests, apparently volunteers, were in South Africa and Australia from around 1820.

In 1837 Propaganda addressed bulls to the archbishop of Dublin detaching the mission in South Africa from that of Mauritius, and making it a separate vicariate apostolic, and shortly afterwards bulls were issued to a Fr Griffiths appointing him bishop of the vicariate. He went on a preaching tour in Ireland seeking recruits, and one or two priests went to South Africa with him. From South Africa the new bishop wrote to Archbishop Murray requesting that the Irish Sisters of Charity be sent out. The Irish Sisters of Charity sent a community to Australia in 1838 (*9; 13; 367*).

In 1840 Dr Cullen in Rome was asked by Propaganda to

try to secure more priests for the missions. After discussing the matter with Archbishop Murray, he reported that the chief obstacles were lack of money for education, no college (presumably no *endowed* college in the Romans sense) for the missions and a lack of Irish vicars apostolic under whom Irish priests would be willing to serve. Requests for priests continued to come from South Africa and, in addition, from Nova Scotia. Dr Murray informed Dr Hamilton that he did not know where they were to come from. About this time the foreign mission college, of which more later, was mooted. Dr Griffiths does not seem to have got his convent just then.

The Presentation Sisters had a convent in Madras in 1842, and one in Newfoundland as early as 1833. The Loreto Sisters set out for Calcutta in 1841 where they were welcomed by the Irish bishop of that diocese and by the Governor-General, Lord Auckland. Forty-two sisters were to die there in the next twenty years. In 1845 the Loreto Sisters went to the British-owned French-speaking island of Mauritius and to Gibraltar to assist the Irish Franciscan bishop there. In 1879 they went to the Transvaal, but a foundation in Spain in 1851 was uncharacteristic. The Irish Sisters of Mercy had convents in St John's, Newfoundland in 1842, in Liverpool in 1843 and in New York, Perth, Pittsburg and Chicago before 1850. Dr Cullen noted that before 1840 Irish priests had gone to the East Indies [India?], to Australia and to the Cape of Good Hope, so these convents can be seen as direct results of the expansion of Irish priests overseas.

The introduction of the Society for the Propagation of the Faith, founded in Lyons in 1822 by Pauline Jaricot, also made Ireland mission minded. In 1838 a Fr O'Toole came from Paris to establish it in Ireland, and at his request Archbishop Murray convened a meeting in September and was the first person in Ireland to subscribe to the new institute. Before his death in 1852, £70,000 had been subscribed in Ireland for the support of missionaries abroad, an average of £5,000 a year. The association's magazine, the *Annals*, sold 75,000 copies in 1841.

A missionary college for educating priests for the missions was founded in Drumcondra, Dublin by Fr Hand with the personal encouragement of the ubiquitous Archbishop Murray, who personally named the college All Hallows. After an initial period when alumi went to the tropics, the college began to concentrate on Britain, Australia, New Zealand, Canada, South Africa and the USA. The near-fatal life in the tropics may have been the cause.

Though numerically perhaps not as great as in the twentieth century, Irish missionary activity abroad was considerable. Irish influence however probably reached a peak by the end of the nineteenth century when Maynooth, in Dr MacDonald's opinion, was the undisputed head of a worldwide spiritual empire. The increasing maturity of the Churches in America, Australia etc. in the following century naturally tended to lessen the role of the parent Church. We should note that the missionary effort was ·completely unstructured, each individual or group going where it liked when it liked, bound only by canon law. The prestige of the Irish Church was the sole source of its influence, but the spread of Irish-type Churches throughout the Empire and further indicates the effectiveness of this influence. And it was effective. If a full study of developments in canon law were made — especially leading up to the revision of the Code by Pius X — it might well be found that the whole Church was 'hibernicised' rather than Ireland being 'Romanised'. There were two reasons for this: the extreme reluctance of Irish bishops at home or abroad to give up ancient rights and customs, and the suitability of Irish customs developed under the penal laws to missionary conditions.

Changes in the Parochial Work of the Clergy

Unlike the building of monasteries, churches etc., changes in the life of the parish are hard to document because of lack of exactly comparative material over the entire period. Certain matters were noted as innovations at the time, and on these we rely. Ronan notes that in 1841 Fr James Young introduced the custom of having Benediction of the Blessed Sacrament on one Sunday of the month. His brother had already introduced this custom to St Michan's, and it is reasonable to suppose that the custom of having Benediction dates from about this time. It is not stated if the Benediction was after last mass or was a separate service in the evening. In Newry sometime during Dr Blake's rule, the 'Nine Fridays' were celebrated officially, and Benediction was given on Friday mornings after the half-past eight mass. On Easter Sunday there was Benediction after last mass, and vespers, sermon and Benediction in the evening.

In 1840 Archbishop Murray commended the zeal of those Dublin priests who were now spending Saturday evenings and Sunday mornings voluntarily in the confessional. Sometime, probably at or after mid century, Dr Blake *prescribed* the hours the priests were to stay in the confessional during Paschal Time. In 1836 Dr Blake instructed the vicar-general to get a certain priest to put a confessional into the church and to say mass every day. The increasing presence of confessionals should probably be connected with regular hours of attendance by the priests in them.

It is also noteworthy that the priest was asked to say mass every day. Ulick Bourke notes that Dr MacHale said mass every day for the last sixteen years of his life (1865-81), but before that about thrice a week. J. A. Murphy notes that around 1800 there might be as many as a hundred station masses a year in populous parishes. There were few private masses of devotion, so this would mean mass in the parish on two or three mornings a week. It would seem that around mid century it was felt proper for a priest to say mass every day (Appendix B).

In 1830 Dr Kelly of Dromore thought that marriages within the forbidden degrees even with a dispensation should not be celebrated in the church, which would seem to imply that marriage was celebrated in a church at least sometimes at that date. In 1844 Dr Murray called Dr Hamilton's attention to the form of ceremony of the marriage in church as described in *The Tablet*, and wished to see that followed.

Fr Young introduced the custom of *kneeling* at mass into Finglas about 1840, which indicates approximately when this practice was introduced. The custom of allowing people to bring up secular affairs during mass was abolished in Dromore around 1830, which again gives us an approximate date. It is unclear when the custom of leaving the chapels open all day began, for early in the century they were closed after morning mass. It is difficult to determine if masses on Sunday became more numerous. An attempt was being made to cut down on the practice of each priest saying two masses on Sunday. On the other hand also there was a growing number of masses in chaplaincies and gaols and such places. Katharine Tynan notes a puritanical campaign in the 1860s and '70s to stamp out crossroad dances and other rural gaieties, with no attempt to replace them. At the very end of the century, Fr James Cullen, the temperance worker, stressed the need for priests to organise suitable amusements. Novel reading and 'fast' dances were increasingly disapproved of, not to mention the theatre. But despite murmurings, the priest's authority was sacrosanct. Miss Tynan thought Cullen lacked human qualities. With regard to the activity of the clergy in the first half of the century, indirect evidence for an increase comes from the growing number of activities carried on in the parish in the form of building new churches and seeing to their constant improvement, the development of the confraternities, parochial libraries, agencies like the Society for the Propagation of the Faith and the Society of St Vincent de Paul. There seems to have been an increase in the numbers approaching the sacraments, probably due to the influence of the confraternities. The priests were also given the role of supervisors of the schools and guardians against attempts at proselytism. But as noted earlier, the teaching of catechism was now done by school teachers. Later, other activities of a non-religious nature were added which kept the priest in constant contact with his parishioners, for example chairmanships of agricultural co-operatives, sports clubs etc. It is not clear from this formal recognition of the strategic role of the priest if his influence was greater than earlier in the century.

Changes Affecting the Laity

There seems to have been a considerable change in the habits of *social* behaviour in Ireland in the course of the nineteenth century. Macaulay in 1872 notes the greater sobriety of conduct and the absence of faction fights and of disturbances at wakes. But he attributes the improvement partly to education, partly to the better enforcement of law and order, and partly to the improved example of the better classes. This latter point is important:

> The rollicking, reckless, fighting, fox-hunting, squire or squireen, the half-pay captain of dragoons, professional duellist, gambler and scamp, the punch-imbibing and humorous story-telling priest, the cringing tenantry and lawless peasantry; how unreal and unrepresentative all these characters seem now! Before Charles Lever died last year most of his pictures were out of date. It is Ireland of the past he depicted. . . . Yet Charles Lever was a true artist of days not long gone by (*345*).

A. M. Sullivan noted a change in social habits also: 'More steadiness of purpose, more firmness and determination of character, mark the Irish peasantry of the new era.' Sullivan connects this with the temperance movement and notes that there was a greater general sobriety, a turn to religion and a lessening of crime. Godkin too noted that the gatherings which led to drunkenness and immorality had been largely suppressed by 1865, at least in rural areas, and he gives full credit to the Catholic clergy for their part in bringing about the improvement. Godkin also noted a more aggressive policy on the part of Catholics:

> The Roman Catholic revival during the last quarter of a century in Ireland has taken a direction in regard to doctrine and worship which may be regarded as an innovation of very grave import.
>
> The doctrinal system which prevailed up to the present generation was what might be called — to adopt a Protestant phrase — 'Low Church'. The tone of controversy, where it was adopted, was rather apologetic, and the policy defensive rather than aggressive, and there seemed to be everywhere a desire to present what Protestant regarded as errors in the system in a mitigated form.

He goes on to note that the Catholic clergy enthusiastically combatted the Bible readers, infiltrating Bible meetings in order to read out the speeches of O'Connell and Shiel, but doctrinally also there was an increasing emphasis on specifically

Catholic interpretations of dogma, transubstantiation, veneration of the saints and especially Marian dogmas. The Catholic churches were everywhere more visible, no Catholic opened a pub on Sundays, nor was a fair or market held on a Catholic holy day.

During the pontificate of Pius IX, especially following on the misfortunes of that pope, there seems to have grown up widely a sense of loyalty to the papacy which was not there before. Of course in the early part of the century the Irish Church was in conflict with the papacy, a respectful but very firm conflict, before and after the Quarantotti Rescript. Evidence is found in the *Life* of Dr Dixon of Armagh, the primate.

The only public meeting that Dr Dixon ever attended was one held in a church in Drogheda in 1859 to express the sympathy of the clergy and laity for the misfortunes of the pope. Dixon said:

> I may say perhaps that it is the first time in my life I have attended a public meeting and it may be a long time before I will do so again. . . .
>
> You must remember we are assembled in a sacred place — though the Blessed Sacrament is removed — but at the same time an appropriate place to assemble in for the cause which has brought us together.

Dixon organised the Papal Brigade to go to fight in the Papal States and about a thousand volunteers were recruited. In 1849, at the time of the pope's first exile, the archbishop of Dublin collected almost £2,700 for the pope in his diocese. Dr McNally of Clogher collected £400. After 1870 the collection for the pope, called 'Peter's Pence' was established on a regular basis. While some decisions by Rome in the 1880s brought a certain unpopularity, the general pattern was soon re-established (*580; 573; 268*).

In 1825 Primate Curtis hoped to be able to collect £1,000 from Ireland towards the rebuilding of the basilica of St Paul, promising twenty guineas personally and expecting like sums from the other bishops. He added that gallican opinions were not taught in Maynooth and that all the Irish bishops were loyal to the Holy See. After the Veto controversy and the evidence before the parliamentary committee that year, some people in Rome might have had doubts. Curtis sent money from the bishops only. As he had been prominent in organising the Catholic Rent in his diocese, he may not have wished to add another collection especially when the Rent was already interfering with the normal charitable collections.

So on the evidence available we cannot conclude that there was a swing from anti-papal feeling or from virtual gallicanism to outright ultramontanism. From the 'Veto' till the 'Plan of Campaign', there was resistance to papal interference in political matters, just as there was lay resistance to clerical interference. Ultramontanism in the form in which it existed in France at Solemnes or in England at the Brompton Oratory, with an exaggerated devotion to all typically Roman practices, never existed at any time in Ireland. And as is well known, it was the assurance by Dr Russell of Maynooth that in Ireland the clergy avoided the more typical Latin excesses which led Dr Newman into the Church. This good sense typified Irish priests.

By the end of the century the numbers attending mass on weekdays was noticed by strangers. Direct comparison with earlier in the century is not possible because of conditions prevailing in rural Ireland, and lack of information as to what proportion of a district attended a convenient station mass. Notice was also taken of the number of communicants, especially men. This had been commented on too at the beginning of the century, but the general impression is that there was a significant increase in 'devotional' masses and communions. The practice of having masses said for the dead and of praying for the souls in Purgatory in general seems to have been another devotion which was to become a characteristic of Irish Catholicism (*374; 290*).

9

Changes Involving the Hierarchy

In this chapter I will deal with those aspects of the Irish
Church which involved national problems or national proposals, and which the bishops decided to treat in a uniform
manner. I will also deal with such questions as appertain
more properly to the activity of bishops within their own
dioceses, even though there was no particular national
strategy agreed on. Finally, some things which involved
clergy from all ranks are included here.

I have dealt, for the sake of convenience, in an earlier
chapter with the structural changes in the Church involving
the bishops, the development of the Conference of Bishops
and the holding of national synods.

The Appointment of Bishops, the Veto and Domestic Nomination

The first major point with which the Irish hierarchy had
to deal after the Act of Union was the question of the
appointment of bishops. There were two points involved in
this. The first was a claim put forward by some British
ministers that in the event of Catholic Emancipation
being conceded, the government would have the right
of *Veto* over any appointment they disliked. The other was
the claim by parish priests to be allowed to choose the names
to be forwarded to Rome. There was thus a political element
and a religious element. The whole got entangled in the
prolonged campaign for civil emancipation (*60*).

The question of the appointment of bishops was much
discussed at the beginning of the century. Dr Doyle made a
particular study of the discipline of the Irish Church on this
point and expounded it in the *Dublin Evening Post* in 1822

in the course of a controversy, and also before the parliamentary enquiry of 1825 as follows.

There was no one method in force in the Celtic or medieval Church. Even if certain powers were conceded to the king, it did not follow that the local chapters obeyed the king. Originally bishops were elected by people and clergy conjointly and then the right was restricted to the clergy and finally to the chapters. The various popes and kings entered into agreements whereby the king was given the right to send a *congé d'elire* to the chapter recommending a person the king wished to see elected. This was done in Ireland in Tudor and Stuart times but no such right was accorded to the Protestant monarchs. The Stuarts even after 1690 continued to 'nominate' bishops even without consulting the chapters. But the popes themselves also nominated, 'sometimes at the entreaty of a nobleman resident in Ireland, sometimes through this or that influence'. From the death of the Young Pretender it was allowed that the pope had the right of original nomination, but in fact he never appointed anyone except a person recommended by someone in Ireland (*170*).

But conceding the right of original nomination to the pope would apparently mean that the chapters lost their right to elect, unless it referred only to dioceses which had no chapter. But it is clear that the chapters had lost the right of *election*, and this was never restored. It is not clear when they lost this right. Such chapters as existed in the early nineteenth century often assembled to *choose* a name to send to Rome (i.e., not to elect). The pope, hearing the wishes of the chapter and of the other interested parties, himself made the appointment. Any person or group could recommend someone for the vacant see, for the ordinary Catholic could write to the pope about anything. Townsend notes however a decree of Propaganda in 1785 saying that petitions and recommendations from Irish gentlemen would be ignored. This seems not to have been done for a century later. The assistance of a lay lord was still regarded as effective (*12*). At that time it was customary for the clergy of the diocese to meet and send in a recommendation of one or more persons to Rome, and the bishops of the province likewise met and sent in their recommendations, and the opinion of the bishops was felt to have the greater weight (*499*).

The parish clergy certainly had the right to elect a vicar capitular on the death of a bishop. Benedict XIV made it clear that in the case of the death of a bishop, the following rules were to be observed for the election of a vicar capitular. The practice existing in each diocese hitherto was to be observed. Where there was a chapter, and the chapter hitherto had met without other ecclesiastics, it was to do so in future, and was alone to elect the vicar capitular. Where the custom was for other ecclesiastics to join with them, those who always hitherto had attended and voted were to do so for the future. Where there was no chapter, the parish priests, either alone or with other ecclesiastics who always had attended and voted, were for the future to attend and vote (*601*, 30, Bull *Quam in sublimi*, 27 July 1753). This bull apparently gave legal force to arrangements already traditional, but did not innovate or establish uniformity.

Following a proposal by Lord Castlereagh, the chief secretary for Ireland, the episcopal trustees of Maynooth agreed that the Veto was lawful. The government proposal was connected with emancipation and the Act of Union (*60*).

What seems to have been overlooked was the hostile attitude of the civil patriotic party in Ireland. The co-adjutor of Dublin, Dr Murray; the bishop of Cloyne, Dr Coppinger; the bishop of Cork, Dr Murphy; Dr Blake, the future bishop of Dromore; and Rev. Richard Hayes O.S.F. were among the leaders of *clerical* opposition. Rome was prepared to concede the right of Veto and the Irish bishops refused to agree.

Fr Hayes among others, including the bishops, then brought in his plan of 'domestic nomination'. Hayes' plan, put before the Sacred Congregation, was as follows: the parish priests, including members of the chapter, were to elect three persons. The bishops of the province were to add a note on the merits of each. Propaganda was to appoint one of the three. For co-adjutors, the bishop was to propose whom he wanted to the parish priests and canons, who would agree to accept or not by voting. The bishops of the province would add their opinion and Rome would appoint (*60*). With regard to the Veto, Cannon remarks:

> In the face of the uncompromising attitude of the Irish hierarchy and laity the Pope did not insist on the proposed concessions. Having received the bishops' letter, Pius VII directed the Prefect of Propaganda to inform the Irish prelates that he would approve domestic nomination if a method acceptable to all could be found.

Negotiations with Rome dragged on. 'There is no hurry at all — *sat cito si sat bene* — Rome is never in overgreat haste for us, nor should we for her. I fear she is very easy about what gives us so much trouble' (*578*, Curtis to Murray, 20 April 1823). Curtis was of the opinion that all mention of the government should be omitted but wanted Troy's and Murray's opinions. Murray and Curtis wished to have the franchise among the clergy limited as much as possible. Writing to Murray, Dr Doyle said:

> ... the glory of God and the interests of our Church would be advanced in proportion as the power of electing would be removed from the lower clergy and restricted to the bishops; but this is an impression which if acted upon would not be well received in Rome, and would have to meet at home every species of obloquy and opposition.
>
> Therefore, preferring what is more practicable, to what appears to me most wise, I would divide the right of election between the first and second orders (as they are called) of the clergy.
>
> For this purpose I would preserve the chapters where they are, and create, or re-establish them. ... On the demise of the Bp. [*sic*] I would have the Dean and chapter to assemble, and proceed to elect in the legal manner three persons to be recommended to the Holy See.
>
> I cannot but feel something of regret that the H. See [*sic*] should be so tenacious of her privilege as not to suffer us even to treat with her about our discipline — that she should consider us in all respects a prostrate Church as we are a prostrate people, and withhold from us all right to elect our own pastors. ...

God grant she does not reserve the power she is so anxious not to communicate for the purpose of entering into engagements with others who should not be entitled to her confidence (*545*).

If Doyle was looking for full canonical right of election, this was never conceded by Rome, then or since (*578*).

The proposals finally put forward by the Irish hierarchy in the names of the archbishops of Armagh, Dublin and Cashel suggested that *all* and *only* the parish priests should be convoked and that they were to select three names. The bishops of the province were to hear the results of the election, to approve or disapprove of some or all of them and change the order if they liked. If they disapproved of all three, they were to seek permission of the Holy See to have the parish priests proceed to another election. Cardinal Cappellari replied for Pius VII saying the following modification would make the proposals acceptable: that canons, where they existed, should also be called; that the words election, nomination and postulation should never be used, but only terms suggesting commendation; the words *dignus, dignior* and *dignissimus* should be omitted, but there should simply be a mention of the merits of each candidate; that the documents should be in the form of a petition to the Holy See; and finally, that if the bishops rejected all three, the pope himself would provide, without another election. The absolute right of the pope to appoint was safeguarded (*Directory*, 1843).

Dr Whyte has given figures for appointments within and without the *terna* up till Pius IX. Leo XIII was regarded as being more unwilling than his predecessor to go outside the *terna*. (Each pope gives directives to the Roman Congregations, informing them of his general policies. This is called the *stylus curiae*. It does not imply personal intervention.) In 1925 there was a return to Dr Doyle's opinion and the bishops were given the dominant role, while the post-Vatican II period saw a return to appointing from the *terna*.

It should be noted that *Cum ad Gravissimum* merely settled a legal point within the dioceses. Lobbying by interested parties or governments continued. Rome rarely appointed a priest as bishop in Ireland if the British government objected to him. It is unclear if the British government was always consulted, or always made representations. It would seem that the Roman Secretariat of State would have preferred a formal consultation procedure, but this was rejected in favour of an informal link by the Foreign Office. Propaganda seems to have been neutral, and at most periods Irish government affairs were of low priority in the British cabinet. In 1829 Sir Robert Peel resolutely refused to recognise the jurisdiction of the Holy See in any way in the United Kingdom, and refused to include safeguards like the 'Veto' and 'Exequatur' in the Emancipation Act of 1829. On the other hand, Greville says that Gregory XVI rarely appointed against the wishes of the British government (*399; 12*).

The 'Second Reformation', Proselytising and Religious Controversy

The Second Reformation is the name given to the amorphous movement in Ireland inspired by similar movements in England which began early in the nineteenth century. Its aims were to convert non-Protestants to 'Christianity' and to convert Protestants to a more 'evangelical' life. For these aims it relied chiefly on the distribution of the Bible. The movement was worldwide and usually called the biblical or evangelical movement. The founding of the Hibernian Bible Society in 1806 marks the beginning of the movement, but Bowen prefers 1820 as a more accurate date for the onset of the Second Reformation.

Some attempts at least were made to spread the Bibles throughout Ireland and to convert the Catholics. Even though we have two studies by Bowen on this subject it is still difficult to get an exact idea of the extent of the attempt to convert Catholics. We do not have any clear idea, for example, of how many parishes in Ireland saw a serious attempt being made to convert Catholics or to turn Protestants to a more scriptural mode of life. But for the purposes of this study, no factual investigation is necessary; it was sufficient for it to have been believed that the biblicals were everywhere active. Mostly this may have been scaremongering, and Dr MacHale had to assure the pope that the biblicals were active in only six or seven parishes in his diocese. What is of interest is the sudden burst into controversy on the part of the Catholic clergy. As Thomas Wyse put it: 'A new and somewhat fantastic spirit of polemical chivalry then burst upon the country; every dogma was made a good plea for battle.' This was the great era of public theological dispute and polemical sermons.

The biblicals were alleged to be attempting to proselytise Catholic children in the schools. Evidence that they were actually doing so is hard to come by, at least as far as the pay or hedge schools, which formed the vast bulk of the schools, were concerned. In a survey of the twenty schools in Wicklow parish, some Catholic and some Protestant, there was no evidence of proselytism (*582*). The allegation was sufficient, however, to make education an important element in the campaign for Emancipation.

> The priest saw that he lived in a day when instruction could not be refused; the only point with him was how it could best be given, and in his own defence he founded Catholic schools.
>
> The cause of education became identified with the cause of Emancipation. It formed a principal object in the collection of the 'Rent' (*545*).

One does not get the impression that the Catholics took the Protestant threat seriously. On the other hand they seemed to have welcomed every attempt of the biblicals as an opportunity not only to engage the enemy in battles they could not lose because of popular support, but also to carry the war into the enemy's camp. The priests bought copies of the *Dublin Register* in which were printed the speeches of Shiel and O'Connell, infiltrated the Bible meetings, and read the pro-Emancipation speeches to the captive audience (*198*).

The scale of the effort can be judged by the claim that the number of converts to the New Reformation up until 1828 was only 2,357. The onset of the Tithe War in the 1830s doomed any attempt at mass conversion. Occasionally there were scares. In 1852 the biblicals were announced to be solidly entrenched in the very parish of the archbishop of

Dublin, Dr Murray. Three thousand or even six thousand poor children were alleged to be in their schools. Numerous and crowded meetings of the clergy met to decide on action; the confraternities, the Society of St Vincent de Paul and the Christian Doctrine Societies were all urged to take action. The Catholic journals deplored the situation. The statements of the Irish papers were repeated by those on the continent and reached the ears of the pope. When an actual count was made of Catholic children attending *any* Protestant school, it was found that they totalled one hundred and fifty, and in most cases the schools were Protestant pay schools where no attempt was made to proselytise.

The well-meant endeavours of various evangelical bodies to convert the Catholic poor poisoned relations between the Churches till the end of the century. Catholics did not distinguish between legitimate attempts to preach the gospel and underhand attempts to secure adherents with offers of clothes, soup or jobs.

The Education Question

The Catholics had no school system of their own apart from some hundreds of Catholic charity schools, and no real way of supporting them. There were other schools supported by the government. The Kildare Place Society was sufficiently neutral in its attitude towards Catholic children to allow Catholic children to attend, and O'Connell himself sat on the board. Then there came the growth of the 'Second Reformation' and the allegation that the schools of the Kildare Place Society were being used for purposes of proselytism (*21; 3; 146; 22*).

In 1819 Propaganda issued a warning in the form of a letter from Cardinal Fontana to the bishops of Ireland, which letter was still referred to in the footnotes giving the *fontes* of each canon in the 1917 Code (*Codex Juris* can 1374).

... information has reached the ears of the Sacred Congregation that Bible schools, supported by the funds of the Catholics, have been established in almost every part of Ireland, in which, under the pretext of charity, the inexperienced of both sexes, but particularly peasants and the poor, are allured by the blandishments, and even gifts of the masters, and infected with the fatal poison of depraved doctrines.

It is further stated, that the directors of the schools are generally speaking, Methodists, who introduce Bibles, translated into English by the Bible Society, and propt up by errors, with the sole view of seducing the young. . . .

Every possible exertion must be made, therefore, to keep the youth away from these destructive schools. . . .

But for the purpose of escaping the snares of the adversaries, no plan seems more appropriate than the establishing of schools, wherein salutary instructions may be imparted to the poor and illiterate country persons.

This letter came from Propaganda and not from the Holy Office whose right it was to deal with all matters concerning the spread of heresy. It was in the form of an encyclical letter, i.e., a letter of the pope to his 'venerable brothers' in Ireland (*Codex*, loc. cit.). It was a cautious document, merely reporting what had been said and issuing a warning that children should be kept away from such schools, if any such schools were actually found to exist, and concluding with the platitude that the best way to deal with the matter was to build Catholic schools. Curtis, the newly appointed primate, wrote to Plunkett:

I have the honour of transmitting to your Lordship the enclosed copy of Cardinal Fontana's circular letter to the four archbishops, which was received in our meeting of the 29th ultimo.

In my letter of the 10th instant to his Eminence, I mention some particulars, in which the information given to the Sacred Congregation appears incorrect, concerning heterodox proselytising schools, as they have been silenced and put down in many places by Catholic schools, which the prelates endeavour to erect and encourage, as the best antidote against such attempts (97).

As Thomas Wyse remarked, it was not until the threat of proselytism became imminent that the priests set up Catholic schools. These schools would of course be set up only in the vicinity of the proselytising schools.

Who supplied the information to Rome? If one reads the second and third letters of Hierophilos written by MacHale from Maynooth in 1820, one would suspect J. MacHale, but Edmund Rice's brother in Rome is another possibility.

How real was the threat of the proselytisers? What was said above on the effectiveness of the Second Reformation should be considered. It is sufficient to note that allegations about the Bible schools in Dublin were reported to Rome by Archbishop Murray's opponents, without there being apparently much substance in the allegations. Allegations were made about the success of the Bible Societies in MacHale's own diocese, allegations which MacHale apparently had no difficulty in refuting (*324; 399*).

For various reasons, one of which was the unsatisfactory state of the hedge schools, the idea of a genuine national system of education, both for the spiritual and the secular advancement of the country, was mooted, and gained adherents both with the government and with the Irish bishops. Fitzpatrick, in a tantalising reference, states, 'We have no doubt that the dissentient prelates at the Synod of 1821 over-rated in their zeal for religion the dangers with which they imagined it was threatened.'

It was not until 1826 that we have a clear statement of the definite views of the hierarchy. In 1821 Doyle had written to Sir Henry Parnell:

In the counties of Carlow, Kildare, and the Queen's County, very nearly all the Roman Catholic children attend school during the summer and autumn, and are taught reading, writing and arithmetic, but their masters are in many instances extremely ignorant, their school-houses are mere huts, where the children are piled on each other and the sexes promiscuously jumbled together.

For want of space the Lancastrian plan, or that of Bell cannot be introduced; and if there were space, we have not the funds to buy forms, books, or to pay a master capable of instructing.

In the winter months the children do not attend. . . . Of these three counties I may safely say that nine-tenths

of the farmers' children and all those of the better classes
receive education of a very imperfect kind, and imparted
in a very defective way by men, in most instances, incom-
petent to teach.

The children of the poor in the country are entirely
neglected; in the towns many are left in absolute ignorance. . . .

These counties, I presume, might present an average
view of the state of Roman Catholic education throughout Leinster and Munster . . . but in Connaught (which I
visited chiefly to ascertain the state of the peasantry) they
are buried in destitution, filth, ignorance, and misery.
I believe that in the North, below Drogheda, their state
is not much better (*175*).

We may note Doyle's objection to the promiscuous jumbling
of the sexes. For the rest of the century, education was
strictly segregated. About 1900, a teacher of Irish in
Portarlington was rebuked by the parish priest for holding
mixed classes. The teacher told the parish priest to mind his
own business. The language movement often provides interesting criticisms of official clerical attitudes.

Rev. Michael Collins agreed that Catholics would accept
a neutral system even if they preferred a religious system.
A letter in favour of the Patrician Brothers in the archives
of Propaganda in 1823 describes their system of education.
All denominations were taught. No Bible or catechism was
used as a textbook. The Catholic children were taught
their religion after school hours. 'All other communions
were permitted to resort to those whom their parents may
wish to instruct them on religious concerns.' The contrast
with the Christian Brothers is striking. In a letter to
Dr Blake in 1825, sending money for the rebuilding of
St Paul's, Dr Curtis made it clear that no Catholic children
would be allowed to receive any religious instruction from
non-Catholics (*170; 601*).

Edward Stanley (Lord Stanley, Earl of Derby) defined
the policy of the Whig government in 1831 as the provision
of 'a system of education from which should be banished
even the suspicion of proselytism, and which, admitting

children of all religious persuasions, should not interfere with the peculiar tenets of any' *(32, 313)*. The Board of National Education sought to accomplish its purpose on a basis of 'joint secular and separate religious instruction'. Archbishop Murray accepted a position on the Board of National Education and reported favourably on the liberal character of the other members of the board. Dr Murray apparently was anxious that the Catholic schools in his diocese should be placed under the board. The Christian Brothers, on his persuasion, tried the system but dropped out. The Sisters of Mercy apparently agreed with Dr Murray but were in no haste to join the system. The Presentation Sisters in George's Hill resisted the archbishop for many years until 1849, but most of the other Presentation convents seem to have joined quite rapidly *(450; 451)*.

There were various objections to the system, apart from the fact that it did not allow the display of Catholic emblems or the saying of prayers during class time. The Catholic bishops as such were not allowed to appoint the Catholic masters and mistresses; they were not allowed a Catholic training college for the training of Catholic teachers; and they were not allowed a veto over the books used. It may very well be that these points were sufficiently provided for in practice, but in 1839 the archbishop of Tuam and the bishops of Ardagh, Clonfert, Elphin, Achonry, Ferns, Kilmacduagh, Meath, Galway and the administrator of Killala held that the system contradicted the principles agreed in 1826 *(549)*.

On the question of control over textbooks, Akenson argues that rather than being aroused by the lack of religious content, concern was generated principally by the *indiscrimateness* of that content:

> One of the most important things to realise about the Irish National School textbooks is that they were not godless or secular in the modern sense of the word. Actually, they were crammed full of moralising and religiosity, and differed from denominational textbooks only in their religious content being neutral as between Christian denominations.

Prolonged disputes over one or other aspect of education were carried on as long as the British government remained in Ireland, and the system in practice became denominational. Suspicion and distrust of Protestant intentions prevailed. But the basic form of the settlement remained what had been established in 1831. It in fact survives to this day. The government was determined to set up a non-denominational system when a denominational system would have been preferred by all the main religious denominations. There was no reason, for example, why a simple cash grant could not have been made to voluntary schools. But the government wished to avoid denominationalism at all possible cost. The basic lines of the struggle did not ever change, whether the dispute was over model schools, intermediate schools, or the Catholic University. The Irish bishops never yielded an inch over what they regarded as their just claims. Further points are examined in the sections on the Synod of Thurles in this chapter and on religious and charity schools in chapter 8 (*493; 32; 300; 374; 517*).

The Priest in Politics

Though Lecky remarked that the British government first brought the priest into politics over the Veto, yet Dr Plunkett of Meath at the time of the revolution seems to imply that there was an intense interest in politics among the Irish clergy. 'Some of your clergy canonise, *if not belied*, with unqualified praise, the whole of the proceedings of the late National Assembly in France, whose majority were clearly under infidel influence.' This would seem to indicate that Irish priests in 1792 were as interested in secular politics as the French clergy (*97; 483*).

In the Veto and Emancipation controversies up to 1829, the three main political strands (as well as the terrorist one) were already clearly established. The first was the militant revolutionary republican tradition deriving from Tone, Emmet and Lord Edward Fitzgerald. Up to mid century the leadership was mainly Protestant, after which time it became more and more Catholic. The second was the Whig aristocratic tradition associated with the figure of the earl of Fingall. It was closely allied with the English Whigs, and its means of achieving its aims were strictly parliamentary. The third strand was synonymous with the name of Daniel O'Connell. It worked through parliament, co-operated with the government only when it felt like it and relied chiefly on mobilising public opinion outside parliament. Non-violent agitations, demonstrations and 'national associations' were its most prominent features. Developments of this were the tactic of independent opposition and obstruction in parliament. The Irish clergy were divided into those who wholeheartedly went along with O'Connell and those who felt that co-operation with the Fingallian Whigs was possible and necessary. Thoroughgoing Whigs seem to have been rare among the clergy. All through the century the clergy seem to have been basically O'Connellite, but with increasing sympathy along with the rest of the nation for the republican tradition. When Archbishop Cullen refused to attend functions at Dublin Castle, only four Dublin priests continued to attend (*12*).

Rome was prepared to concede a 'Veto' on episcopal appointments to the British government. The Irish patriotic party and many of the clergy opposed this. Though O'Connell's chief aim was the repeal of the Act of Union, it suited him to agitate for the remedy of as many grievances as possible. The most important of these as far as the clergy were concerned was the inequality in the allocation of government funds for education, especially when proselytism was supposed to be widespread in the schools. Wyse remarks:

> The priesthood no longer refused co-operation in every expedient of constitutional annoyance. They seized with alacrity every opportunity of legitimate attack: they seconded every proposition, they lent their aid to the execution of every proposal. . . . The cause of education became identified with the cause of Emancipation. It formed a principal object in the collection of the Rent.

The primate, Dr Curtis, took a lead in organising the collection of the Rent in his diocese. Curtis, it may be noted, was a distinguished professor in Salamanca at the time of the Spanish revolt against the French in 1808. The Spanish bishops and clergy took a leading part in the revolt, even

acting as generals of armies. Curtis afforded every assistance
to Wellington's armies. Dr Doyle, then a student at Coimbra
in Portugal was, like the other students, inducted into the
Portuguese army. The Irish students seem to have been used
as interpreters and liaison officers.

Only occasionally before 1826 did priests take an open
part in elections, but in 1826 they became very active and
remained active for the next hundred years, despite some
efforts to withdraw them in the early 1830s after Emancipation was achieved. After Emancipation, as O'Farrell notes,
O'Connell's policies consisted of constitutional agitation
(over Repeal) and defence of Catholic interests. At this
period in his life O'Connell was a sincerely religious man.
O'Farrell comments that Cullen reversed O'Connell's order
of importance. Though O'Connell and many later politicians
wished to see the priests engaged in political activity, there
was always a stream of Catholic laymen, both republican
and constitutional, who did not. Though O'Connell always
expected the clergy to follow lay direction in secular politics,
this was not a role happily played by leading clerics in the
second half of the century.

It is difficult to establish precisely what proportion of the
priests actually took part in politics. Whyte mentions an
election in Mayo in 1832 where one-fifth of the clergy
participated. But little clerical activity was reported for
1835, 1837 and 1841. In 1854, thirty priests, half of them
curates, were reported to be backing one candidate, and
fifteen the other. But were they from one diocese? In 1843,
the twenty-four signatories on the published requisition for
a political meeting in Dublin were all those of the local
priests, which would seem to argue a high level of clerical
involvement in the area. A little later, Dr Murray could rely
only on one-third of his priests, but there may have been
other factors. Significant too is the number of votes cast
in the *terna* for the politically-minded Dr Cullen who
favoured moderate participation of the clergy in politics. The
votes were twenty-three, nine and eight. Forbes confessed
that he was unable to establish what proportion of the
clergy were active. Cardinal Lambruschini pointed out that
from the evidence supplied to him they were few in number,

but Broderick feels the cardinal may have been under-estimating (*534; 62; 367*).

The number of priests engaged in overt political acts like canvassing or driving voters to the polls probably varied directly as a major religious issue was seen to be involved. The clergy as citizens had a right to participate in politics, but as clergymen they were in a different position. Canon law did not deal with the matter except in the most general terms. In fact the standard theological authors of the period, La Croix, Antoine, Ligouri and Dens, do not deal with the peculiarly British phenomenon of popular elections.

But one can look at priests in politics rather as being involved in tumultuous public assemblies like hunts or race meetings.

> I know of nothing more detrimental to the peace and prosperity of a district than an election for members of parliament, conducted as such elections usually are in Ireland. The worst passions of the people are aroused to their utmost pitch on both sides, and sectarian animosity and virulence seem, demon-like, to possess the whole community (*500; 367*).

When Dr Blake refused to allow chapels to be used for political meetings he referred to the clamour, clapping, hissing, groaning and other 'damnatory demonstrations'.

There seems to have been no controversy about the right of any priest to give counsel to his parishioners privately with regard to elections. The Synod of Leinster (1831) forbade (*a*) the use of churches, or any chapel therein (*sacellus*) for public meetings of the laity; and (*b*) any proclamations from the altar, except the banns or such like (*62, 58*). The bishops also made clear in 1834:

> that whilst we do not intend to interfere with the civil rights of those entrusted to our care, yet as guardians of religion . . . we do hereby pledge ourselves on our return to our respective dioceses to remind our clergy of the instructions we then (1830) addressed to them, and that we most earnestly recommend them to avoid in future any allusion at their altars to political subjects,

and carefully to refrain from connecting themselves with political clubs, acting as chairmen or secretaries of political meetings, or moving or seconding resolutions on such occasions, in order that we may exhibit ourselves in all things, in the character of our sacred calling, as ministers of Christ and dispensers of the mysteries of God (*549*).

According to Dr Nolan, the new bishop of Kildare and Leighlin in 1834, the priest was bound to instruct his people. 'We are bound to give them our assistance', he stressed, 'and it is necessary to explain to the electors the real nature of the question they are called on to determine by their votes' (*62*, 63). As examples, Dr Nolan gave whether voting for this one or that would allow proselytism, would prolong the Church establishment or would restore or continue the ascendancy. Dr Nolan pointed out that the clergy were bound to avoid political activity in general, but in the current emergency (the return of the Tories) they were bound actively to give their counsel. If confined to this only, no one was likely to object. As Dr Doyle put it, referring to his service in the Peninsular army,

> 'There are times', writes the bishop, 'and circumstances, when a priest is justified — nay when he is obliged to mix with his fellowcountrymen and to suspend his clerical functions whilst he discharges those of a member of society' (*175*, I, 32; *The Irishman*, 4 May 1872).

The statement is worth noting for it was a careful theological exposition of the relative claims of the duties to God and to Caesar on the priest's time. Though direct proof is not available, it seems that the priests who took an active part in politics were generally O'Connellite in policy and sentiment while those who abstained tended towards the Whigs.

What precisely did the priests do? Whyte notes them acting as chairmen of meetings, speaking at meetings, addressing the people at or after Sunday mass, allowing the candidate to address the congregation and allowing the chapel yard to be used. They also canvassed and transported voters to the poll and scrutinised voters at the hustings. Contrary statutes, when they existed, could easily with a little casuistry be evaded. A priest could legitimately take voters to the polling town if not to the polling booth. Prohibitions against attending meetings could be got round by standing conspicuously in the next field, or sitting in a gentleman's carriage. One notes Fr Lavelle and his bishop, Archbishop MacHale, pushing casuistry to its limits, and successfully for the most part (*109*).

Apropos of this, we can note Archbishop Croke advising his priests to distinguish between 'law' and 'fact', and ruling that the local clergy were the only fit judges of this latter. A later generation might have been inclined to think that the distinction was valid but that Catholic *laymen* should be left to judge. Cardinal Cullen, though professing to follow Rome, was in fact advocating a 'Free Church in a Free State', something which was explicitly condemned by Rome at the period.

Statutes promulgated by Dr Cullen for the province of Dublin forbade speaking on political matters in church. Priests were forbidden to attend purely political meetings, and public controversies between priests were also forbidden. The Armagh provincial statutes of Dr Dixon (1854) recommended that in elections for poor law guardians or members of parliament, the clergy should be solicitous that the faith of the poor and the rights of the Church should be protected:

> But we consider that these matters should be dealt with outside the churches, without tumult, without breach of charity, and with due submission to the bishop of the diocese lest there be dissentions among the clergy, and with that moderation which is altogether proper to the clerical state, and leaving to everyone in matters of doubt the right of thinking for himself on the matter.

The matter was however complicated in the 1840s by an intervention by Rome. What is puzzling about this intervention is not that it took place, or the form in which it took place, but rather why the then primate, Archbishop Crolly, treated it seriously. Rome issued two injunctions with regard to the participation of the Irish clergy in politics. The documents contained no new point of *law* with regard to clerical participation in secular affairs, and so could only be concerned with the *fact* of whether *in the circumstances*

some Irish priests were excessively addicted to politics. The
British government and others might want a curb put on the
speeches and writings of Dr MacHale, and Rome may have
felt it necessary to issue a general warning. This could be
treated as a mere diplomatic warning, and seems so to have
been treated by Crolly and all the other bishops. The reason
for regarding the injunction of 1839, the first one, as official
diplomatic verbiage, besides the fact that it was apparently
so regarded by the whole Irish hierarchy, is that Rome was
extremely reluctant to pronounce on a point of fact when
the local bishops disagreed on its interpretation, without a
very prolonged and very thorough examination of the dis-
puted fact (*62*).

The second injunction came in 1844, issued by Cardinal
Fransoni, at the request of Gregory XVI himself. Broderick
is of the opinion that the presumption in Rome was that
Repeal was a purely secular issue. Error in point of fact
could of course be rebutted *either* by showing that there was
a proportionate cause, *or* that the activity of the priests was
not excessive. Crolly regarded the instruction from Rome as
peremptory (within the limits still ever valid of Constance
and Florence), and to be obeyed, while the Repealing bishops
set about rebutting the charges (*62*, 195).

MacDonagh slightly overstates the case when he says that
'all "secular" activity for whatever cause had been unreservedly
condemned'. Rome would not and could not condemn all
secular activity: such a concept was unjuridical. In 1839,
Cardinal Fransoni expressed a strong wish (*optarem
vehementer*) that the priest would have nothing to do with
political *controversies*, and that when speaking in public
he would avoid the use of any language which might imply
that he was addicted to political controversy (*62*, 101).

The relevant words in the actual instruction from Rome
were *adeo a politicarum partium studiis et saeculi negotiis
prorsus alienos minime demonstrent*, which I would trans-
late as 'They are not seen to avoid political party strife and
secular affairs.' *Studium* can have many meanings: a forceful
meaning seems called for. *Saeculi negotiis prorsus alienos
minime demonstrent* seems to be little more than a stylistic
variation of *A saeculi actibus se facere prorsus alienum* of the

monastic Rule of St Benedict. The *saeculi negotia* can be read and should be read with *politicarum partium studia* (*odiosa sunt restrigenda*).

What makes the matter peculiar is that the primate was made responsible for 'efficaciously admonishing' any priest or bishop in Ireland who did not obey the instruction of the Holy See. This was outrageous, and makes one believe that the instruction, at least the second time, was a personal *faux pas* of the pope. The instruction placed the primate in an impossible position. On the one hand he had a clear instruction from Rome and was made personally responsible. On the other hand he was given no authority whatsoever to interfere in the diocese of another bishop. Dr MacNally, replying to the above letter, refused to admonish a priest in his diocese, Clogher, pointing out that the Holy See had made the primate responsible for doing so. Yet it was clearly impossible for the primate to 'admonish efficaciously' a priest of another diocese. Dr MacNally replied:

> Your Grace will however permit me to place before your consideration, whether considering all the circumstances it might not be as well to pass over unnoticed in this particular instance any unmeasured language which in their zeal against the Bequests Act might have fallen from these gentlemen, lest Your Grace's admonition might be construed into a desire to prevent the expression of public opinion upon the measure itself, and if such construction, however erroneous, should be put upon Your Grace's admonition, it would, beyond all doubt, increase a hundredfold the painful excitement which now universally exists, and which, while things remain in their present position, all Your Grace's exertions and influence would in vain attempt to allay.
>
> From Your Grace's letter it appears that you look upon these meetings held to petition against the Bequests Act as mere public political meetings, but Your Grace knows that the great majority of the prelates, now, I believe, to the number of seventeen, including the humble individual who writes, and almost all the clergy and people have declared their conviction that the dearest interests of

religion are involved in that measure, and that in petitioning against it, they are doing what duty obliges them to do
in defence of their holy religion by seeking the repeal of an
Act anti-catholic in its . . . (573).

There was much sense in Dr MacNally's advice. First, he
thought that the primate would do well to ignore what was
said and done in the heat of the painful excitement which
existed. And secondly, he should remember that the priests
and laity had good reason for regarding the issue as a religious
one, for no less than seventeen of the bishops thought
likewise.

The Irish bishops accepted the papal instruction. There
was nothing of the 'solemn pontifical jest' about this (351,
49). The problem was about *interpreting* it. Some of the
bishops understood the instruction to refer to a prohibition
upon taking any part in public meetings, or being present at
dinners; others considered that only excessive addiction and
imprudent language was meant (*politicis negotiis nimium
addicti*). Cantwell and Higgins noted the hypothetical nature
of the condemnation 'si relata subsisterent; si ita essent'
(if what is reported is true, if things are so). Though a perfectly valid argument, such an interpretation would seem
to fit the first instruction rather than the second. The precise
and categorical condemnation of the agrarian 'plan of campaign' in 1888 was more difficult to wriggle out of (62).

The Repealing bishops then gave as their opinion that
there was a necessary role for the clergy in the political
circumstances of the time, a view some years later confirmed by Rome in approving the Armagh statutes, the only
provisos being that the intervention of priests in politics
should be outside the churches, without tumult, without
violation of charity and with due subjection to the bishop
(Armagh, *Acta et Decreta*, 1854; Propaganda changed the
wording in approving these statutes wherever necessary.)
Participation in land agitation, in as much as it could be
regarded as involvement in secular affairs, followed the same
principles.

MacHale seems to have acted as a gadfly to the government
and to others, and the controversy as to whether he or his

clergy were excessively addicted to public political meetings, or spoke imprudently at them, overshadows the fact that MacHale devoted very little of his time to political agitation. That MacHale, unlike Cullen, took little part in politics is confirmed by a remark in the *Drogheda Conservative* in 1869, concerning the new primate. Dr Kieran, it was suggested, resembled MacHale rather than Cullen in that he interfered little in politics. MacHale, too, was very careful not to allow clerical disputes over elections, and if the priests of his diocese could not agree on which candidate to support they had to remain aloof from the contempt altogether. Gavan Duffy remarked that the priests in a diocese usually followed the bishop's lead (*399; 12*).

MacHale was a target for allegations. He complained that a few years earlier his clergy were constantly accused of making denunciations of landlords from the pulpit, 'albeit no such denunciations ever took place, nor was a single murder of the kind committed at any time under such excitement'. Also he said it was constantly spread abroad that the biblicals were over-running his diocese and whenever any Catholic joined them it was reported he was from Tuam, when in fact there were proselytisers in only six or seven parishes in Tuam. In 1854 Propaganda inserted into the statutes of the provincial synod of Tuam the resolutions of the hierarchy concerning the conduct of priests during elections. But this tells us nothing of what the Tuam clergy actually did during election time (*399; 268*).

Archbishop Croke claimed that he was immersed in diocesan activities and devoted little time to politics. As in MacHale's case, his position as archbishop lent great weight to his pronouncements. On the other hand he seems to have devoted much effort towards securing the appointment of nationally-minded bishops.

The continued controversy about the extent to which it was lawful for priests actively and *publicly* to campaign in politics masked the real issue, namely to what extent priests were engaged in politics. It is clear that the priest or bishop who spends most or all of his free time in counselling his flock in political matters, in arranging with other priests or laymen how meetings should be conducted, in writing to politicians, in drafting resolutions and so on, is much more 'excessively addicted' to politics than the priest who occasionally attended a public Repeal meeting.

But it would seem that if participation in politics is understood in the first sense, the great majority of the clergy were involved. Non-political priests in Ireland must have been few and far between. Dr Murray, for example, was a Repealer, supported O'Connell and paid the Tribute (*530*). He celebrated a solemn pontifical mass of thanksgiving, followed by *Te Deum*, with a prominent Dublin priest Repealer preaching on the occasion of O'Connell's release from prison. He personally favoured a domestic legislature, but did not think that mere moral force or agitation would achieve it.

> The array of military force that paraded so ostentatiously before our church on Sunday seems to have been intended as an indication that our clergy are objects of peculiar suspicion (can we wonder at it?), and that in case of outbreak they would be among the first victims to be aimed at.
>
> I long foresaw, and it required no spirit of prophecy to do so, that if the agitation were persisted in, the whole power of England would as far as necessary be employed to crush it. But I was ridiculed as overtimorous (or something worse), and the dream of moral influence as able to accomplish everything was clung to in opposition to the plainest dictates of common sense.
>
> I was quite as much alive as any of the agitators to the benefits which a domestic legislature would be capable, if peaceably obtained, of conferring on the country, but I trembled to think of the effects of a struggle to obtain it by means of physical force (Murray to Hamilton, 13 October 1843).

One person at least was not carried away. As Murray said, these remarks were only common sense. As in the case of mixed education, Murray realised that the government was inflexible, and so made the best of it. On the question of the Charitable Bequests Bill, Murray took the obvious precaution of enquiring of the government what exactly was meant by the proposed legislation, and his opposition changed to acceptance. With regard to the Queen's Colleges,

Murray recognised that they were going to be built anyway, so one should have Catholic priests associated with them (*563*). Murray was level-headed and pragmatic; this appears even more clearly in a letter to Dr Cullen:

> You say it was greatly to be regretted that they (the Confederates) received so much encouragement when assailing O'Connell.
>
> It is a lamentable truth that the Confederates did receive encouragement when assailing O'Connell from quarters which should have cast them off with honour. But it is unfortunately true that they had gained over many to the belief that O'Connell was not sincere in his professed expectation of carrying his Repeal by moral force, and also that they themselves were only acting on the lessons which he inculcated but which he had not the courage to carry into effect.
>
> They laughed at his pretended peace principles after having so often heard him rousing the masses of the people by the most inflammatory harangues against the constituted authorities of the country, pointing to America and other countries (Murray Letters 32/5, Murray to Cullen, 10 March 1849).

Murray went on to state that it was true that O'Connell hoped, or said he did, to keep the angry feelings in check, but it was clear, as the late preparations for armed rebellion showed, that this was not true. And Murray added, O'Connell was supported in all this by priests. These letters show that Murray, when he opposed the policies or tactics of O'Connell, or agreed to particular government policies, could not in any way be regarded as a non-political priest.

MacNally pointed out to Crolly that seventeen of the bishops and *almost all of the clergy* and people had declared that the dearest interests of religion were involved in the Charitable Bequests Bill. Dr Higgins stated that every bishop in Ireland was an ardent Repealer. If the word 'ardent' is left out, this may well have been true. Or to put it another way, by mid century Unionism was virtually unsupported by any priest. (This does not necessarily refer to either earlier in the century or later in the century.) The fierce disputes at mid century between the supporters of MacHale and those of Murray should rather be seen as disputes over points of tactics. They turned on whether a particular form of political activity was legitimate for priests, or whether particular concessions should be made to the government's intentions, for example to accept the national schools or the Queen's Colleges.

It is difficult to find simple terms to describe the two factions in the clergy. The 'patriotic' or 'nationalist' faction denounced their opponents as 'Castle bishops' or 'Castle Catholics' on no other grounds, it would seem, than that they behaved with courtesy to and co-operated with the Castle authorities, whatever their own long-term ambitions for Ireland. Indeed some of the clergy *may* have favoured the union; a greater number, like Archbishop Murray, may have tolerated it. It would seem, however, that a majority favoured taking active steps to end the union. Modern nationalism, involving a strong belief in a national ethos or *geist* and a national destiny, dates in Ireland from the Young Ireland period. There does not seem to have been any fundamental difference of opinion with regard to the basic Irish Catholic self-image and definition of the Irish situation for, despite allegations to the contrary, all the bishops and clergy seem to have been patriotic in outlook.

One of the factions crystallised around MacHale; one of his earliest writings contains the quotation '*Aut ulla putatis dona carere dolis Danaum?*' ('Do you think that Greek gifts are ever lacking in trickery?' 2nd Letter of Hierophilos). In 1848 MacHale and Higgins advised Pius IX, '*time Anglos et dona ferentes*' ('Fear the English, even when they are bringing gifts'). According to Dr Cantwell:

> It was folly – it was insanity to hope for justice at their hands [the English government], and every true Irishman devoting his energies to the re-achievement of our legislative independence, ought for the future to take 'no compromise' for their motto. Look at the religious persecution which the Catholic members of the army were, at the present day, compelled to assist (*97*).

According to Dr Higgins, 'English Catholics – aye and

English priests – are the corrupt tools employed by Peel.'
Suspicion of Protestant England was not *altogether*
unwarranted. Another member of MacHale's group wrote:

> Everyone with whom I have been speaking thinks it
> strange that the bishops have not come forward in a body
> to repel the horrible calumnies against the priests, which
> the English press, with the most diabolical malice, still
> continue to circulate (573, Dr O'Hanlon of Maynooth).

Dr Cullen wrote about events in Rome:

> I think Englishmen, and English money, are moving the
> people here. The parsons and other black Protestants
> who are here are all delighted with the hope of seeing the
> Pope's temporal power destroyed or curtailed (367).

Comments from the other side are scarce. With regard to the
Charitable Bequests Bill, Murray noted that Dr Crolly was
prepared to give the bill a fair trial, whereas he himself was
not. Murray changed his mind on this point. He recognised
fairly the activities of the British government during the
Famine, and especially the policies of Sir Robert Peel:
'Hitherto poor Sir Robert has been our Joseph.' Crolly
pertinently remarked with regard to mixed education that
the danger of proselytism and perversion of Catholic children
to Protestant beliefs could either be so remote as scarcely to
be said to exist, or it could be so real as to make the school a
'lion's den and a fiery furnace of perversion'. Only experience
could tell, and the experience in Belfast was that in the
mixed schools attended by Catholic children no single case
of perversion had ever occurred. Dr George Crolly notes
that his uncle, the primate, did not even go as far as Dr
Doyle or Dr Curtis in complying with the prejudices of
Protestants.

The nationalist clergy were not noted for the sympathy
with which they protected the interests of the Protestants,
or took heed of their prejudices. On the contrary. As
O'Farrell notes, they were determined to ignore the Protestant element in Ireland and to seek a Catholic state, run by a
party Catholic in ethos and personnel, motivated by Catholic
principles, 'a holy party working towards a parliament of

saints' (*388*). Later in the independent state, generosity towards the Protestants came not from any Christian or ecumenical gestures of the clerical party but from the heirs of the semi-anticlerical republican movement which Cardinal Cullen strove so hard to crush.

The nationalist priests were to secure a decisive victory at the Synod of Thurles, but disputes as to whether priests could engage in particular forms of politics or countenance violence persisted until the departure of the British (and as far as Ulster is concerned, till the present). The theological and canonical principles were plain enough in themselves. Doubtful points could have been dealt with on the principle that where there is doubt there is liberty. Protesting groups always use that principle anyway. The application of the principles was not always clear, so Rome for the most part contented itself with reiterating the principles and evading the point. Specific condemnations such as those of the Queen's Colleges or the plan of campaign were rare. Despite a widespread and deliberately orchestrated popular outcry, one can presume it is likely that Rome made no specific condemnation until it was clear that the great majority of the Irish bishops were in agreement. Though the Land League now has an honoured place in Irish history, it is clear that many lay politicians, including Parnell, thought it had passed legitimate bounds, both theological and con-stitutional.

Most of the Irish bishops except Cullen seem to have taken a pragmatic and level-headed view of the activities of the Fenians even when they disagreed with them, and recognised their *bona fides* and loyal Catholicity. Bishop Moriarty merely condemned the Fenian 'godfathers' who recruited the gullible from a safe distance and left their poor dupes for hanging and transportation with appalling consequences for their dependants. Given the efficiency of the Castle spies, Moriarty's appreciation was probably realistic. Cullen's notorious suspicion of Young Irelanders and Fenians does not seem to have been shared by many bishops. He remained militantly O'Connellite when O'Connell's ideals were going out of fashion. He seems to have dropped the idea of Repeal, however, without accepting that political action for the foreseeable future should be within the framework of the Union. Nevertheless, O'Connellite politics as interpreted by Cullen were to remain dominant till the rise of the home rule party. His suspiciousness does not seem to have been of a pathological nature but to have sprung from the ideological beliefs of 'Catholic Ireland', namely that the holy people were everywhere threatened from without. Cullen's priests were equally dissuaded from associating with Protestants, Dublin Castle officials, the nobility, even Catholic Whigs like the then earl of Fingall, not to mention the Fenians. Only one Dublin priest, the famous Fr Healy of Little Bray, cheerfully ignored the successive archbishops of Dublin who followed Murray. Needless to say, he was never promoted. It may be of some significance that on Cullen's death the Dublin clergy chose Dr MacCabe who was supposed to resemble Archbishop Murray in his politics, and after his short reign they chose the advanced nationalist, Archbishop Walsh. But there may have been personal factors. MacCabe, though liked as vicar-general, got a reputation as bishop for blundering while Walsh as President of Maynooth had a reputation for clearsightedness and efficiency.

A question has been raised as to whether the Irish bishops were notably 'politicised' between 1840 and 1850 (MacDonagh). It is alleged that the bishops who agreed to the Veto in 1799 were a humble, accommodating body of men, ready if hard pressed to yield to a demand for royal nomination, and again that by 1852 clerical influence in politics had reached its peak. The evidence against the eighteenth-century bishops is based merely on an unsubstantiated denunciation by Jack Lawless who opposed those bishops on the point. There is no evidence that they were hard pressed, or that they saw any difficulty in their agreeing to what Rome clearly wished to concede. One bishop, Dr Hussey of Waterford, was very outspoken on political matters. The other bishops unanimously protested that if the Veto meant injuring the Catholic religion, they would prefer to endure the penal laws again. During the long controversy between the Vetoists and the anti-Vetoists, two bishops, Coppinger of Cloyne and O'Shaughnessy of Killaloe, were outspoken in favour of O'Connell's controversial tactics. The vigorous Primate Curtis had no hesitation in denouncing O'Connell when he strayed into ecclesiastical territory, while Doyle's confrontation with O'Connell over the 'wings' is famous. If there was politicisation it was only with regard to tactics.

That clerical *influence* on political affairs declined after 1870 is a point which has been more carefully argued by Dr Whyte. Various reasons are advanced for this. One was the rebirth of the Irish secular political machine which almost totally collapsed after the death of O'Connell. Another was the divisions among the clergy themselves. The indicators of the decline in clerical influence chosen by Whyte coincide with the rise of a strong Protestant personality in secular politics, namely Parnell, the growth in *central* party organisations which the bishops had not yet had time to infiltrate and a serious split in the movement after the Parnell scandal. None of these causes were likely to be permanent. Also, the indicator chosen by Whyte, the ability of the clergy to secure the election of a particular candidate, did not necessarily measure the full extent of their political influence. Each candidate may have felt it necessary to bow to the mitre. One should not assume that because for various reasons the influence of the Catholic clergy over *elections* declined, their political influence declined equally (*268*).

When we speak of influence we must ask the question: influence for what? There was no clerical faction or interest group distinct from those of the lay Catholics. The priests initiated no policies: they *followed* lay trends. They were, however, concerned that religious questions should have primary importance, and the political priests believed their personal intervention in politics was necessary to this end. A home rule priest could justify his activity, not on secular grounds, but on the grounds that home rule was essential for the defence of Catholic interests. There were as many political strands among the priests as among the laymen, except that the priests *never* supported terrorism. Only once, under Cardinal Cullen, did the clergy attempt to lead and direct but every lay leader had to conciliate a majority of the clergy.

Did political activity decline? The various indicators used

by Whyte are all excellent, but none of them is essential. If the priests did not take a publicly observable part in politics it in no way implied that they were not active. The decline in external activities, speaking, ferrying canvassers etc. may have reflected no more than a greater heed to the ecclesiastical statutes; a realisation that such activities on the part of the clergy were no longer necessary; or even a relative rise in the social status of the clergy which meant that they were no longer confined to the more menial aspects of politics.

There remains therefore the distinct possibility that as far as political awareness and private counselling went, the level of political activity of the clergy did not change between 1800 and 1900, though public political activities may have waxed and waned, and clerical influence may have varied because of external factors. It should be noted that there was also a tradition among some lay Catholic politicians deploring the presence of priests in politics.

The next question is the attitude of the clergy to the use of physical force. Physical force was not in itself ruled out by common Catholic theology, and Dr Doyle made it clear that a priest, in a case of extreme necessity, might lawfully shoulder arms. Dr Doyle was probably aware of, and apparently did not condemn, the activity of Dr England of Charleston in collecting 40,000 men in 1828 against the eventuality that Emancipation would be denied. It is not clear in what way Dr England intended to use this force, but we can probably assume that he expected a civil war to break out. Later in the century the primate, Dr Dixon, took the initiative in collecting a military force to defend the Papal States (*175; 127*).

The theological principles with regard to the use of force were traditionally that there must be a just and proportionate cause, that no other means except violent ones were possible, that the minimum amount of force consistent with winning be used, and that there must be a *reasonable expectation of success*. If this latter condition were not fulfilled, men were being killed without any real hope of achieving anything substantial. It naturally involved a concrete appreciation of the situation at any given time, and for Ireland this in practice meant that England could only be attacked when engaged in a major European war. This was not true in the 1840s and 1860s when the question was discussed.

O'Connell broke with the Young Irelanders or Confederates over the question of the use of physical force. Yet the split seems to have focused on whether it was right to *threaten* to use force, in the expectation that the ministry would yield, rather than on the actual use of force. The model seems to have been the Volunteer Convention of 1782 which apparently secured the legislative independence of Grattan's Parliament with a threat of force, as opposed to the revolutionary uprising of 1798.

The Young Ireland leader, William Smith O'Brien, does not appear to have envisaged an actual uprising beforehand until he acted precipitately in 1848. According to the newspaper *The Felon's Track*, the most militant of the bishops, Dr Maginn of Derry, offered to take the field at the head of the priests of his diocese, if the insurrection were held back until after the harvest; there is no need to assume, however, that he intended anything more than the threat of armed force. Maginn himself envisaged a reconciliation of Old and Young Ireland, and considered that united, the British government would be faced with the combined strengths of the two factions, the one warlike and self-sacrificing which could do and dare anything, while the moderate party acted as a check on it. Dr Blake of Dromore was another bishop who thought that the views of Old and Young Ireland could be reconciled within the one organisation, but this was denied by O'Connell who stated emphatically that those who held that physical force could be used could not remain in his organisation. Dr Murray could not see any difference between O'Connell's views and those of the Confederates, and believed that both were holding the threat of the use of physical force over the government's head, the one more openly than the other. He was also sceptical about a belief that the government would not call the bluff. It is interesting and curious that shortly after 1848, MacHale, Cantwell and Higgins were in favour of armed intervention in the Papal States, while Dr Murray was opposed. It would seem, however, that at the time of the Young Irelanders there was considerable clerical sympathy for their views on holding a *threat* of force over the head of the government. MacHale, incidentally, was totally opposed in 1848 to the 'revolutionary principles' of Duffy, the Young Irelander (*367; 573; 554; 397; 399*).

The only time the question of the actual use of physical force came up was during the Fenian activities of the 1860s. What actual clerical support there might have been for them and their views was obscured by the violently anti-clerical line taken by the Fenian leaders. The famous Fr Lavelle preached the traditional right to rebel against an unjust or unlawful government. There seems to have been considerable clerical sympathy for the Fenians even if they were regarded as 'misguided'. Both O'Leary and Sheehan mention that priests gave absolution to the men going out to fight. This happened also in 1916 (*301*). Tynan notes that the regulars absolved even in Cullen's time. MacHale had some sympathy with the Fenians and their supporters, and vigorously defended his clergy against the incursions of Cardinal Cullen west of the Shannon, but there is no indication that he ever changed his lifelong principles that the remedy for Ireland's grievances was repeal of the Act of Union and the granting of an independent legislature to Ireland, and in the meantime an independent opposition in parliament. The condemnation of the Fenians in 1870 was on the grounds, however, that they were a secret society proscribed by the Church like the Freemasons and *Carbonari*. Though condemned in the 1820s, it was not till nearly a century later that the Freemasons began to figure prominently in Irish Catholic demonology (*109*).

Finally, it should be noted that the Irish clergy in the nineteenth century were loyal to the crown and the constitution. If any of them wanted an independent parliament, they still wanted it under the crown. MacHale was a strictly constitutional agitator. The same was true of the rest of the bishops. Republicanism never seems to have been an issue (*62*).

It is worth making a note on the sources for this section. Both the Irish newspapers — notorious in the last century for their partisan distortions — and appeals and reports to Rome must be treated cautiously. The newspapers were

accused, indeed, by Dr George Crolly of deliberately suppressing any news favourable to Primate Crolly at the height of
the Queen's Colleges controversy. Crolly also accused James
Maher, Dr Cullen's uncle and one of the leading nationalist
propagandists, of 'barefaced perversions of the truth and the
most unscrupulous fictions'.

Dr Whyte remarks that after 1850 a much greater flow of
information is available from the reports of Dr Cullen to
Propaganda. This supposes that Cullen's reports to Propaganda
are reliable. Whenever I have been able to check Cullen's
statements independently, I found that they reflected at the
very least a highly personal point of view. One priest, a
supporter of Dr Murray, accuses Cullen of 'blackballing every
priest and bishop in the Irish Church', and this possibility
must also be kept in mind. Cannon notes that with regard
to episcopal meetings we have only Cullen's version, and adds
cautiously 'if we can rely on the objectivity of these accounts'.
O'Reilly's *Life of MacHale*, though partisan, serves as a useful
corrective to Cullen's versions.

George Crolly's *Life* of his uncle was written deliberately
to counteract the slanders of the Rev. James Maher. William
Meagher intended writing a fuller work as an apologia for
Dr Murray, basing it on the 'piles' of the late archbishop's
papers. He was unable to get his hands on these papers
because of 'insurmountable difficulties'. He does not accuse
Dr Cullen of making such difficulties, though much of the
relevant documentation was to hand in the diocesan archives.
Trevor, too, notes Cullen's endless complaints to Propaganda
regarding Newman, who, however, did not write to complain
of Cullen: 'There was no counterblast to this continual
denigration.' There is some evidence that those Dublin priests
who supported Dr Murray had their promotions retarded by
Dr Cullen (*502; 12*).

Tithe and Land Agitation

This was a question which on the face of it was social
rather than political and in which the clergy could with good
conscience participate. Terrorism directed against tithes
and various features of landlordism were a noted feature of
Irish life. Early in the century the genuine grievance of the

Irish Catholic tenants with regard to paying the tithes to the
clergy of the Established Church was widely recognised
inside and outside parliament. But the royal coronation oath
was seen as an obstacle to any remedy, for the king swore
to uphold the Established Churches.

Sympathy with those suffering wrongs did not mean
sympathy with those who took the law into their own hands.
Dr Doyle roundly condemned agrarian violence:

> Where is the landlord amongst you who is an oppressor?
> Where is the employer who is not humane? . . . and if you
> could point out exceptions are they not as rare as the
> stars that fall from heaven?

Though when revising this pastoral some years later he
omitted this passage, it should be noted that as an eye-
witness he once wrote it. How many later writers quoted
Castle Rackrent as the sole authority? Again he wrote:

> Who are those who would undertake to subvert the laws
> and constitution of this country? Persons without money,
> without education, without arms, without counsel, with-
> out discipline, without a leader; kept together by a bond
> of iniquity (*175*).

I have come across no mention of any of the practising clergy
who supported agrarian terrorism, though the Banims
mention a 'Fr Tackem' in this connection. Rather, the clergy,
early in the century, saw eye-to-eye with the landlords, at
least the good landlords, whose viewpoint was expressed
by Trench.

In the early 1830s there arose a spontaneous resistance to
paying tithes and Dr Doyle lent his influential support to
those who were avoiding payment. He did not countenance
physical resistance but actively supported passive resistance
by such means as refusing to bid at an auction of distrained
cattle. Clerical attitudes changed. In the 1840s Dr Murray
and Dr Crolly, replying to Rome, deny any influence of
priests in favour of terrorism and murder, and attribute
these evils to the cruelty of the *Domini soli*, the landlords,
and the tithe proctors, though admitting the need for an
impartial investigation. Whyte and Larkin give full accounts

of clerical participation in the tenant right movement at mid century, and later in the Land League. These were largely political movements, though in theory distinct. No special comment is called for beyond what was stated in the previous section. The most important feature was the manner in which the clergy, normally the most conservative where property was concerned, came to side with the tenantry. This is not the place to analyse whether they were correct to do so: that is a question for political economy or economic history. Ultimately the emotional desire of the tenantry to secure their smallholdings on reasonable conditions prevailed. The clergy sympathised with this, but Dr Doyle seems to have been both the first and last priest to consider the matter objectively.

We may perhaps comment here on the fact that the clergy never seem to have become involved in the parallel trade union movement. Why this happened is not clear. It certainly had nothing to do with Church teaching on property rights, for that would have affected the land movement even more. Perhaps it was because many priests came from families of smallholders, and few from the 'operatives' who formed the trade unions. Or perhaps it was because the clergy sided with O'Connell and not with the emerging trade union leaders. Again, the socialist or class movement gained little support in Ireland, presumably because nationalism was so predominant.

The Synod of Thurles

This had little to do with reforming the Irish Church. Rather it was called to settle a crisis which had been building up over the previous fifteen years. As early as 1820 Dr MacHale, not yet a bishop, had taken a strong line of distrust with regard to government policy on education, but open disagreement with the other bishops did not come until the system of national education was established and MacHale himself was an archbishop. Serious disagreements appeared among the bishops with regard to national education, to the role of the priests in politics, to their attitude towards the government over charitable bequests and university education. The matter was complicated by disagreements as to how far one should support O'Connell and still more Young Ireland. Factions crystallised around Dr Murray who supported the government, and MacHale who did not.

> It wasn't a question of disagreements that were confined to the bishops' meetings. Resolutions and reports of the meetings appeared in newspapers and gave rise to much public debate in which bishops, priests, and laity took up opposing positions.
>
> The difference of approach centred round the attitude to be adopted towards government institutions which gave Protestants power to make arrangements that vitally affected Catholics (*73*).

Catholic education became an obsession in clerical, and especially hierarchical circles from the 1830s onwards. Priests were to control the schools. The bishops were to control education policy. The priest presidents of Maynooth or the Catholic University were to be excluded from decision-making by the bishops, lay participation in the direction of the Catholic University resisted at all costs, attempts by Catholic lay teachers in national schools to achieve some influence denounced, efforts by the Christian Brothers to get some freedom for their order from the bishops resisted. Why this happened is not clear. The original excuse was alleged proselytism, but as the century went on, alleged free thought, communism etc. could be substituted.

Cannon notes that successive British governments were unable or unwilling to provide Catholic schools for Catholic children for a variety of reasons. But the basic reason was clear and unchanging, as Cardwell explained to Cullen:

> If those demands were conceded, the national system would be overthrown, and a system of sectarian education substituted for it, calculated to revive social divisions in Ireland, and to stimulate feelings which it is the object of every just and liberal government to allay (*374*).

The revival of sectarian education was precisely what a 'just and liberal government' did not want.

As Archbishop Murray explained to Propaganda when the question of translating MacHale from Killala to

Tuam was allegedly contested by the British government in 1832:

> I must confess indeed, most eminent Lord, that prelate, otherwise most worthy, sometimes uses too sharp a style, as it seems to me, when he writes about political matters.
>
> It must be remembered nevertheless that he is surrounded by poor persons languishing in want and misery, and if he adverts to the causes of this misery more sharply than I would wish, I think it should be attributed to his sense of duty towards the poor and to a zeal which burns for religion, although for a little while perhaps it went beyond the limits of prudence, as some believed. . . .
>
> I am very happy to be able to add my testimony to the votes of the bishops of the Province of Tuam concerning that prelate, learned, pious, eloquent, and deserving well of religion (*62*).

MacHale never became reconciled to the system of national education. In 1832 his predecessor as archbishop of Tuam, Oliver Kelly, wrote to him:

> The new Board of Education, so far as it has gone works well to the extent of the means placed at its disposal, which, as yet, are very scanty. His Grace, Dr Murray, who is a most efficient member, assures me that the dissenting members are very liberal. . . .
>
> If the present government holds its place, I have no doubt the Board will become permanently useful. But if the Tory party succeeds in ousting the Ministry, it can easily be seen that the Kildare Street folk will again resume power (*399*, I, 196).

A little later Kelly again wrote to MacHale expressing the hope that on his return to Ireland he would have reason to be reconciled to the new board. The new system did not in fact incorporate the principles laid down as essential at the meeting of the bishops in 1826.

In 1837 MacHale wrote a series of articles in the press denouncing government policy, especially its educational policy, and in the following year abolished the national schools system in his diocese, as far as lay in his power. In the same year, 1838, MacHale denounced the system to Rome and in this he was supported by the other bishops from Connaught. Murray wrote to Hamilton:

> Perhaps it would be only fair to the Connaught bishops that their sentiments on the National Education System such as they were six years after its establishment should be known to Rome. If those sentiments have undergone an unfavourable change, the reasons which produced it will be better understood (*563*).

At the same time Murray sent on the books used in the national schools which the Connaught bishops had complained about to Rome. In October Murray, for unknown reasons, answered MacHale in the press (23 October 1838). Why Murray took this step is not obvious. There may have been pressure put on him from the government or other members of the Board.

The matter came up in January 1839 at the annual conference. The bishops voted sixteen to nine in favour of retaining the national system in their dioceses. A minority, dissenting opinion for presentation to the Holy See was signed by the bishops of Tuam, Ardagh, Clonfert, Elphin, Achonry, Ferns, Kilmacduagh, Meath and Galway and the administrator of Killala.

One of the most important of the adherents to MacHale's cause at this period was Dr Higgins of Ardagh, an extremely active prelate. Dr Higgins was probably the most learned member of the hierarchy in the first half of the century, far surpassing the learned Dr Doyle in the number of years he spent in formal theological education. Dr MacHale regarded Dr Higgins as the best authority on canon law in the British dominions, a point to be kept in mind, for it was probably true, in all the disputes in the next fifteen years. It is safe to assume that as the bishops relied on O'Connell for opinions on civil law, so the entire Repeal faction relied on Higgins for opinions on canon law. And between the two there was nobody in the empire who could match them, or from whom Rome could ask for a more independent evaluation. The other notable adherent was Dr Cantwell of Meath who was, along with Dr Higgins, to be one of

O'Connell's leading supporters in the Repeal movement (*366; 97*).

It must have come as a shock to the majority of the bishops when Rome condemned the system of national education, but the Pope, Gregory XVI, declined to sign and referred the matter back. Rome's final decision in 1841 was to leave the matter to each individual bishop to decide. MacHale's party was defeated on this issue (*28; 400*).

Chronologically, the next issue dividing the factions was that of the priest in politics. In 1839 Rome issued a general warning, but the issue did not become crucial until the bishops, led by Dr Higgins, began actively to associate themselves with the Repeal movement in 1843. This dispute, which dragged on for several years, has been already dealt with.

After defeating O'Connell by calling his bluff at Clontarf to see what was behind the implicit threat of force, Sir Robert Peel set about introducing legislation for the better government of Ireland. Motions against state provision for the clergy came up in the episcopal conferences of 1837, 1841, 1843, 1845 and 1848. Sir Robert Peel's idea was rather to allow the Catholics to endow their own clergy, and this formed the basis of the Charitable Bequests Bill:

> The essential object of the Bill was to encourage private endowment of the Catholic clergy. To achieve this, it was necessary to offer stronger guarantees for the impartiality of the statutory body administering such endowments. The existing Board of Charitable Trusts had since its inception earlier in the century been composed exclusively of Protestants, though three-quarters of the trusts were Catholic (*187*, 421).

Archbishop Walsh states that O'Connell thought it necessary to hinder the bill for political reasons. O'Connell gave an opinion on the bill, that it was a new penal law, and this afforded an opportunity to those clergy who supported Repeal to attack the government. Dr Murray was much opposed to the bill, as several letters to Dr Hamilton show. Dr Murray referred O'Connell's opinion to the lord lieutenant, who referred it to the crown lawyers, who said that

O'Connell was mistaken in his interpretation. Crolly, Murray and Kennedy of Killaloe accepted seats on the board, and were fiercely attacked in the press.

> ... the publication of anonymous letters attacking with great bitterness those bishops who were sufficiently clear sighted to see through the clouds of sophistry by which the view of so many Catholics in Ireland — ecclesiastics as well as laymen — was being obscured, and who were also sufficiently courageous to do what they felt to be their duty regardless of insult and of all personal considerations (*519*, 96).

Higgins, MacHale and the reckless propagandist James Maher who supported O'Connell with 'customary vigour of language', opposed the board. They were joined by Paul Cullen and Tobias Kirby, the rector and vice-rector of the Irish College in Rome, 'both of whom supported in strong language opposition to the Bill' (*366; 519*).

The matter was brought up at the annual conference of bishops, and a motion by Crolly of Armagh and Egan of Kerry proposing that the matter be left to each individual bishop was adopted. MacHale appealed to Rome unsuccessfully.

The next clash between the two factions in the clergy was over the proposed Queen's Colleges. The principles underlying the proposed state provision of higher education in Ireland were identical with those already accepted for the primary sector. The bishops who objected to the proposed colleges did so on three grounds: one, that children were living away from home in one case, and living at home in the other; two, if there were three colleges, a single bishop could make a decision and set a precedent which would in fact bind the other bishops whereas if there was only a single college it could be subjected directly to the hierarchy; and three, by preserving a united front they could exact better terms. Technical differences in the wording with regard to appointments or dismissals of staff may also have been a factor in treating the two cases as not identical (*2*).

There was another point. With regard to national education, it was agreed by all except MacHale that there was no alternative to accepting what the government offered. With regard to a proposed Catholic university, opinions differed. Murray did not think that sufficient money could be raised. MacHale and Higgins went to considerable trouble to prove that there was no difficulty in raising such a sum, in view of the very considerable sums raised annually for the past thirty or forty years. On the Catholic University of Louvain, it should be noted that Louvain was an ancient university and had a right to confer degrees. MacHale's proposed university had not (*601; 400*).

Murray tried as far as possible to stand aside from the controversy, which may have been a tactical move. He pointed out that none of the colleges were in his diocese or province. This was of course implicitly to assert the right of each bishop to act independently and affirm the principle of non-interference in another province. Crolly made it clear that he was concerned only with the college within his province, and not those in other provinces.

Rome condemned the colleges, but her reasons for doing so are somewhat suspect. Political factors on a European scale may have been involved. There is no need to doubt the statements in the following letter:

> My informant assures me that he (Pius IX) was greatly averse to the condemnation of the infidel colleges, and we are indebted for that blessing to Cardinal Feretti's hostility to England, and to his insuperable repugnance to English intervention in the internal affairs of Italy.
>
> Feretti procured the condemnation of the colleges for the purpose of creating an alienation between the English government and the Pope. The agents of England are straining every nerve to effect Feretti's removal from office, and it is apprehended that their efforts will prove successful (*573*).

The British government did not give up its attempt to have the decision reversed. Despite allegations, by Dr Maginn for example, that Murray was busily promoting the cause of the colleges in Rome, this does not seem to have been the case. A Dublin priest, favourable to Murray's cause, was in Rome at the time and was given letters of introduction to various people, when he went '*pio affectu ductus*' (for reasons of devotion, i.e., on pilgrimage), and was not sent by Murray. The lack of references in the sources to any part played by Dr Murray seems to indicate that he did not interfere in the question, but kept to his stance that the colleges concerned other dioceses and other provinces. On the other hand, references indicate that Lord Clarendon, the lord lieutenant of Ireland, and Lord Minto, Lord John Russell's envoy in Italy, used the Irish Carmelite bishop of Corfu, Dr Francis Nicholson, as their go-between.

Rome's decision was based on the serious intrinsic dangers to the Catholic faith of students attending them (*Gravia intrinseca pericula*) (*367; 493*).

In 1857, Propaganda issued a statement with a view to reconciling the different responses given in the cases of the national schools and the Queen's Colleges. The statement alleges that in the case of the national schools, an experience of ten years had shown that they could be used safely. This, however, does not explain why ten years' probation could not have been given to the colleges (*557*).

The debate was in fact carried on in England for a further decade after 1850 with regard to Catholics attending Oxford and Cambridge, finally resulting in a prohibition of attendance by Catholics. In 1895, Leo XIII at the request of Cardinal Vaughan of Westminster, reversed the decision of Pius IX and allowed Catholics to attend those universities. As Snead-Cox remarked, the prohibition of 1867 (like that of 1847) was based only on the intrinsic danger of mixed education, and as long as this was the only objection the universities were practically open to Catholics, as individual priests or bishops could say that in this case or that the danger was remote.

Referring to the English case, Dr Butler says:

> If the archbishops and bishops had pleaded for toleration there is no reason for doubting that it would have been given as easily in '65 as it was in '95.
>
> Propaganda throughout showed itself ready to be guided by the voice of the authorities on the spot.

So also Trevor, who makes the point that the English

ultramontane clergy were misleading Propaganda.

Rome apparently did not call a national synod specifically to settle the matter. Even though the resolution moved by Dr Cantwell urged the deferring of business until a national synod could be convoked, *in obedience to the wishes* of Rome, the mind of the Holy See seems to have been expressed in the most general terms (*549*).

When Propaganda issued the second rescript dealing with the amended statutes of the Queen's Colleges, it largely repeated what was said in the first rescript: the danger of the colleges; the desirability of a Catholic university; concord among the clergy. In the second one, however, mention was made with regard to this latter of the advisability of holding clerical meetings in due canonical order. Otherwise there would always be differences of opinion, and the meetings would rather resemble secular meetings than ecclesiastical ones. It also held that the acts should be sent to Rome for approval (*493*).

Now these were precisely the criticisms which Paul Cullen had of the manner of holding the conferences of bishops, i.e., that when the meetings were held after the manner of civil meetings the best speaker had the most sway. Such meetings led to an increase of disputes rather than a decrease and there was lack of a properly constituted authority to which all the members should be subject (*73*).

The close resemblance of the sentiments would seem to show that either Cullen was copying Propaganda, or the sentiments of Propaganda were inspired by Cullen. Already in May (the rescript was published in October) Cullen informed Dr Maginn: 'It is the wish of His Holiness that the bishops should hold their next meeting in synodal form. The majority will then be able to do something efficacious. It is the only way to impede further aggressions (*367*, III, 44). Whether the pope or Cullen first thought of the idea is immaterial: Cullen made the sentiment his own.

Archbishop Crolly died on 9 April 1849, and those of MacHale's faction made every effort to get one of their own party chosen as primate. In November, when Rome's choice was still undeclared, Cantwell and MacHale moved that a synod be convoked. In December Paul Cullen's appointment was announced on the recommendation of MacHale, Slattery of Cashel and Cantwell. The machinations of the bishops on this occasion to obtain a particular nomination for political reasons set a precedent which was often to be repeated (*602; 580*).

On 6 April 1850, Cullen was appointed apostolic delegate and may have been ordered to convoke a synod. As this was very close to Cullen's view that an apostolic delegate should preside over every meeting of the bishops, it is reasonable to assume that the mover behind this decision of Rome was Cullen himself. MacSuibhne states that Cullen was ordered to convoke a synod but does not give the source. Pius IX states, in the letter of 6 April 1850 appointing Cullen apostolic delegate, 'so that in that name *also* he might convoke a synod' (*qui eo quoque nomine synodum convocet*). This formula left the relationship between the pope and the Irish Church, undecided until 1870, unchanged (*367; 73; 553*).

The most important point on the agenda was to establish a uniform discipline throughout Ireland on the subject of the Queen's Colleges. After 1870, this matter could be treated by a simple act of the pope, but Propaganda was wary of having another rescript treated as Monsignor Quarantotti's had been. By having a synodal decision, and that approved by the pope, a uniform discipline could be enforced, and the position of Crolly and Murray that each individual bishop could be allowed to negotiate with the government would thereby be excluded.

Despite what Cullen was reported to have said afterwards, there is no indication that Rome had prejudged the issue. In his letter of 6 April to the Irish bishops, the pope expressed a desire that a discipline *consonant* with the already expressed rescripts should be established (*consentanea ac uniformis*). In the rescript of Propaganda of 18 April, Rome expressed the wish that the prelates 'would show all due respect to the Holy See and its responses (*si a debito erga Apostolicam Sedem ejusdemque responsa obsequio vel minimum deflectent*). This in practice meant that Rome would not tolerate the *unilateral* rejection of one of its rescripts. *Any* decision made by the Irish bishops on the matter would have to be referred back to Rome, and meanwhile the fact that a council was held did not mean that in the interim the rescripts were inoperative, suspended or cancelled. A priest could not therefore accept office in the colleges (*553*).

Cullen and MacHale had to think of something else to do in the synod besides formally accepting the rescripts:

> We must enter most accurately into all questions concerning education, and all other such matters that affect the faith of the people, and the liberty of the Church.
>
> It will also be necessary to treat of the condition of the poor.
>
> But we cannot avoid, I daresay, making some regulations for the clergy, secular and regular, and commencing to remove any abuses that have sprung up in the times of persecution (*367*).

These letters show that reform of discipline was something of an afterthought and a piece of window dressing. The word 'commencing' shows the care one must exercise in reading Cullen. Establishing a uniform discipline had in fact been agreed upon in principle twenty years previously. It is not clear how seriously the other bishops took the provisions on the reform of the Church. Most of the items, like the furnishing of churches or the provision of parochial glebes, were already within each bishop's power to decide. Cullen's complaint of non-observance may have had some foundation in fact (*124*, 7ff.).

One piece of information with regard to the conduct of the synod seems to have been leaked to the press:

> Dr Kennedy was a powerful orator, and when speaking in support of the Queen's Colleges, Dr Cullen requested him to resume his seat. 'By what right does your Grace tell me to sit down?' demanded the bishop. 'By authority of the Holy See of which I am the Apostolic Delegate', replied Dr Cullen. Dr Kennedy seemed transfixed. 'I bow to that', he said, 'but not to you' (*367*, on the authority of the reliable Fitzpatrick).

Those who opposed Cullen and MacHale wrote to Rome

pointing out that whereas the synod had been called to discuss the uniform discipline of the Irish Church (i.e., concerning the Colleges), the apostolic delegate · disallowed discussion. Fransoni replied evasively that he could not find fault with anyone who read and approved rescripts of the Holy See, and added *post-factum* that the synod had only been called to find uniform ways of carrying the rescripts of the Holy See into practice. The decrees of the synod were confirmed by Rome.

With regard to the other prescriptions concerning the discipline of the Irish Church, the only points on which Cullen expected opposition were those on the placing of baptismal fonts and confessionals with grilles in the churches. Murray agreed to these points, with the proviso that they not be introduced immediately but as opportunity arose. Cullen and the majority of the bishops supported and reiterated Rome's decision on the national schools.

Right to the end of his life, these decrees of Thurles gave Cullen the opportunity of blackballing any supporter of Dr Murray, or indeed any priest he did not like. For example, Cullen wrote to Propaganda objecting to a priest who was first on the *terna* on the grounds that he would not be disposed to put into effect the reforms of Thurles regarding the administration of the sacraments. The priest himself, Fr O'Sullivan, had no doubt that Cullen's opposition came from the fact that he had been a supporter of Dr Murray; he commented that Cullen blackballed every priest and bishop in the Irish Church. The placing of confessionals and fonts in the churches were customs which were being gradually introduced at the time. There seems little doubt that Cullen was misleading Propaganda on the real state of the Irish Church after 1850, though not deliberately. Some writers have relied heavily on Cullen's reports to Rome in his early years as a bishop in Ireland, and have thus painted a blacker picture than that which emerges from an examination of the full range of evidence. Cullen's writings, especially his letters, show him to have been inclined to see matters in stark black and white terms, and to be deeply intolerant of opposition. He was a complex character and his statements should be treated with some caution.

The war of attrition with the government over university education, as over primary education, continued into the next century with a similar result: the system tended in practice to become denominational (*404*). In 1875 the bishops forbade attendance at Trinity College. A strong attempt during Cullen's lifetime to set up an independent Catholic university was virtually abandoned on his death.

The Work of the Episcopal Conference

From 1829 until 1852, we have a considerable amount of information about the activities of the episcopal conference, but not always as much as we would wish, for the minutes record only formal resolutions. Before 1829 and after 1852 the decisions of the bishops have to be gleaned from other sources. Those decisions of major importance concerning the public were usually published in the newspapers.

Some of their activities seem merely adventitious, resulting from the fact that the conference seemed to be the logical place to discuss certain questions that arose and not from any considered plan of the bishops. Among these were the supervision of Irish colleges on the continent, their endowments and the discipline of their students. The bishops devoted much time, effort and expense to these colleges and their special financial and disciplinary problems. The bishops were involved, too, in setting up a national book society. They also devoted much consideration to the question of the reduction in the number of holy days. The question of the veto engaged the bishops for many a long year. So too did the question of a suitable system for state-supported education.

We can assume that the application to the whole of Ireland of the Tridentine decree *Tametsi* was discussed. In 1824 Dr Doyle wrote to Propaganda indicating that the decree was promulgated in the whole of Ireland except in the ecclesiastical province of Leinster, in the diocese of Meath and in the wardenship of Galway. He wished to see a uniform discipline in this matter over the whole of Ireland. In theory, marriages before couple-beggars were valid in these areas, invalid elsewhere, and runaway couples could go to Dublin instead of the famous Gretna Green. Doyle feared resistance from 'turbulent' priests, and suggested to Propaganda that it write to the metropolitan of Dublin suggesting the measure. The decree was formally promulgated in all Ireland on 2 December 1827, and came into force thirty days later, 1 January 1828.

The bishops wished to see some of the minor fasts abolished and certain indulgences extended to the whole of Ireland. Murray twice made the point to Propaganda that he had to consult the other bishops, as they wanted to see a uniform discipline throughout Ireland.

Two questions appear in the archives in this period. One was the question of bination, saying two masses on a Sunday, and the other was the question of ordaining 'titulo missionis'.

It was noted in the archives of Propaganda at this time that the Irish priests, by the authority of some decree of Rome the origin of which could not be found, had the right of celebrating mass twice on Sundays and holy days. It is not clear who reported this to Rome, or for what reason, but the Tuam statutes of 1818 forbade the practice *without licence*. The national synod at Thurles forbade the practice except with the permission of the bishop (Thurles *Decreta*, 25).

The custom in Ireland was to ordain priests on the title of the mission. The 'title' was the guarantee of the means of support which a priest had to have to prove that he could maintain himself decently after ordination. In 1828 Dr Blake reported from Rome that the Irish bishops had no authority to ordain their subjects merely on the 'title of service' in an Irish parish, i.e., with the right to dues and casual emoluments. The title remained, however, until 1909 when the title 'diocesan service' was officially recognised.

The conference set up a committee of four bishops to study the discipline of the Irish Church with the remit 'to take into consideration the discipline of the Irish Church and to report thereon, with a view to rendering it as uniform as circumstances will permit, and more in accordance with the canons'. The Right Rev. Drs McLoughlan, Coen, Egan and Keating formed the committee. They reported that they found it difficult to get exact information. Baptism was generally administered in private houses. The holy eucharist was sometimes administered at stations of confession where mass had not been celebrated. Some clergymen carried the eucharist around on their persons. Mass was often said in private houses and often priests said two masses on a Sunday. In some cases the vestments were poor. Priests lacked soutanes. Confessions were heard in private houses and many priests dined at these stations and even accepted the dues. Some did not even wear a stole.

Some priests, it was alleged, showed unwillingness to administer extreme unction without previous remuneration, and priests seldom repeated their visits to the sick. In many instances due care was not taken in selection of candidates for orders. Banns for marriage were seldom published and frequently people were married without going to confession. These allegations are rather vague and it is surprising that the bishops were not better informed about what was done in their own dioceses.

The committee made the following recommendation: no adults should be presented for confirmation unless previously well instructed; mass should be celebrated at each station of confession; no clergyman might dine at the station house on the occasion of a station; no dues should be accepted in the confessional; the pyxis holding the eucharist was to be folded in a corporal and kept in an inside pocket when the priest was away from home, and on his return deposited in a suitable place under lock and key; examiners were to be appointed in each diocese to examine candidates for the seminary; no priest should hear confessions till examined by the examiners; those being married should go to confession within three days before the marriage; any priest who withheld his ministry on the grounds of not receiving the fees should be punished; an instruction should be given by each parish priest and curate on Sundays and holy days; the clergy should not attend theatres, races, hunts or balls (*549*).

The report was, of course, confined to clerical behaviour and the conduct of worship. It does not report any grave abuses but deals with several points where the bishops wished to see improvement. The conference itself had no authority to make laws or to establish a uniform discipline. A national synod may have been envisaged around 1830. One was proposed in 1818 but judged inexpedient by Rome (*73*).

The recommendations in the report are interesting for they show us the approach adopted by the bishops to reform, an approach which has remained unchanged ever since. There were no radical changes proposed. Nor was any sweeping proposal made to bring in all of the *jus novissimum* which had never been promulgated. Rather they wanted to make the discipline as uniform in Ireland as the times would permit, and as much in accord with the canons as Irish conditions made advisable. Reluctance to change ancient custom on the part of the clergy could be an important factor in this regard. The discipline of the Irish Church was already fairly uniform, so the changes proposed might seem to the layman rather trivial. But as they concerned the professional conduct of the cleigy, it affected them more directly. No attempt is made to override the authority of each bishop in his diocese. Reform of canon law was not seen as an urgent priority. It would seem, however, that later Cardinal Cullen did make some conscious attempts to introduce the *jus novissimum*, but it was not a project likely to gain wide support among the clergy. Reform of canon law was carried out on a piecemeal basis to the end of the century, usually as the result of some pressures brought by particular priests like Dr Walter MacDonald. The 'new code' was adopted *en bloc* in 1917 (*46*).

The recommendations remained such at least as far as the conference was concerned, but they seem to have formed the basis of the canons in various provincial synods held soon after. Resolutions of conference had no binding force whatsoever, as may be noted in connection with the famous resolution withdrawing the priests from active participation in politics after emancipation. It simply expressed the bishops' opinion that such activity was not for priests. Each individual bishop was of course free to make a local statute on the point if he felt it necessary. The bishops' joint pastoral did not specify what precise forms of electoral activity were discountenanced, it presumably being obvious to the laity and clergy what innovations the emancipation campaign had brought. The older forms of participation such as collecting the rent or ostentatiously voting were continued even by the primate. Murray issued a diocesan prohibition in 1830.

Synods and Statutes

This section concerns the regulatory activities of the bishops, each within his own diocese, and of the groups of bishops in a province in provincial synods as well as in the national synods.

A problem arises with regard to the sources for this section, for printed collections of diocesan statutes often incorporate earlier statutes. We can, however, reasonably accurately date the reforming activities of Dr George Plunkett of Elphin and determine their scope, for we have a report from the bishop to Propaganda dated 1826. He had held synods in his diocese, made regulations concerning the conduct of the clergy and enforced the wearing of clerical dress. In the administration of the sacraments he had enforced the wearing of soutane, surplice and stole. He introduced an anteprandial law forbidding alcoholic drink before dinner so that now but one drunken priest remained in the diocese.

Wherever the biblicals had set up a school, his priests set up a rival one. The priests taught the Christian doctrine every Sunday before mass and confraternities were established to teach it after mass. Nobody ignorant of the Christian doctrine was admitted to the sacraments. The bishop personally administered confirmation every year. Clerical conferences were regularly attended and the priests went over most of their theology once a year. 'The whole of the foregoing system I have introduced and enforced' (*264*). Later priests noted that if most of the theology could be revised in a year, it must have been fairly simple.

Dr Higgins of Ardagh held a synod in 1834 but I have been unable to trace any record of any statutes that were passed. The bishop of Limerick apparently made diocesan regulations concerning the life of the clergy, and found that he could not enforce them on the regulars except where it was already the common law of the Church.

The 1817 statutes in Tuam, if they can be relied on with

regard to the date, were as follows: the clergy were to attend theological conferences; confessions were not to be heard without the licence of the hishop; the clergy were to preach; they were to reside in their parishes; only approved books were to be used in the celebration of the sacred rites; mass was not to be said twice on a Sunday without licence; wandering priests (*sacerdotes vagi*) were not to be admitted to works of the ministry; the bishop could appoint a curate to an old or infirm priest; a priest stirring up a faction and riot (*factio et seditio*) or any doing so in his favour made the priest ineligible for the parish; no lay patronage to be allowed on any grounds; the priest was to say mass for the people on suppressed holy days; the parish priest was to keep parochial records; a fornicating priest was to be suspended; no priest was to hear the confession of an accomplice in sexual matters; if a priest was guilty of drunkenness, he was to be suspended after a third admonition; no priest was to go into a public house to drink, nor to dance when women were present (*neque saltare coram foeminibus*); he was to avoid race meetings and public handball contests (*pilae palmariae lusum publicum*) or even private games on a Sunday; priests were not to attend theatres; candidates for the priesthood were to be watched over for a year before being accepted; at least two years of theology in some academy were to have been studied before ordination (Tuam *Statuta*).

Some of these statutes have an archaic ring about them, being in fact citations from the Council of Trent. Such are statutes against the *clerici vagi* and those enforcing the typical editions of the liturgical books: the contemporary object of the statute on *clerici vagi* may have been excessively strolling friars. Such statutes may have survived from an earlier date. Others, we know from contemporary sources, were very relevant in the early nineteenth century. M'Kenna in his history of the diocese of Clogher states:

The northern bishops were then engaged in a strenuous effort to eliminate various abuses which had crept into the administration of the Church in penal times.

One of the most serious and troublesome of these was a custom which had grown up of appointing to a vacant parish a native of that parish, who could reside with his relatives, and where a native was not available, the selection of a few of the leading families got the preference.

Gradually, the people in some parishes assumed that they had a right to select their own pastor, and that the functions of a bishop were confined to formal approval of their selection. . . . The bishops, who had no legal standing in the country, having no power to enforce their ecclesiastical authority, had generally been obliged to take the line of least resistance.

I have noted above some indications that the bishops did not in fact have as clear a right to nominate to parishes as some of them claimed. The bishops may have accepted the nominations not because they could not enforce them in civil law, but because they could not enforce them in canon law — the right of presentation of the original endower, or monastic patron, and their heirs or lawful successors never having being extinguished. It is interesting to note statutes both against lay patronage and popular clamour.

The statute on preaching repeats the Council of Trent but was apparently relevant to the situation at that time, with its emphasis on the instruction of the faithful. The question of bination is referred to in the archives of Propaganda of the period. The statute against drunken priests reflects that in Elphin and Dr Murphy's sweeping legislation against the use of alcohol. The statutes against entering places of public amusement or public drinking reflect the Leinster legislation (Dublin *Statuta* 1831). Greater care was now being taken in the selection of candidates for the priesthood. Two full years of theology were regarded as a minimum. Archbishop Murray in 1827, in a letter to Dr Blake, noted that out of twenty-one priests ordained in Maynooth for various parts of Ireland, no less than eleven were called to orders by their bishops at the end of their second year of theology.

Absent from these statutes is one on clerical dress, a point which Plunkett of Elphin stressed, and which receives a whole chapter in the Leinster statutes. Also absent is a statute restricting the amount of land a priest could hold, and various other statutes on the life of the clergy. The regulations introduced by Dr Doyle were not necessarily typical in every detail of those introduced elsewhere.

The statutes of the Synod of Cashel were much more elaborate. They dealt first with the proper administration of the sacraments, with baptism, confirmation, the eucharist, the mass, masses for the dead and with parish churches. Confession and related matters, reserved sins, censures and indulgences were dealt with. The value of the Confraternity of the Blessed Sacrament is stressed. Then comes the anointing of the sick, holy orders and matrimony. After the section on the due care in the administration of the sacraments comes a section on the life of the clergy. The duty of preaching is stressed, while chapters are devoted to theological conferences, confraternities and parochial schools.

The next section deals with the diocesan officials, the vicar-general, the vicars-forane, the diocesan examiners and synodal judges. Vicars-forane were to be appointed in both dioceses (Cashel and Emly) and synodal judges whose function it was to settle disputes, and diocesan examiners who were to examine regulars, curates and students in theology. Though these statutes show the kind of legislation that was being considered at the time, we cannot conclude that vicars-forane had not been appointed before regularly, or that synodal judges were appointed regularly thereafter.

The best known of the reforms in the various dioceses is that of Dr Doyle, just because it is dealt with in Fitzpatrick's biography. The ideas of Dr Doyle were incorporated largely into the Leinster statutes in 1831. Dr Doyle first stressed the life of the clergy.

The precise rationale behind this desire to supervise strictly the life of the clergy is not clear. All that was essentially required was that abuses should be eliminated and incentive given to reach and maintain high standards of professional competence, as is done in the regulatory activity of professional bodies. A further point seems to be included, namely the *witness* to eternal values given by a distinctive celibate clergy, the more so as the theology of the Council of Trent stressed the special kind of priesthood of the clerical order.

The clergy were to keep away from any public spectacles,

or places of public resort or amusement. This included horse-racing and hunting. Doyle allowed a parish priest to attend race meetings in his own parish, with a view to keeping order. Doyle re-introduced the wearing of distinctive clerical dress. (It should be noted that as fashions changed since Roman times, there never was any one distinctive dress for secular priests everywhere. The religious orders, clerical and lay, from the early Middle Ages at least, were recognisable by the fact that they wore a hood or cowled garment.) The Leinster statutes did not prescribe a form of clerical dress. A long skirted garment reaching the ankles (*vestis talaris* or soutane) was not prescribed except during the administration of the sacraments. The use of the breeches and upper jacket was therefore allowed. The colour should always be black or dark (grey? *niger aut sub-niger*). Both the Armagh statutes and those of Thurles make the point expressly that the garb should be such as to make the clergy readily distinguishable from the laity. On the avoidance of places of public resort, Meagher noted that the intention was to bring the Irish church into closer conformity with the canons while Doyle himself said that no zealous priest would object to avoiding those places that the Church declared unsuitable for his profession.

One obvious abuse to be rooted out was the squabbles by relatives over the possession of ecclesiastical goods on the death of a priest. In 1789, in a visitation, Dr Plunkett insisted that the sacred vessels, chalice, pyxis etc. should have the name of the parish inscribed, and every article belonging to the parish should be inscribed in a book so that they could come into the hands of the parish priest's successor. Doyle was very severe with clergy who failed to make a proper will, as was also Dr Blake of Dromore. The difficulty was caused by the state of the laws which did not recognise Catholic parishes as possessors of property.

Doyle limited the holding of land by parish priests to fourteen acres (Dublin *Statuta*, fifteen acres). The reason for this, according to Fitzpatrick, was that some of the clergy in Kildare and Leighlin had rented up to a hundred acres and were agriculturalists rather than pastors of souls. The statute was included in those of Thurles.

Chapter 3 of the Dublin statutes deals with the study of theology, and the clergy were required to read some every day. This was also in the Carlow statutes. The study of theology was reinforced by the resuming of the custom of holding the summer clerical conferences on theology. These had lapsed in Kildare and Leighlin in the troubles of 1798 and apparently had not been restored. In Meath apparently only one conference had to be abandoned on account of the troubles, though there were four military engagements in the county. Dr Plunkett promptly suspended a parish priest whom he suspected of abandoning his post. In Ferns, despite the precaution of getting the agenda printed by a Protestant printer, there was some suspicion that they were being used to foment the rebellion. The fact that theological conferences were not resumed in Kildare and Leighlin until 1820 lends some weight to Fitzpatrick's remarks about the easygoing or careless nature of the administration of Doyle's immediate predecessors.

Doyle began his episcopal career by preaching a retreat for over a thousand priests, half the clergy in Ireland, including nearly all the bishops. The retreat lasted ten days and Doyle preached three times each day. The sole source of information on this important event I have been able to find is Fitzpatrick. The magnitude of the enterprise shows that it must have been a common decision of the hierarchy.

The custom of having the clergy make an annual retreat seems to have begun about this time. When exactly this custom began is not clear, but a form of retreat was held in some French dioceses at least in the eighteenth century (*483*). In Dublin in 1823, a directive of Archbishop Troy instructed the secular and regular clergy to make an annual retreat of ten or at least eight days. Doyle preached to several hundred priests in Maynooth in 1825. The annual diocesan retreat for the diocese of Dublin began in Maynooth in 1820. In 1822 Dr Murray handed over a sum of £90, being the contribution of sixty-one priests, mostly from Dublin, at a rate of £1 10s. 0d. each, to cover the costs of the retreat.

It is difficult to trace the spread of the custom or obligation, of making an annual or biennial retreat, as there were several possibilities open to a priest. He could attend a retreat in a neighbouring parish, or go to some religious house, or go to Maynooth. Cullen claimed to have introduced the retreat into Armagh and as far as formal exercises went may well have done so. It was not until 1889 that a statute was introduced setting aside one week for parish priests and one for curates, though a general obligation to make a retreat had been in force in the province at least since Dr Dixon's provincial synod in 1854 (*18; 20*).

Neither these statutes concerning the life of the clergy nor the reports given above suggest that the clergy in Ireland were morally corrupt, or *in general* neglectful of their duties. Rather, they suggest that in some cases particular instances of inappropriate conduct needed to be corrected, and also that a more 'clerical' image was desired.

Much of the legislation concerned the manner of conducting divine service. Dr Plunkett noted that neither soutane, surplice nor stole were in use in Elphin for the administration of the sacraments when he came to the diocese. He insisted on their use. The use of soutanes before that seems to have been comparatively rare. The Leinster statutes prohibit the saying of mass *in public* without a soutane (*549; 155*).

There was also the problem, not confined to Ireland, of dirty vestments; it occurred in Naples and in France (*40; 503*). Dr Plunkett of Meath in his early visitations (*c.* 1780) complained constantly of the poor vestments and altar vessels and linen. Doyle used to tear up and burn any vestments he regarded as unsuitable for worship. In one case he found the vestments stored in an old turf basket, and the priest whose vestments were thus torn and burned by the bishop was in fact a wealthy man. A statute in the Dublin *Statuta* warned against dirty vestments of poor quality. It is not clear how widespread was the habit of using dirty or poor vestments. The report of the episcopal committee on the discipline of the Irish Church which noted that few priests had soutanes merely says that 'some' make use of poor-quality vestments.

One Irish custom Dr Doyle wished to see eradicated was the holding of 'stations'. The parish priest read out the names of those houses in his parish which he would visit for the purpose of hearing confessions and saying mass. Often a hundred people would assemble in a small house to perform their devotions. The parish priest and his curates were given a hearty meal and sometimes the dues were paid at the same time as the parishioner went to confession. Stations, as Carleton indicates, could be used by non-Catholics who wished to cast aspersions on Catholic practice. But they apparently had an irreplaceable pastoral function and accordingly their practice was not forbidden in the Leinster statutes. Doyle, however, seems to have suppressed the custom of the priest dining at the station house. A priest, though forbidden to *dine*, could however *break his fast*. The Armagh provincial statutes refer to the laudible custom of holding stations at Christmas, but say that mass should never be omitted at the station of confessions (*19*).

Dr Doyle insisted on the exact observance of the rubrics in the celebration of liturgical worship. The Dublin statutes of 1831 exhort that the divine office should be read in a careful, reverent manner and the mass also said in reverent manner. The Synod of Cashel laid special stress on the reverent singing of the funeral service. The Dublin statutes of 1831 prescribe that the acts of contrition, of faith, hope and charity, and the prayer before mass were to be said before mass on Sundays and holy days. The *De Profundis* after mass is mentioned early in the nineteenth century by Kennedy. Carelessness about rubrics was not confined to Ireland. St Alphonsus had to deal severely with it in his Neapolitan diocese in the preceding century.

The Dublin statutes prescribed that churches were to be well kept and clean and all secular acts were to be prohibited within their walls (*Saeculares omnes actiones, vana et adeo profana colloquia, deambulationes, strepitus, clamores*: talking, walking about, noise, shouting). Political meetings had been held in churches, as was teaching. In Clogher even threshing had been carried on in the church. About 1780, Dr Plunkett mentions dirt around the altar, children and even older people talking in church, the altar not being sufficiently raised, the people coming too near the altar. Lover mentions the fact that people could reply to the priest when he spoke of a secular matter from the altar. When still a newly ordained priest, Dr Doyle had denounced the habit of reading notices about lost and found objects from the altar. Dr Thomas Kelly, when bishop of Dromore around 1830, forbade the custom in that diocese.

In 1841, allegations were made that priests were saying mass with their spurs on, that the altar vessels and vestments were mean and the chapels and altars were dirty (*Directory*, 1842, p. 256). In reply, it was testified that in Kildare and Leighlin the chalices were of silver and in some cases even in country areas, of gold. Some of the chapels in the larger towns had monstrances, ciboria and thuribles. In Cashel the sanctuaries were clean; the sacred vessels of gold or silver (chalices), or silver (ciboria, pyxes, oil-stocks); the altar linens and vestments generally unexceptional; the chasubles, stoles and maniples of the richest material. The clergy even in country chapels wore soutanes when celebrating. One priest in Killaloe admitted that riding boots were worn by the clergy during mass, but not spurs, and another remarked, 'The reviewer seems to be describing the state of religion in this country some fifty years ago – certainly not what it is at present.' One wonders how accurate this last comment was. The amount of dirt which is regarded as tolerable by one generation may well offend the standards of another generation. At the end of the century we have the famous remark about the 'clane dirt', i.e., altar wax in *My New Curate*.

As the main purpose of holding national synods was to deal with some urgent national problem, it follows that the legislation of such synods was quite secondary. They derived their authority only from the confirmation of the pope and so became a kind of intermediate canon law. There was no machinery for enforcing them, and provincial synods seem to have been held after each of them to make the necessary adjustments in the provincial statutes. It is clear that the more bishops are involved, the more difficult it is to get agreement, and Irish bishops were notoriously reluctant to interfere with each other's rights.

The legislation introduced at Thurles was clearly secondary and it is not clear how much of it was intended as window dressing. In 1882 an attempt was made to produce an up-to-date standard version of the catechism for the whole of

Ireland. What resulted was a revision of Butler's catechism, called the Maynooth Catechism, which was ignored in many dioceses. It survived to our own day. (With regard to it, a teacher in a country primary school in Armagh asked why it spoke of 'theatrical representations and other amusements in which sacred things are ridiculed' when 'bad plays' would have done for all that country children knew.)

In an extremely clerical and autocratic era, the synods at all levels were dominated by the bishops and their theological advisers. Apart from presenting a united front to the British government on such matters as education, it is hard to see what point there was in holding them. The synod in 1925, after the departure of the British, was held ostensibly to consider the implications of the new code of canon law (1917).

10
Finances

General Aspects

The Church in Ireland was not supported by the state nor had it any lands or endowments (*510*). There was no central treasury or consolidated fund either within Ireland or within each diocese in which all monies were lodged. and from which all expenditures might be paid. The cost of each item was raised separately, the support of the priest, the capital cost of the church, the running costs of divine service, the salary of the schoolmaster, the expenses of a confraternity, the support for an orphanage, the support of the personnel of a convent, the expenditures on the charities run by the convent and so on. In general, without the express consent of the donor, any money collected for one purpose could not be used for any other purpose.

The Catholic Church in Ireland was essentially a voluntary society, and had to meet all its expenses from the more or less voluntary contributions of its members by sale of work, or by appeals to the general public. There seems to have been an obligation on the people to contribute in money or in kind to the support of their pastors, and on the basis of this obligation bishops could ordain priests who had a right to suitable support *titulo missionis*. There was also an obligation, directly on the priests and bishops, and indirectly on the laity, from the common canon law of providing sacred vessels and linen of an appropriate quality. There does not appear to have been any canon *ordering* the construction of a church, any relevant legislation being rather concerned with restricting or preventing the building of churches.

The Support of the Parochial Clergy

In the Latin Church the clergy were forbidden to engage in various trades and professions, though certain others, like teaching, which were 'liberal' rather than 'servile' (Latin *liber, servus*, a freeman, a slave) were allowed. Before being ordained, they had to give evidence of how they proposed to support themselves in a manner proportionate to the dignity of their station during the whole course of their lives. In the common canon law there does not seem to have been any direct obligation on the ordinary faithful to contribute to the support of their pastors. A priest could indicate that he had sufficient patrimony, a permanent chaplaincy, a benefice etc. Benefices were the normal means of supporting the clergy.

I have not come across any clear examples of surviving or new benefices in Ireland, though it would be strange if there were not some, especially when endowments could be made overseas. There is a reference to the 'revenues of the abbey of St Fintan'. Glebe lands, one of which had the form of a 'bishop's lease renewable, assigned over to the clergyman' existed in at least two cases in Tuam. There were a few cases of pew-rents, and seat-rents, but revenue from this source was scant as the rent was low and the seats few. I have come across no instance of an attempt to collect tithes (*578; 170*).

Corresponding to the title of ordination of the 'mission' was a corresponding obligation, numbered in Ireland among the 'Precepts' of the Church, to contribute to the support of the pastors. This was paid twice a year in the form of 'dues'. According to Sir Thomas Wyse, about whose evidence there is admittedly some doubt:

> There is no general ecclesiastical law to enforce the payment of these trifles; but as the mode was struck out in what has been denominated the Council of Kilkenny under Rinuccini, it has continued ever since to be practised, and from custom has acquired the force of law.

The first half of the seventeenth century is likely enough as the time of origin of this innovation. Clerical revenues came in three different forms: first, the dues; second, offerings made 'on the occasion' of the performance of a sacred rite; and third, when the priest acted as notary, in giving dismissorial letters, certificates of baptism etc. (*340*; Appendix B).

The average level of income around 1800 was estimated at about £65, exclusive of the cost of keeping a curate, which would imply a net income of around £100. But incomes varied from some parishes in Leighlin with an income of over £300 to some in the wardenship of Galway with less than £25. By 1825, O'Connell thought £150 per annum a high average. Lord Killeen thought £500 good for Dublin, £300 good for a country parish, while parishes in Meath were worth £100 to £150, and this is comparable with O'Connell's estimate, Killeen giving the upper end of the scale. At mid century MacHale and Higgins also take £150 as being the average for the clergy, but as they multiply this by 4,000, the income of curates, and possibly regulars, must be included in the average. This would imply a higher figure for parish priests (*601*, vol. 29, *Libellus* of MacHale and Higgins on the finances of the Irish Church. How they reached the figure 4,000 is a mystery). At the end of the century, Walter MacDonald estimated the income of a parish priest to be £260 (the revenue from a large parish with two curates to be £520). These estimates are little more than educated guesses, though the figures cited for 1800 may be more accurate than the others, being based on an official questionnaire sent out by Lord Castlereagh. The bishops who made the returns would have a fairly accurate idea of the *relative* wealth or poverty of particular parishes.

An estimate of the relative wealth of the Irish parishes was made about 1860 by Archbishop Leahy, with a view to setting up a levy to support the Catholic University. The proposed levy per parish in the various dioceses was as follows:

	£		£
Armagh	6	Cashel and Emly	8
Meath	10	Cork	8
Derry	3	Killaloe	6
Clogher	5	Kerry	5

Raphoe	3	Limerick	8
Down and Connor	4	Waterford and Lismore	7
Kilmore	5	Cloyne	8
Ardagh	6	Ross	5
Dromore	4		
		Tuam	5
		Clonfert	5
		Achonry	3
Dublin	20	Elphin	5
Kildare and Leighlin	6	Kilmacduagh and K.	5
Ossory	7	Galway	5
Ferns	6	Killala	3

(Leahy Papers, Proposed Expenditure on the Catholic University, 1 April 1861)

The reputed wealth of Dublin, more than three times the estimated national average, is clear. There is also a wealthy group of southern dioceses, with a proposed levy of £8 and a poor group of northern and north-western dioceses. Meath was estimated to be the richest diocese outside Dublin.

For comparison, in the early part of the century, MacDowell gives the following earnings: an agricultural labourer £15 per annum, a skilled artisan £20—30, porters and messengers £25—30, lowest paid clerks and minor officials £50. Situations with an income of £100—150 were regarded as appropriate ones for the sons of gentlemen to start in. Over two hundred government officials had incomes of over £200 and another one hundred and thirty had incomes of £500. At around £40—50 came curates, ensigns in the army and doctors and lawyers at the beginning of their careers. Teachers in the pay schools got from perhaps £7—14 (*582; 585*). The incomes of farmers varied, but it was estimated that a man who rented six acres could net £17 after paying the labourer (*Limerick Reporter*, 24 September 1839). Lynch and Vaizey estimate an annual income of £40—50 for small farmers.

Subsistence for a child was estimated at two pence halfpenny a day, or £3 16s. 0d. per annum. Five pounds per annum could be regarded as subsistence level for an adult. At the other end of the scale were salaries like that of the viceroy at £20,000. Protestant bishops in Ireland had £17,000 (Armagh), £14,000 (Derry), £10,000 (Clogher). Of the nobility and landed gentry in Ireland, the earl Fitzwilliam had £18,000 and Lord Cloncurry £9,000. (Lord Durham once memorably defined £80,000 as 'the sort of income a man could jog along on.') Sir Robert Peel, on succeeding to the title, had £40,000. In England, even late in the century, Bishop Vaughan regarded £90 sufficient for a rector and £40 for his assistant. Assistants in some dioceses got £25 (*350*).

Did clerical incomes rise in the course of the century? The evidence, such as it is, £260 for a parish priest around 1900, given above, would seem to indicate that it did rise. But if GNP was rising at the same time, it is more important to enquire if clerical incomes rose more rapidly than the average.

A rise of 1 per cent in per capita GNP will lead to an increase of 28.2 per cent in twenty-five years, 64 per cent in fifty years and 110 per cent in seventy-five years. An annual rise of 1.5 per cent gives 45 per cent in twenty-five years and 110 in fifty years. The figures I have cited do not indicate that the income of the clergy was rising more rapidly than the national average.

It must, however, be noted when quoting figures for the wealth of individual priests that the priest could have wealth from other sources besides his parish. One way to get wealth was to inherit it. Or he could get an income from farming. Even if the priest, after the reforms of Dr Doyle, was restricted to fourteen or fifteen acres, he could still have a revenue of up to £40 from this source. The peculiar nature of Irish clerical incomes meant that they were not included under the prescriptions of canon law concerning income from benefices. In canon law, a beneficiary was obliged to pay to the poor the *superflua beneficii* from the *reditus stabiles* after deducting what was required for *congrua sustentatio*, i.e., after deducting 'what was necessary to maintain himself properly', the beneficiary had to pay the 'remainder' from the 'stable revenues' of the benefice to the poor. Though diocesan legislation increasingly regulated clerical incomes not derived from benefices, the legislation did not apply to non-clerical income.

The Support of the Bishops

The ordinary income of a bishop was derived from one or more parishes which he held *in commendam* (by this was meant that each bishop individually was given authority by the Holy See to take the revenues of the parish, while paying a curate to perform the duties). He also received the *cathedraticum* or contribution from the parish priests (*340*).

In 1800 the average income of an Irish bishop was estimated as being £300, ranging from £550 in Cork to £100 in Kilmacduagh. In 1825, Dr Kelly of Tuam estimated his income to be above £500, while Dr Doyle put his at £450–500, saying that this was less than that of some other bishops. In 1835 episcopal revenues were estimated to be between £500 and £1,000. Dispensations and licence fees could also augment the bishop's income, and many bishops thought that 40 per cent of their income came from that source (*340*).

Dr Doyle also had the income from a suppressed abbey. A bishop, like any other priest, could have a private income. Besides his personal income, the bishop might receive money, sometimes in great quantities, for disbursements to various charities. The bishop, of course, was merely the administrator of these.

In the nineteenth century, the bishops appear to have kept considerable state. They had to buy their pontifical vestments and these were expensive. In Dublin, the successive archbishops lived at good addresses; in Kildare and Leighlin a mansion, Braganza House, was purchased for the bishop, who then had to maintain it; a bishop in Clogher, Dr Kernan, spent over £4,000 on a house. But as Dr Doyle remarked, a bishop was beset on all sides with requests for financial assistance and he was obliged to contribute to every charitable institution.

It is difficult to decide if certain episcopal expenditures were paid for by the diocese or by the bishop's family. A sum of £370 was spent on Archbishop Everard's funeral. MacHale had little or no personal income, so his extensive journeys on the continent must have come from the revenues of the diocese, if not from relatives and friends. Who paid Dr Murray's and Dr Higgins' expenses when they were sent abroad by the Conference of the Irish bishops? Or who paid Cardinal Cullen's legal expenses?

Offerings for masses, either for individual masses or for
foundations, could form a part, even a considerable part,
of the income of a priest, or an institution like the Irish
college. I have come across no reference to 'foundations'
of masses, i.e., a capital sum set aside from the revenues
of which stipends for a stated number of masses were
annually derived, in Ireland itself in the first half of the
century, but one is mentioned in connection with the Irish
college in Paris. Another is mentioned with regard to the
Irish college in Rome (*578; 553*). Towards the end of the
nineteenth century, from 1875 onwards, bequests for
masses became very common and largely replaced income
from direct contributions. Funeral offerings were peculiar
to northern dioceses (*349; 189*).

The Support of Curates and Chaplains
    The curate was paid by the parish priest. He was paid
a small fixed stipend out of the parish priest's revenue.
Carleton mentions a curate getting £50 per annum. John
Dunn refers to a curate getting one-fifth of the dues plus
his keep, and as one curate was kept for every £200 revenue
from the parish, the curate had £40 plus his keep. Forbes
noted that a curate could either get £20—30 plus his keep,
or a share of the parish revenues, a quarter or a third, depending on the number of curates. But Forbes also noted that
a curate, if popular, could receive many personal gifts. The
Leinster statutes allocated to the curate one-fifth of the
parish revenues, or if there were two curates, one-eighth
each. A curate could augment his income by teaching (*340;
170*).
    Another source of clerical income was the chaplaincies.
First, there were the official or government chaplaincies.
About 1810, the government began to authorise payment
of chaplains to gaols at a rate of £30 per annum. As the
century advanced, these chaplaincies became quite numerous
and could be held either separately or by a parish priest or
curate already employed in parish work (*Directories*, passim).
Convents too, if they could afford one, paid a chaplain.
In one case we hear of, the convent was prepared to offer
£60 while the chaplain could get an additional £20 per

annum for saying mass in the workhouse on Sundays and holy days. Warrenmount Convent paid their chaplain £50. The chaplaincy was normally a perquisite of the clergy of the parish where it was situated (*563; 579*).

Besides these, there were also a few priests on pension. An old priest, Rev. Mr Keenan, was paid 12 guineas per annum in Clogher. Others with pensions, which were a charge on a given parish, were mentioned in various places. Those priests teaching in colleges got a stipend of some kind. Dr Doyle, when teaching in Carlow, had £20. Those teaching in Maynooth at mid century had £211. 12s. 8d. (*181*, II, 321; the odd figure was caused by the government increasing the salary by a fraction of the original).

The Support of the Regular Clergy

The income of the regular clergy came from collections at their own church doors, and if that proved insufficient, members of the order were sent 'questing' for alms. Some revenue may have come from 'property houses, funded property and monied interest'. The Jesuits kept a school, while the monks of Mount Melleray had a farm and also kept a school and performed certain works of the ministry (*170*).

The Support of Nuns and Teaching Brothers

Any girl who wished to become a nun had to have a dowry. The provision of a dowry seems to have been the rule in Ireland, and in the absence of other means of subsistence it is difficult to see how the nuns could survive. It was, of course, always open to somebody else to provide sufficient funds for the support of one or more nuns. The important point was that the nun, like the priest, would have a guaranteed support for life. But there seems to have been a certain looseness in interpretation, and the dowry seems to have been at times spent instead of being invested (*160*).

The workings of the system and its drawbacks are illustrated in a problem presented to Dr Murray. A sister wished to go to another convent, but the convent she was in could not let her go as they were dependent on the interest from her dowry to pay off the debt on the convent. The superioress told Dr Murray that if Sister Fitzgerald went, her £40 per

annum went with her, leaving only '7 Govt. Deb. Interest of
£29 p.a.' and 'Bank or Govt. Stock Int. of £6—7 p.a.'. Sister
Crowe's people had promised £500, but to date were only
paying £25 per annum; another novice had only £10 per
annum; the rent of £40 and the chaplaincy of £40 would
amount to more than their entire income if Sister Fitzgerald
left.

Dr Murray got an inventory of the convent's assets:

	£ s d	£ s d
52 Debenture Interest	4. 4. 0	210. 8. 0
1 Debenture Interest	4. 0. 0	4. 0. 0
3 Canal Interest	4. 0. 0	12. 0. 0
1 Pipe Water Interest	6. 0. 0	6. 0. 0
Sister Fanning's Interest on bond of £800		40. 0. 0
Sister Drumgoole's for six years		40. 0. 0

and so for the other sisters to a total of £739. 1. 1.

This money had to be invested to give an annual return,
which could be risky. The Carmelites in Tallow had £1,320 in
government stock which was yielding only 2 per cent, and
when the interest was as low as that there was scarcely
enough income to support the nuns. Accordingly a bond was
received from a gentleman at 5 per cent for the whole lot.
But it was then discovered that this gentleman's estate was
so encumbered with previous mortgages that there was not
enough income to pay the nuns. A collection was made for
the nuns to which the pope contributed £50, and the local
bishop £250. The Presentation nuns in Waterford lent £1,200
to T. Wyse MP at 6 per cent, but lost all when mortgages on
his property were foreclosed (*421*).

Not all the income was from securities or bonds. John
Cremin, a Cork butter merchant, left money to his daughters
in religion 'charged and chargeable with powers of distraint'
on his lands, to the extent of £500, and an annuity of £20:
'I charge and encumber my farm and lands at Kilcully' (*598*).
The expected dowry of a Presentation sister was mentioned
as being £500. Income from the National Board was not used
to support the sisters, nor was the penny-a-week collection in
schools of the Christian Brothers used for their support.

The income of the Poor Clare convent at Newry amounted to an 'annual sum of £15 for each nun including the four lay-sisters', and came from 'whatever pecuniary means she [the nun] may possess or her friends supply' (*598*). References to dowries for lay sisters are wanting but we can presume they were not required, otherwise there would be few or no lay sisters. At least early in the century, convents with boarding schools had a very considerable income, the Ursulines being able from their profits in Cork to afford £30,000 for an estate. Later, the Loreto sisters were reputed to have paid £17,000 for an estate (*170; 479*).

The Christian Brothers too had dowries, and because of the problem of shifting the dowry around, Edmund Rice pooled them all.

The Support of Catholic Charities

Besides the charities in the usual sense, collections for the missions and the pope are included here. The charities run by convents, but not the support of the convents themselves, come into this section. Money was obtained from fashionable charity sermons, fashionable bazaars and systematic collection of subscriptions. Bequests became common later in the century. Ladies devoted time to fund-raising. Lady Killeen assisted the fund-raising committee of the Poor Clares. Catharine McAuley engaged the services of the lady mayoress, the Ladies Paget, Lady Templemore, Dowager Lady Ventry, Lady Leitrim, Lady de Bathe, Lady E. Chichester, Lady Talbot, Lady Esmonde, Lady Gosseste, Lady Kingsmill, Lady Alexander, Lady Jarvis Whyte, Lady Crofton and Lady O'Donnell O'Hara. Not all of these ladies seem to have been Catholics. Some appear to have been connected with the viceregal lodge. Two successive vicereines, the Marchioness Wellesley, who was an American Catholic, and the Countess Mulgrave, along with their consorts, patronised her bazaars. For sale in the bazaars they received gifts of fancywork embroidery by the Duchess of Kent and her daughter the Princess Victoria, the future Queen (*451*).

Charity sermons too were fashionable occasions.

In subsequent years preachers of this charity in Townsend

Street included the archbishop of Armagh, Dr Crolly, and Dr Blake, then bishop of Dromore.

On these occasions the dingy chapel took on the air of a gala day, with all the approaches blocked with long lines of waiting carriages; the annual sermon was an afternoon function, and when the preacher mounted the pulpit he found himself facing a gathering of fashionable and wealthy Catholics drawn from every quarter of the city (*451*).

Other methods of fund-raising were more prosaic. The orphan society of St James and St Joseph was supported by the exertions of a few charitable young men who devoted a few hours on each Sunday to the collection of a penny-a-week from the working classes. Those who did not bring in their subscriptions were waited upon by the collectors. This same method was used by the St Vincent de Paul Society. Ronan asserts, but without citing a source, that the income from the penny-a-week collections exceeded that from the fashionable sermons. According to Margaret Aylward's biographer, the return from collections and sermons began to decline after about 1870, but this was compensated for by an increase in charitable bequests. (On the legal aspects of bequests, see *517*).

The estimated annual income of charities in 1868 was £250,000 compared with £340,000 for the support of the clergy (*265; 268*).

The Support of Education

Many Catholics were paying something at least towards the cost of educating their children. The amount might be small, one or two pounds a year. Sometimes the children brought a penny-a-week to school. Fees in colleges and seminaries ranged from £20 to £40. Carlow College charged 45 guineas. Expenses in Maynooth were estimated at £50 for the first year and at least £12 a year afterwards when the student enjoyed a burse, but about £70 in the first year and £33 thereafter if he did not. About two hundred students were being educated on burses on the continent (*170; 225; 140; 585*). The regular clergy educated their own members out of their own resources in Rome and elsewhere. Doyle notes, however, '. . . and beg you to inform me whether you will receive this young man, and where he is to be sent to serve his novitiate. I need not add that the necessary expenses will be defrayed by his father' (*175*).

The provision of burses was a capital-intensive business. Bishop Murphy transferred £1,000 to Maynooth and got two burses. The Irish Church depended quite considerably on income from investments. Money from the Irish College in Rome was invested in stock, and a fall in price caused £1,500 to go down to £1,490. This led to the inevitable question:

Apropos, how is all this explained at Rome on the anti-usury principles? Do tell me how this is understood.

Unfortunately I have not got Blake's reply. The general lines of the answer accepted later were that in a commercial society money was virtually productive — in a primitive or non-commercial society it was not — and so interest could be understood as a share in the trading profits (*553*).

Maynooth, the 'Royal College', was the only ecclesiastical college directly supported by the government (Maynooth includes the later 'Dunboyne Establishment'). Some students had to pay fees and the bishop also provided burses. This support ended after disestablishment on the payment of a lump sum.

Capital Expenditure

In the nineteenth century about 3,000 churches were built or re-built in Ireland, i.e., about three per parish. MacHale and Higgins estimated that 2,000 were built in the thirty years preceding 1848. They estimated the cost of these at £1,500 each. Some years later, Myles O'Reilly estimated the cost to be £1,700 each, while the *Freeman's Journal* in 1868 estimated the cost to be an average of £1,736 for 1,842 churches built since 1800.

When a chapel was to be built, the ubiquitous committee was formed. It assessed every man in the parish, and in addition a general collection was made in the locality among both Catholics and Protestants (*170*).

Under the heading of capital expenditure can be placed the costs of church furnishings. Among these were vestments, crucifixes, religious engravings, altar linen, antependants for the altar, altar stones, chalices, remonstrances, thuribles, other sacred vessels 'in the gold, silver, plated, and jewellry line', candlesticks, bibles, missals, rituals (i.e., the official book dealing with rites), breviaries, tabernacles, altar charts, asperges, book-stands and bells. By 1836, statues and pictures, according to Barrow, were not common in chapels, except those of convents and friaries. Furnishing the interior of the chapels was a continuing process (advertisements in *Directories*, passim).

There were also other expenditures connected with the chapel, the addition of a high altar, a chapel yard, a proper road to the church, gates for the chapel yard, walks in the chapel grounds, external rendering and waterproofing and even stabling. Fr Peter Daly recounts the building of a sacristy, a porch, a belfry, a chapel wall, a gallery and a cemetery wall (*601*).

There were also the current expenditures on upkeep, painting, repairing of broken windows etc., as well as the direct costs of worship, the cost of lighting, candles, altar wines and breads. The appropriate means for paying for these seems to have been the weekly 'penny collection' at the church door, though profit from the cemetery could also be used for this purpose, in addition to paying the costs of security for the cemetery against body-snatchers.

The other main headings of capital expenditure were summarised by MacHale and Higgins in 1848. They estimated that eighty convents had been founded since 1810 at a total cost of £240,000, an average of £3,000. The cost, we may assume 'prime cost', of founding a convent was given by Fr Peter Daly in 1840 as £1,435, made up of £1,100 for the interest in the lease of ground, £25 for conveyance, £130 for a 'House of Mercy' and £180 for convent, chapel and schools. This last figure included only the costs of the carpenters and painters making necessary alterations to the existing house (*451*). The eventual cost could quite easily be doubled. With regard to the cost of his convent, Fr Daly notes contributions of £461, £100, £100 and £50.

On monasteries, they estimated an expenditure of £200,000, on schools they estimated another £200,000, that is twenty schools at an average cost of £10,000. By 1870 it was estimated that the college of St Kieran had cost the diocese between £40,000 and £50,000. Finally, MacHale and Higgins give a figure of £200,000 for poor schools, schools of the Christian Brothers and so on.

Total capital expenditure for the previous thirty years they estimated at £3,940,000 (out of a total expenditure of over £21 million). O'Reilly's estimate of the same period was around £3,485,000, i.e., taking three-fifths of O'Reilly's estimate for fifty years (*265*, 858).

The Resources of the Irish Church

The above-mentioned expenditures show that Catholics in Ireland even before the famine had considerable financial resources.

In Dublin, O'Connell estimated that more than half of the commerce in 1825 was in Catholic hands (*170*, 168). De Beaumont estimated that in 1829 nine-tenths of the funds in the Bank of Ireland belonged to Catholics.

The calculations on farm profits shows that a farmer with as little as five acres could have a disposable surplus (such a farmer was clearly marginal, and in a bad year might be reduced to beggary). Those with less than five acres in 1841, at the height of the population pressure, amounted in Ireland as a whole to 70 per cent of the population, but in eastern Ireland those with five acres or more amounted to only 40-42 per cent of the population. As Ó Tuathaigh says: 'It is not true that there was an absolute shortage of capital in pre-famine Ireland.' Or as L. M. Cullen says:

In fact, it is impossible to state that the rural community as a whole was impoverished in pre-famine Ireland. Farmers may well have suffered in the years of lowest prices. They were not, however, totally without resources even in the worst years.

The resources in the post-Famine era are not in doubt or contention.

11
Conclusions

The first and most overwhelming conclusion is that there was no 'reform' of the Irish Church in the nineteenth century, whatever about earlier. It was orthodox in doctrine though slightly tinged with Gallican and rigorist formulations. Its attitude towards the Holy See before and after 1870 was one of independence as far as the theology and canon law could be stretched. Attitudes over the veto and the Land League were identical.

Its organisation was complete and uniform over the entire island. This uniformity was quite astonishing and it was a feature which was noted time and time again. What was done in Cork was done in Dublin and Donegal as far as the essentials of organisation, rites, beliefs, practices, attitudes or devotions were concerned, due allowance being made for the constraints imposed by local conditions. There was no difference between urban Ireland and rural Ireland, Gaelic Ireland and English-speaking Ireland, Northern Protestant Ireland and Southern Catholic Ireland. The organisation was Tridentine. This too was very surprising. All the essentials of the legislation of Trent had been applied at times more rigorously than Trent intended. There was one basic catechism, the Roman Catechism; one basic rite, the Roman Rite; one way of educating the clergy, Tridentine-type seminaries; one basic type of parish, that which was recommended by Trent; one image of the Church loyal to the pope.

The structure of the Church was highly simplified. The original cause of the simplification was the application of the penal laws, but there was much resistance to redeveloping the complicated structure of the continental churches. (The

American daughter-church retained more of this simple, efficient structure.) In the course of the century, cathedral chapters were introduced, or as in America, alternative arrangements were made. From 1800 onwards there were no constraints on the development of the Catholic Church as long as it confined itself to religion, so external pressures can be discounted.

There was an adequate number of priests, although not always as many as enthusiastic bishops wished, for the ability of parishes to support extra priests was limited. There was a temporary crisis caused by the closure of the continental seminaries. The priests themselves were worthy men for the most part. Their besetting sin was drink. It is a matter in which it is virtually impossible to get exact comparative statistics, but there is no reason to believe that the secular clergy at least were any worse then than they are now or at any time in between, when allowance is made for statistical variations. The evidence available is not statistical but merely the common reports of observers.

With regard to the morals of the laity, the same conclusion is reached. They were no worse then than now and the same exceptions which apply nowadays applied then, the evil influence of drink and party faction. Drink may have been less of a problem earlier in the century because of the lack of cash in a rural economy.

With regard to the regular clergy, they were not bad men, but ill-trained and lazy. The bishops had already in the previous century taken strong steps to deal with the problem.

There were chapels and recognised mass places in every parish, services were held with great regularity, and a system of 'stations' existed to accommodate those who could not easily get to mass. Attendance at mass and reception of the sacraments seems to have been at a higher level than was usual at the time in Catholic countries on the continent. Personal piety was regarded as being at a satisfactory level, as was instruction in religious beliefs.

Yet enormous changes came over the Irish Church in the course of the century. They clearly did not constitute a 'reform', for that implies pre-existing abuses. They did not spring from the inspiration of the contemporary evangelical movement, for they were totally different in character. Nor were they inspired by a Benthamite utilitarianism, sweeping away old, inefficient 'useless' customs. Rather the feature which most characterises them is a tendency to emphasise 'Catholicism'. If in previous centuries the practice of religion in these islands tended to harmonise with Protestant practice, now it did so no longer. Catholic schools were built, as were Catholic orphanages, libraries, and other institutions distinguishable from their Protestant counterparts. Large, splendid and expensive churches and cathedrals were built in prominent places. Previously, the mass-house was scarcely distinguishable from the meeting-house: now they rivalled those of the Established Church. Clerical statutes seem to be aimed at emphasising the peculiar dignity and status of the sacramental priests. Much effort has been devoted in this book to establishing exactly when each development began.

Not all the changes fit exactly into the pattern. The most obvious stranger was Fr Mathew's temperance movement whose inspiration was derived from Protestant temperance circles in America. Then there was the revolution in devotions. This phenomenon appeared in England and Ireland about the same time, i.e., in the early decades of the nineteenth century. More study would be required to establish if it began in other countries on the continent at the same time. It consisted of the gradual addition of emotional 'devotions' to the straightforward moralistic religion prevailing in the three kingdoms up till then. Its origin is obscure but it would seem to be an offshoot of contemporary romanticism, emphasising emotional rather than rational aspects of religion.

The chief source from which new devotions and practices were derived would seem to have been France, though Ireland had no particularly close links with France during the century. Rather it would seem that the French Church was particularly inventive and progressive, and the Irish Church copied the up-to-date ideas. Italian, and specifically Roman, influences are hard to trace. Italian-trained priests were few in number and Italian-based orders lacked influence. (The Franciscans were a spent force throughout the century.) Despite the phalanx of bishops trained in the Peninsula led by Primate Curtis, Archbishop Murray and Dr Doyle, influence from that quarter seems negligible. The strongest external influence on the Irish Church in the nineteenth century, as in the preceding one, would seem to have been the English Church. Small though it was in numbers it was extremely dynamic in all sorts of ways. Of all English influences, the greatest, though most hidden, was surely from the Bar Convent in York which trained the foundresses of the Irish Sisters of Charity and the Loreto Sisters. The other major source of influence came from English writers. One has only to mention Fr Faber, Dalgairns, and Gallwey.

But it must be emphasised that the great revival was of native origin. It accompanied the Catholic political resurgence of the early nineteenth century, as it was to do again a century later. It should also be noted that I have traced the origins of all the changes and developments to the first half of the century. Readers may notice that I differ from Professor Emmet Larkin on this as on other points. Some of the differences may be a matter of emphasis, for example as between when a devotion was first introduced and when it became widespread. It should be noted, too, that when a devotion was regarded as widespread in the last century it does not mean necessarily that it achieved the penetration arrived at in this century. Some of the differences may be due to differing interpretations of scanty evidence, as for example with regard to the morals of the clergy. Whenever evidence was scarce or doubtful I have always indicated this.

Though the evaluation here may be more subjective, I differ from him in evaluating the achievement of Cardinal Cullen. In my estimation Cullen's predecessor, Archbishop Daniel Murray, was the greatest bishop in Ireland in the last century, and probably since Oliver Plunkett. If his name is not well remembered it was because he kept clear of politics. The bishops who are remembered were without exception famous for their interventions in political matters. Readers will have noted how often changes in Dublin — and Dublin was the spearhead of the changes — took place under the personal direction of the archbishop. One can mention the founding the three religious orders of nuns, the re-establishment of the Irish College in Rome, the founding of All Hallows, the foundation of the Irish Vincentians and the making of their college at Castleknock virtually the diocesan minor seminary, the welcoming of Fr Mathew, the introduction of devotions to the Sacred Heart, the first attempts at parish missions, the introduction of the Association for the Propagation of the Faith: in all of these we find him playing an active and guiding part. His policy on education was far sighted, and though defeated by the nationalists at Thurles, his stand was vindicated many years later by Leo XIII (see Appendix E).

Some word must be said about points which were not treated in this book. The reasons for the omissions are various. Great work was done by all the clergy during the Famine. This I regard as part of their ordinary ministry, heroic in the circumstances, but what we would have expected. Also it was common to the clergy and female religious workers of other denominations. The Irish bishops played their part in the First Vatican Council, voted with the majority and accepted the decrees. Their performance was not notable even compared with the English bishops. There was considerable discussion over the disestablishment of the Irish Church. The matter was largely political, but even so the Irish priests cannot be said to have distinguished themselves by their charity or ecumenical spirit. Their attitude merely reflected the bitterly anti-Protestant spirit of the period. In general, blow-by-blow accounts of events in which priests were involved are not given, for this is a sociological study, not a history. When therefore the point has been sufficiently explained earlier, no further reference is made to similar events later except in passing. The role of the clergy in the days of the Land League, important though it is to the historian, is not treated in full, but reference is given to various theological points: the acceptance of Roman decisions, the role of the priest in politics, or the attitude towards agrarian crime indicated. The plan of the book results in illustrations tending to come from earlier in the century when the new point first occurred. The second half of the century was repetitive, not innovatory.

Most, if not all of the innovations, as was shown in the

course of the book, manifested themselves before 1850. The conclusion drawn was that the Church went through two phases in the course of the century: a phase of innovation and a phase of consolidation. (It may be that this followed more general trends in British and Irish society.) Why exactly the fount of innovation dried up is unclear. There are some signs that innovation was reviving towards the end of the century as a prelude to the greater developments in the next century. By the end of the century it would seem that devotionalism was beginning to yield its primacy to a spirituality based on the sacraments; that a renewed and better organised campaign against drink was getting under way; that a stricter enforcement of canon law, especially in the field of canonical trials and tribunals, was commencing; that censorship of books was beginning to be enforced; that priests were beginning to take an interest in social questions. The full flowering of these trends came in the twentieth century. But between 1850 and 1890 innovation seems to have ceased, as the developments of the preceding half century were assimilated. Though the change occurred about the time of Cullen's arrival, it would be difficult to prove he was the cause.

By the year 1900 the Irish Church was no longer a minor, tolerated, though respected sect in the United Kingdom, but was at the centre of a worldwide sphere of influence and prestige. It was the heyday of the expansion of the white races, when all the rest of the world looked to Europe and much of Europe looked to the United Kingdom. As far as Catholic affairs were concerned, Maynooth was the centre of the English-speaking world. Between the prestige of the English-speaking peoples and the stubborn adhesion of the Irish to their own customs, it is safe to say that the Irish in various subtle ways made an immense impact on the Church at large. If one were to study tendencies in the codification of canon law, one might perhaps find that there was a question not of a Romanisation of Catholic Ireland but a Hibernisation of the Roman Church.

Appendices

APPENDIX A

Methodology

In a study like this material must be drawn from a wide variety of sources and be of very differing kinds. The researcher has two aims: completeness and objectivity. To achieve these, some theoretical framework is essential within which he can develop his arguments. Such a framework cannot be chosen arbitrarily but must be carefully matched to the nature of the subject being investigated. From the variety of sociological perspectives one must select the one which is most likely to lead to the twin aims of completeness and objectivity.

Preliminary investigation shows that the Catholic Church in Ireland was not merely a system of beliefs, values and attitudes. It possessed a considerable organisation. An approach at the level of structural functionalism or systems theory was therefore indicated. None of the existing theories was found to be adequate in practice so various approaches were at times used pragmatically. As goal-orientated activity seems an important area to be investigated, this study inclined rather towards functionalism than towards systems theory. The major structures of belief and organisation were first investigated. Then the activities of Church members were studied, and the lesser structures which were developed to support these. Finally, change in society was investigated; this proved an important topic. (For other approaches to the problem of investigative framework see Wallis, Whitworth, Beckford and Robertson.)

In general a positivist stance was adopted. No assertion was made unless there was positive evidence for it. The usual *caveat* must be entered that mere absence of evidence is not in itself a proof. Where evidence was scarce or doubtful it is noted as such.

The use of a wide variety of sources meant that they could be used as checks against each other for bias. The usual rules for identifying bias in sources were consistently applied as well.

The need to explore all the areas identified by the theoretical framework militated against a strict sampling approach, as did the very divergent natures of the sources. But the source material was so extensive that some limitations had to be placed on the use of each kind of material. A pragmatic approach was taken. For example, it was deemed necessary that archival material should be used, but not for all dioceses throughout the whole century. Nor was the type of material preserved identical in each archive. Cases of over-representation were easy to spot: the papers of Cardinal Cullen in the Propaganda archives; the history of Dr Doyle in the printed sources; and Carleton's account of descriptions of the Catholic religion in the Clogher valley. In these cases of clear over-representation, conscious compensation was required. (I am indebted to Dr J. H. Whyte for pointing out these biases in earlier drafts of this book.)

From an immense sea of divergent material, how can one be sure that one is not selecting material to confirm an imaginary picture in one's own mind? I gave great weight to Popper's theories on this point, but Popper is concerned mainly with the testing of theory, not with the establishment of facts. Here the theoretical framework showed its usefulness. It indicated and limited definite areas of research. Take, for example, structures. One asked had the Irish Church a structure, or more than one structure; were all elements covered by the structure, or were there unstructured elements? As each question was raised by the theory, so were the sources combed for answers. The results of this series of questions revealed that the Irish Church was a unit, its overall structure was one merely of sentiment and it was divided into four independent equal legal structures. Also many elements were unstructured, for example trends in devotions. The theoretical framework thus indicates all and only areas of sociological interest. It should be noted that some people might imagine that this particular approach precludes the discussion of strain and conflict. An examination of the book will show that this view is mistaken. Conflict can be and often is structured.

APPENDIX B

'The dues payable to a priest were as following, *viz.*:

A charge of 2/6 on each house or family, gross total of families 800	£100. 0. 0
Collection of corn worth 1/3 from each house	50. 0. 0
Collections on Christmas Day and Easter Sunday by a rule in the parish, 6d each time off each house	40. 0. 0
Confession of the younger people in the parish, making an average of two in each family at 6d each at Christmas	40. 0. 0
Ditto at Easter	40. 0. 0
40 marriages at £1. 8/2 each	56. 6. 8
150 baptisms at 3/4 each	25. 0. 0
Legacies on death, average 40, at 10/- each including the price of a Mass to remove the soul from Purgatory	20. 0. 0
Charge for anointing 1/1 each time, average number of times 200	10. 16. 8
Making offices for sick or diseased cattle at 1/1 for each office, average number 150	8. 2. 6
Private Masses for private intentions, price varying	13. 0. 0
	£403. 5.10

To be deducted:

The old priest's charge	30. 0. 0
Forty half-guineas to be paid to the bishop out of marriages, his charge being half-a-guinea for each marriage in the diocese	22.15. 0

Two guineas to the bishop as an annual rate for the Holy Oils	2.	5.	6
Two ditto for dinners at his own table	2.	5.	6
Two ditto for procuring oats for his horses	2.	5.	6

£59.11. 6

£345.14. 4

Income £300 leaving a balance of
as set off against bad debts and paupers.

45.14. 4

Such, gentlemen, are the charges made in the parishes of the diocese of Killala, as you may learn by consulting a pamphlet published by the Rev. Charles Bourke.' (The meals given to the priest and his servant and the oats for his horses are not included in the above. *Saunders' Newsletter*, 4 April 1827. There seem to be errors in the addition.)

The above was published by a clergyman of the Established Church, a former Roman Catholic parish priest who was now a curate in Drogheda, to prove that he had not conformed for gain but had lost financially to a considerable extent. His name was Rev. Thomas William Dixon.

A few points worthy of note. The first is the value of the guinea in pounds Irish (£1. 2s. 9d. sterling). The other is the fee payable for confessions at the stations. The advisability of abolishing such a fee was discussed by bishops. To avoid the idea of simony, the fee could be construed either as a voluntary gift or to recompense the priest for his trouble in going to the station. The latter interpretation, from the context, seems likely.

There was a second priest in this parish, the retired parish priest, but the accounts seem to indicate that he rarely if ever officiated, for no deductions are made for actual services rendered. In my calculations in the text I assumed an average parish to have a population of six thousand including children (being a Catholic population of six million divided into a thousand parishes), but assumed an average of two priests, including the regulars, per parish, a total of two thousand. In this parish, which seems to have been of ordinary size, the parish priest seems not to have had regular assistance. It would seem however that by comparing the figure given here with the estimate I gave in the text, there must have been on average two annointings or administrations of the last rites for each person who was buried.

APPENDIX C

Pastorini's Prophecies

'Another point I can only just allude to is the circulation of Pastorini's Prophecies; no one knows who does it — yet it is done and extensively . . . the peasantry have a firm persuasion that in 1825 Protestantism is to meet a decisive overthrow.

'Some of the most dangerous passages of the exposition have, with this in view, been selected and printed on a single sheet . . . and dispersed through all the cabins of the Catholic peasantry.'

'The Opening of the Fifth Seal' (*Apoc.* 6:9, 6:10, giving an account of the souls of the martyrs lying under the altar). Pastorini refers this passage to the martyrs in the reigns of Henry VIII and Elizabeth I and concludes that the fifth epoch could be fixed to start in the year 1825.

'The Sounding of the Fifth Trumpet' (*Apoc.* 9:1). 'There was given to him the key to the bottomless pit. To St Peter was given the Keys of Heaven, and to Luther is given the key of the bottomless pit or hell.'

Commenting on verse 5 of this chapter where it was said that the torture was to last five months, Pastorini interpreted this as meaning five x 30 days which signifies five x 30 years, which counting from 1525 brings us up to 1675. But verse 10 says, 'their power was to hurt men for five months; this is another 150 years different from the preceding; it is therefore to be added to it, bringing one up to the year 1825.'

'The Pouring out of the Fifth Vial' (*Apoc.* 16:10). The fifth angel pours out his vial on the seat of the Beast, and his kingdom became dark (abbreviated from *Saunders' Newsletter*, 13 December 1824).

Daniel O'Connell in his evidence to the Committee of the House of Lords gives further details. The book from which the excerpts were taken was written by an English clergyman (Rev. Charles Walmesley) writing under the name 'Pastorini'. It was condemned by Rev. Alban Butler when it came out and was never approved of by any bishop; its style was not suited either to the vulgar or educated fancy, but some mischievous persons were spreading it in Ireland. The year 1825 was due to a misprint. The proper starting point should have been from the Diet of Spiers, 1528-9, and the calculation from 1528, but due to a misprint this became 1825 (*Saunders' Newsletter*, 4 April 1825).

APPENDIX D

The following list of duties recorded by Archbishop Walsh in 1885 when visiting Bray gives a good idea of the pastoral work of a bishop and his position in Irish society in the second half of the century.

(1) presiding at a distribution of premiums to the children of the Catechism classes; (2) receiving an address from the Christian Doctrine Confraternity; (3) another address from the Juvenile Temperance Association; (4) another from the Association of Men in Honour of the Sacred Heart.

Then the scene changed to a platform erected outside the town hall where I had to receive (1) an address from the Town Commissioners of Bray; (2) an address from the clergy of the County of Wicklow (in the three dioceses of Dublin, Kildare, and Ferns) thanking me for defending them against the attacks of Lord Meath; (3) an address from the Meath Branch of the National League; and (4) an address from the Adult Temperance Association of the parish.

The National League was Parnell's political association which Walsh supported. Walsh had something of a reputation at this time among the other clergy of devoting rather too much of his time to politics and too little to his pastoral duties. One can assume that a short address or homily had to be given to each of the eight groups mentioned.

APPENDIX E

Note on the Character of Cardinal Cullen

I did not find that he played a central part in ecclesiastical developments. Though he was a tireless ecclesiastic, he interfered apparently needlessly in the affairs of other bishops. Much of his time was given to politics when this could more profitably have been left to the laity. His writings, such as they are, give an impression of one preoccupied with ecclesiastical munutiae. They do not give an impression of one spearheading a devotional revolution. His suspiciousness, already noticed, of Castle officials, all Protestants without distinction and of Catholic lay politicians, seems to have been shared with many priests of his period. But in Cullen's case this suspiciousness, even of his fellow bishops, seems to have formed the mainspring of his activities.

Bibliography

1. Aalen, F. H. A., 'Enclosures in Eastern Ireland', *Irish Geography* V, 1964-9 (2), 30-33
2. Ahern, J., 'The Plenary Synod of Thurles, I', *Irish Ecclesiastical Record* 1951, 385-403 and 'II', *Irish Ecclesiastical Record* 1952, 1-20
3. Akenson, D. H., *The Irish Educational Experiment*, London 1970
4. Akenson, D. H., *The Church in Ireland*, New Haven 1971
5. Alphonsus Ligouri (Saint), *Instructions to Preachers*, Dublin 1841
6. Alphonsus Ligouri (Saint), *The True Spouse of Jesus Christ*, translated by a Catholic clergyman, Dublin 1844
7. Alphonsus Ligouri (Saint), *Theologia Moralis*, Mechlin 1845
8. André, L'Abbé, *Cours Alphabetique et Methodique de Droit Canon*, Paris 1844
9. *Annals of the Propagation of the Faith*, Dublin 1842, 1843
10. Anon., *Key of Heaven or Manual of Prayer*, Dublin 1836
11. Anon., *The Saxon in Ireland*, London 1851
12. Anon., *Memories of Father Healy*, London 1904
13. Anon., *The Life and Work of Mary Aikenhead*, London 1925
14. Anon., *Joyful Mother of Children*, Dublin 1961
15. Antoine, P., *Compendium Theologiae Moralis Universae*, Venetiis 1802
16. Arensberg, C., *The Irish Countryman*, Gloucester, Mass. 1959
17. Arensberg, C. and Kimball, S., *Family and Community in Ireland*, Cambridge, Mass. 1968
18. Armagh 1854, *Acta et Decreta Concilii Provincialis Armacanae 1854*, Dublin 1855
19. Armagh 1908, *Acta et Decreta Synodi Provincialis Armachanae 1908*, Dublin 1911
20. Armagh 1913, *Statuta Diocesana Armacana*, Dublin 1913
21. Atkinson, N., *Irish Education*, Dublin 1969
22. Auchmuty, J. J., *Irish Education*, Dublin 1937
23. Augustine, Fr, *Footprints of Father Theobald Mathew*, Dublin 1947
24. Banim, M. and J., *Tales by the O'Hara Family*, London 1825
25. Barrett, C., 'Irish Nationalism and Art', *Studies* 1975, 395 ff.
26. Barrington, Sir Jonah, *The Ireland of Sir Jonah Barrington*, H. B. Staples (ed.), London 1969
27. Barrow, J., *A Tour Round Ireland*, London 1836
28. Barry, P. C., 'The Holy See and the Irish National Schools', *Irish*

Ecclesiastical Record, Series 5, XCII, 2, 90-105

29. Barry, P. C., 'The National Synod of Thurles (1850)', *Irish Ecclesiastical Record*, 1956B, 73-82

30. Bartlett, C. J., *Castlereagh*, London 1966

31. Beaumont, G. de, *Ireland: Social, Political and Religious*, W. C. Taylor (ed.), London 1839

32. Beckett, J. C., *The Making of Modern Ireland 1603-1923*, London 1969

33. Beckford, J. A., 'Religious Organisation', *Current Sociology* XXI, 1973, 2

34. Beckford, J. A., *The Trumpet of Prophecy*, Oxford 1975 (a)

35. Begley, J., *The Diocese of Limerick*, Dublin 1938

36. Bell, P., *Disestablishment in Ireland and Wales*, London 1969

37. Bell, Thomas, 'The Reverend David Bell', *Clogher Record* 1967 (vi-2), 253-76

38. Benigni, V., 'Propaganda', *Catholic Encyclopedia*, Vol. XII, New York 1911, 456-61

39. Bernard of Clairvaux (Saint), *De Consideratione, Libri Quinque, Patrologiae Cursus Completus*, Series Latina Prior, J.-P. Migne (ed.), Vol. 182, Paris 1862

40. Berthe, Austin, *Life of St Alphonsus de Ligouri*, Dublin 1905

41. Best, G., 'Evangelicalism and the Victorians', *The Victorian Crisis of Faith*, A. Symondson (ed.), London 1970

42. *The Holy Bible and Apocrypha*, Revised Standard Version, London 1959

43. Black, A. D. C., *Economic Thought and the Irish Question 1817 to 1870*, Cambridge 1960

44. Blanchard, J., *Le Droit Ecclesiastique Contemporain D'Irlande*, Paris 1958

45. Bolster E., *A History of the Diocese of Cork*, Cork and Shannon 1972

46. Bonsirven, J., *Theology of the New Testament*, London 1963

47. Bossy, J., 'The Counter Reformation and the People of Catholic Ireland 1596-1641', *Historical Studies*, VII, Dublin 1969, 155-70

48. Boudenhon, A., 'Primate', *Catholic Encyclopedia*, Vol. XII, New York 1912, 427 ff.

49. Bourke, P. M. Austin, 'The Agricultural Statistics of the 1841 Census of Ireland: A Critical Review', *Economic History Review*, 2nd series, 1965, 18, 376-91

50. Bourke, U. (ed.), *Sermons in Irish-Gaelic by the Most Rev. James O Gallagher*, Dublin 1881

51. Bourke, U., *Life and Times of Most Rev. John MacHale*, New York 1883

52. Bouyer, L., 'Byzantine Spirituality', *The Spirituality of the Middle Ages*, L. Bouyer et al (eds), London 1968

53. Bouyer, L., *Orthodox Spirituality and Protestant and Anglican Spirituality*, London 1969

54. Bowen, D., *Souperism: Myth or Reality?*, Cork 1970

55. Bowen, D., *The Protestant Crusade in Ireland 1800-1870*, Dublin and Montreal 1978

56. Bracey, H., *English Rural Life*, London 1959

57. Brady, J., 'Funeral Customs of the Past', *Irish Ecclesiastical Record*, 1952, 330-39

58. de Breffny, B. and Mott, G., *The Churches and Abbeys of Ireland*, 1976

59. Brenan, M., 'On the Catechism', *Irish Ecclesiastical Record*, 1943B, 392-400

60. Brenan, M. J., *Ecclesiastical History of Ireland*, Dublin 1840

61. Brett, E., *Buildings of Belfast, 1700-1914*, London 1967

62. Broderick, J. F., *The Holy See and the Irish Movement for the Repeal of the Union with England 1829-1847*, Rome 1951

63. Brody, H., *Inniskillane*, Penguin Press 1973

64. Brown, T. N., *Irish-American Nationalism*, Philadelphia 1966

65. Brown, T. N., 'The Irish Layman', *The United States of America*, (P. J. Corish, ed., *History of Irish Catholicism*, VI, 2), Dublin 1970

66. Buckley, W., *Sociology and Modern Systems Theory*, Englewood Cliffs, N.J. 1967

67. Burns, T. and Stalker, G., *The Management of Innovation*, London 1966

68. Butler, C., *Life and Times of Bishop Ullathorne*, London 1926

69. Butler, C., *The Vatican Council 1869-70*, London 1961

70. Calvin, J., *Institutes of the Christian Religion*, London 1949

71. Campbell, J., *A Short History of the Non-Subscribing Presbyterian Church of Ireland*, Belfast 1914

72. Canning, A., 'South America' (P. J. Corish, ed., *History of Irish Catholicism*, VI, 5), Dublin 1971

73. Cannon, S., 'Irish Episcopal Meetings 1788-1882', doctoral thesis, University of St Thomas Aquinas, Rome 1976

74. Carey, F. P., *Archbishop Murray of Dublin 1768-1852*, Dublin n.d.

75. Carleton, W., *Traits and Stories of the Irish Peasantry*, 1 vol. Dublin n.d.

76. Cashel, *Statuta Synodalia* 1813, *Statuta Synodalia Pro Unitis Diocesibus Cassel, et Immalec*, Dublin 1813

77. Catechism (Blake), *An Abridgment of the Christian Doctrine from Dr James Butler's Catechism*, Dublin (Coyne) 1838

78. Catechism (Butler), *Butler's Catechism Revised and Enlarged*, Dublin 1838

79. Catechism (Coyne), *Abridgment of Christian Doctrine*, Dublin (Coyne) 1838

80. Catechism (Gaelic), *An Teagasg Cristuy*, Cork 1830

81. Catechism (Small), *The Small Catechism*, Dublin 1838

82. Catechism (Grace), *An Abridgment of Christian Doctrine*, Dublin (Grace) 1835

83. Catechisms (Presbyterian), *The Confession of Faith: Larger and*

Shorter Catechisms, trans. into Gaelic by the Synod of Argyll, Edinburgh 1725

84. Catechism (Roman), *Catechismus Romanum*, Patavii 1749
85. *Catholic Penny Magazine*, Vol. I, No. 1, Dublin 1834
86. Census 1841, *Report of the Commissioners Appointed to take the Census for the year 1841*, Dublin 1843
87. Census 1851, *Report of the Commissioners Appointed to take the Census for the year 1851*, Dublin 1852
88. Census 1861, *Report of the Commissioners Appointed to take the Census for the year 1861*, Dublin 1863
89. Central Relief Committee, *Transactions of the Central Relief Committee During the Famine in 1846 and 1847*, Dublin 1852
90. Cerfaux, L., *The Church in the Theology of Saint Paul*, London 1959
91. Chart, D. A., *Ireland from the Union to Catholic Emancipation*, London 1910
92. Chart, D. A., *An Economic History of Ireland*, Dublin 1920
93. Chatterton, Lady, *Rambles in the South of Ireland*, 2 vols., London 1839
94. Chesnutt, M., *Studies in the Short Stories of William Carleton*, Goteburg 1976
95. Clough, S. B. and Cole, C. W., *Economic History of Europe*, Boston 1947
96. *Codex Juris Canonici*, Rome 1918
97. Cogan, A., *The Diocese of Meath*, Vol. III, Dublin 1870
98. Cognet, L. J., 'Jansenism', *New Catholic Encyclopedia*, Vol. VII, New York 1967, 820-24
99. Cohn, N., *The Pursuit of the Millennium*, London 1970
100. Cohn, N., *Europe's Inner Demons*, Sussex and London 1975
101. Comerford, M., *Collections Relating to the Dioceses of Kildare and Leighlin*, Dublin n.d.
102. Concannon, T., *The Poor Clares in Ireland*, Dublin 1929
103. Conlan, P., *Franciscan Ireland*, Dublin 1978
104. Connell, K. H., *Population of Ireland 1750-1845*, Oxford 1950
105. Connell, K. H., 'The Colonization of Waste Land in Ireland 1780-1845', *Economic History Review*, 2nd series, iii, 1950-51, 44-71
106. Connell, K. H., 'Peasant Marriage in Ireland, Its Structure and Development Since the Famine', *Past and Present*, 12, 1957 502-23
107. Connell, K. H., 'Illicit Distillation: An Irish Peasant Industry', *Historical Studies*, III, 1961, 58-91
108. Conway, Colmcille, *The Story of Mellifont*, Dublin 1958
109. Corish. P. J., 'Political Problems 1860-78' (P. J. Corish, ed., *History of Irish Catholicism*, V, 3), Dublin 1967
110. Corkery, J., 'Ecclesiastical Learning' (P. J. Corish, ed., *History of Irish Catholicism*, V, 9), Dublin 1970
111. *Corpus Juris Canonici*, A. Friedburg (ed.), Lipsiae 1879

112. Coulter, J., 'The Political Theory of Dr Edward Maginn, Bishop of Derry 1846-1849', *Irish Ecclesiastical Record*, 1962, 104-13
113. Cousens, S. H., 'The Regional Variation in Population Changes in Ireland 1861-1881, *Economic History Review*, 2nd series, 1964, 17, 301-21
114. 'Crawford, William Sharman', *Dictionary of National Biography*, London 1975
115. La Croix, C., *Theologia Moralis*, Paris 1866
116. Croker, T. C., *Researches in the South of Ireland*, London 1824
117. Crolly, G., *The Life of Dr Crolly*, Dublin 1851
118. Croly, D. O., *An Essay, Religious and Political on Ecclesiastical Finance*, Cork 1834
119. Cullen, L. M., *Life in Ireland*, London 1968
120. Cullen, L. M. (ed.), *The Formation of the Irish Economy*, Cork 1969
121. Cullen, L. M., *Six Generations*, Cork 1970
122. Cullen, L. M., *An Economic History of Ireland Since 1660*, London 1972
123. Cullen, Paul, *Pastoral Letters and Other Writings*, P. Moran (ed.), Dublin 1882
124. Cunningham, T. P., 'Church Reorganization' (P. J. Corish, ed., *History of Irish Catholicism*, V, 7), Dublin 1970
125. Curtis, E., *A History of Medieval Ireland*, London 1923
126. Curtis, E., *A History of Ireland*, London 1936
127. Cusack, M. F., *The Life of Most Rev. Dr Dixon*, Dublin 1878
128. D'Alton, E., *History of the Archdiocese of Tuam*, Dublin 1928
129. Danielou, J., *The Theology of Jewish Christianity*, London 1964
130. Danielou, J., *The Origins of Latin Christianity*, London 1977
131. Daniel-Rops, H., *The Church in the Age of Revolution 1789-1870*, trans. J. Warrington, London 1965
132. Dann, G., 'Religious Belonging in a Changing Catholic Church', *Sociological Analysis*, 1976, 37, 4, 283-97
133. D'Arcy, F. A., 'The Artisans of Dublin and Daniel O'Connell 1830-1847, *Irish Historical Studies*, XVII, 1970-71, 221-43
134. Davis, R., *The Rise of the Atlantic Economies*, London 1973
135. Davitt, M., *Leaves from a Prison Diary*, Shannon 1972
136. Deane, P. and Cole, W.A., *British Economic Growth 1688-1959*, Cambridge 1964
137. Deburchy, P., 'Retreats', *Catholic Encyclopedia*, Vol. XII, New York 1911
138. Dens, P., *Theologia Moralis*, Dublin 1832
139. Deshayes, T., *Memento Juris Ecclesiastici*, Paris 1897
140. Directory 1836–, *A Complete Catholic Directory Almanack and Registry*, W. J. Battersby (ed.), Dublin 1836–
141. *Directory* Protestant, *Irish Church Directory 1868*, Dublin 1868
142. *Directory 1817, The Laity's Directory for 1817*, compiled by C. Denver, Dublin 1817

143. *Directory 1821, The Catholic Directory 1821*, H. Young (ed.), Dublin 1821
144. Donlevy, A., *The Catechism or Christian Doctrine*, Paris 1742
145. Dostoievsky, F., *The Brothers Karamazov*, trans. C. Garnett, London 1912
146. Dowling, P. J., *The Hedgeschools of Ireland*, Dublin n.d.
147. Doyle, F. B., 'South Africa' (P. J. Corish, ed., *History of Irish Catholicism*, VI, 4), Dublin 1971
148. Doyle, J. W., *Letters on the State of Ireland*, Dublin 1825
149. *The Life of Rt Rev. Jas. Doyle, DD*, New York n.d.
150. Doyle, W., *A Year's Thoughts*, London 1922
151. Drummond, A. and Bullock, J., *The Scottish Church 1688-1843*, Edinburgh 1973
152. Drummond, A. and Bullock, J., *The Church in Victorian Scotland, 1843-1874*, Edinburgh 1975
153. Dubay, T., 'Retreats', *New Catholic Encyclopedia*, Vol. XII, New York 1967
154. Dublin *Statuta* 1770, *Constitutiones Provinciales et Synodales Ecclesiae Metropolitanae Dubliniensis 1770*, Dublin 1770
155. Dublin *Statuta* 1831, *Statuta Diocesana per Provinciam Dubliniensem Observanda*, Dublin 1831
156. Duggan, E., 'New Zealand' (P. J. Corish, ed., *History of Irish Catholicism*, VI, 7), Dublin 1971
157. Dunbatin, J., *Rural Discontent in Nineteenth-Century Britain*, London 1973
158. Dunforth, D., 'Incardination and Excardination', *Catholic Encyclopedia*, Vol. VII, New York 1910, 704 ff.
159. Durkheim, E., *The Rules of Sociological Method*, trans. S. Solovay and J. Mueller, Free Press 1950
160. Eager, I., *The Nun of Kenmare*, Cork 1970
161. Edgeworth, M., *Castle Rackrent* and *The Absentee*, London 1972
162. Edwards, R. D. and Williams, T.D. (eds.), *The Great Famine*, Dublin 1956
163. Egan, M. J., *Life of Dean O'Brien*, Dublin 1949
164. Egan, P., *The Parish of Ballinasloe*, Dublin 1960
165. Elder, R. (ed.), *The Spirituality of Western Christendom*, Kalamazoo 1976
166. Emerson, N. D., 'The Last Phase of the Establishment' in *History of the Church of Ireland*, W. A. Philips (ed.), Oxford 1933
167. Engels, F., *The Condition of the Working Class in England in 1844*, London 1950
168. Etzioni, A., 'Two Approaches to Organizational Analysis: A Critique and a Suggestion', *Administrative Science Quarterly*, 5, 1960, 2, 257-78
169. Etzioni, A., *Modern Organizations*, Englewood Cliffs, NJ 1964
170. *Evidence on the State of Ireland, Parliamentary Commission to Enquire into the State of Ireland, The Evidence Before the Select Committees*, Excerpts from sessional papers 1826, Vols VII-IX, London 1825

171. Fahey, J., *History and Antiquities of Kilmacduagh*, Dublin 1893
172. Fanning, W. H., 'Confraternity', *Catholic Encyclopedia*, Vol. IV, New York 1908, 223
173. Finnegan, F., 'Irish Confessors and Martyrs', *New Catholic Encyclopedia*, Vol. VII, New York 1967, 641
174. Fitzpatrick, W. J., *The Life, Times and Correspondence of Lord Cloncurry*, Dublin 1855
175. Fitzpatrick, W. J., *The Life, Times and Correspondence of the Rt. Rev. Dr. Doyle*, Dublin 1861
176. Fitzpatrick, W. J., *Memoirs of Richard Whateley*, London 1864
177. Fitzpatrick, W. J., *Correspondence of Daniel O'Connell*, London 1888
178. Fitzpatrick, W. J., *Life of Fr Thomas Burke*, London 1894
179. Flanagan, U., 'Papal Provisions in Ireland 1305-78', *Historical Studies* III, Cork 1961, 92-103
180. Flood, W. H. Grattan, *History of the Diocese of Ferns*, Waterford 1915
181. Forbes, J., *Memorandums of a Tour in Ireland*, London 1853
182. Fortescue, A., 'Exarch', *Catholic Encyclopedia*, Vol. V, New York 1909, 676 ff.
183. Freeman, T. W., *Ireland*, London 1950
184. Freine S. de, *The Great Silence*, Dublin 1965
185. Garcia-Villoslada, R., 'Devotio Moderna', *New Catholic Encyclopedia*, IV, New York 1966, 831-3
186. Gash, N., *Mr Secretary Peel*, London 1961
187. Gash, N., *Sir Robert Peel*, London 1972
188. Gasquet, A., *Parish Life in Medieval England*, London 1906
189. Gibbons, M., *The Life of Margaret Aylward*, London 1928
190. Gibson, W., *The Year of Grace*, Edinburgh n.d.
191. Giddens, A., *Positivism and Sociology*, London 1974
192. Gill, J., *The Council of Florence*, Cambridge 1959
193. Gill, J., *Personalities of the Council of Florence*, Oxford 1964
194. Gillmor, D. A., 'The Agricultural Regions of the Republic of Ireland, *Irish Geography* V, (2), 1964-9, 245-61
195. Ginsberg, M., *The Idea of Progress*, Westport, Conn. 1973
196. Glancey, M.C., 'Christian Doctrine, Confraternity of', *Catholic Encyclopedia*, Vol. III, New York 1908, 711
197. Goddijn, W., 'Catholic Minorities and Social Integration', *Social Compass*, 1960, 7, 161-76
198. Godkin, J., *Ireland and Her Churches*, London 1867
199. Good, J., 'Should Church Let State Regulate Marriage?', *Irish Times*, 27 January 1978
200. Goode, W. J., *Religion Among the Primitives*, London 1964
201. Greeley, A., *The Denominational Society*, Glenview, Ill. 1972
202. Green, A. S., *The Making of Ireland and its Undoing*, London 1908
203. Green, E. R. R., 'Agriculture' in *The Great Famine*, Edwards and Williams (eds.), Dublin 1956

204. Greville, C. C. F., *Past and Present Policy of England Towards Ireland*, London 1845
205. Griffin, G., *The Christian Physiologist*, Dublin n.d.
206. Griffin, G., *The Collegians*, Dublin 1855
207. Griffin, William, *The Life of Gerald Griffin*, Dublin 1857
208. Guedalla, P., *The Duke*, London 1940
209. Guilday, P., *The Life and Times of John Carroll*, New York 1922
210. Gwynn, D., *Father Dominic Barberi*, London 1947
211. Hagerstrand, T., 'Diffusion — The Diffusion of Innovations', *International Encyclopedia of the Social Sciences*, Vol. IV, New York 1968, 174-8
212. Halévy, E., *The Growth of Philosophic Radicalism*, London 1928
213. Hall, Mr and Mrs S. C., *Ireland, Its Scenery and Character*, London 1841
214. Hall, S. C., *Sketches of Irish Character*, London 1844
215. Halsted, T. B. (ed.), *Romanticism*, London 1969
216. Hammond, J. H., *The Village Labourer 1760-1832*, London 1911
217. Harmon, M., 'Aspects of the Peasantry in the Anglo-Irish Literature from 1800 to 1916', *Studia Hibernica* 1975, 15, Dublin 1975, 105-27
218. Harris, N., *Beliefs in Society*, London 1968
219. Harris, R., *Prejudice and Tolerance in Ulster*, Manchester 1972
220. Harrison, P., *Authority and Power in the Free Church Tradition*, London and Amsterdam 1971
221. Havens, G., *The Age of Ideas*, New York 1955
222. Hay, Dr George, *Sincere Christian*, Dublin 1839
223. Hay, Dr George, *Pious Christian*, Glasgow n.d.
224. Hayes, R., *Ireland and Irishmen in the French Revolution*, Dublin 1932
225. Healy, J., *Maynooth College: The Centenary History*, Dublin 1895
226. Heine-Geldern, R., 'Diffusion — Cultural Diffusion', *International Encyclopedia of the Social Sciences*, Vol. IV, New York 1968, 169-73
227. Henriques, U., *Religious Toleration in England, 1787-1833*, London 1961
228. Hilgers, J., 'Sodality', *Catholic Encyclopedia*, Vol. XIV, New York 1908, 120-29
229. Hill, M., *A Sociology of Religion*, London 1973
230. Hill, J. R., 'Nationalism and the Catholic Church in the 1840s', *Irish Historical Studies* XIX, 1975, 371-95
231. Hinings, C. and Foster, B., 'The Organization Structure of Churches', *Sociology*, 1973, 7, 93-106
232. Hinchius, P., *System Des Katholischen Kirchen-Rechts*, reprint Graz 1959
233. Hoffman, J. C., 'Pietism', *New Catholic Encyclopedia*, XI, New York 1966, 355-6

234. Hoffman, R., 'Propagation of the Faith, Congregation for the', *New Catholic Encyclopedia*, XI, New York 1966, 840-44

235. Homan, H. W., *Star of Jacob*, New York 1953

236. Houtart, F., 'Conflicts of Authority in the Roman Catholic Church', *Social Compass*, VI/1/1969, 309-25

237. How, F. D., *Archbishop Plunkett*, London 1900

238. Hughes, J., 'Society and Settlement in Nineteenth-Century Ireland', *Irish Geography* V (2), 1964-9, 79-95

239. Hughes, P., *A History of the Church*, 3 vols, London 1947

240. Hughes, P., *The Church in Crisis*, London 1961

241. Hussey, S. M., *The Reminiscences of an Irish Land Agent*, London 1904

242. Hutchins, P., *James Joyce's World*, London 1957

243. Hyde, D., *Religious Songs of Connaught*, Dublin 1906

244. Inglis, H. D., *A Journey Throughout Ireland*, London 1835

245. James, F. G., *Ireland in the Empire 1688-1770*, Harvard 1973

246. Jedin, H., *Ecumenical Councils of the Catholic Church*, trans. E. Graf, London 1960

247. Johnson, B., 'On Church and Sect', *American Sociological Review*, 1963, 28, 539-49

248. Johnstone, R., *Religion and Society in Interaction*, Englewood Cliffs, NJ 1975

249. Kadloubovsky, E. and Palmer, G., *Writings From the Philokalia*, trans. from the Russian text, London 1962

250. Kane, R., *The Industrial Resources of Ireland*, Dublin 1845

251. Kelly, O., 'Pastoral Letter of the Archbishop of Tuam', *Leinster Journal*, 12 January 1820

252. à Kempis, T., *Imitation of Christ*, trans. R. Challoner, Dublin 1878

253. Kennedy, L., 'The Roman Catholic Church and Economic Growth in 19th Century Ireland', *Economic and Social Review*, 1978, 10, 1, 45-60

254. Kennedy, P., *The Banks of the Boro*, London 1867

255. Kennedy, T. P., 'Church Building' (P. J. Corish, ed., *History of Irish Catholicism*, V, 8), Dublin 1970

256. Kickham, C., *Knocknagow*, 30th impression, Dublin 1949

257. Killanin, Lord and Duignan, M. J., *The Shell Guide to Ireland*, London 1967

258. Killen, W. D., *The Ecclesiastical History of Ireland*, London 1875

259. Knox, R., *Enthusiasm*, Oxford 1951

260. Kohl, J. C., *Ireland, Scotland and England*, London 1844

261. Krause, J. E., 'Confraternity of Christian Doctrine', *New Catholic Encyclopedia*, Vol. IV, New York 1966, 155 ff.

262. Lampson, G. L., *A Consideration of the State of Ireland in the Nineteenth Century*, London 1907

263. Large, D., 'The Wealth of the Greater Irish Land Owners 1750-1815', *Irish Historical Studies*, 1966-7, 21-45

264. Larkin, E., 'Church and State in Ireland in the Nineteenth Century', *Church History*, 1962, 294-306
265. Larkin, E., 'Economic Growth, Capital Investment, and The Roman Catholic Church in Nineteenth-Century Ireland', *American Historical Review*, 1967, 72, 852-83
266. Larkin, E., 'The Devotional Revolution in Ireland 1850-75', *American Historical Review*, 1972, 77, 3, 625-52
267. Larkin, E., 'Church, State, and Nation in Modern Ireland', *American Historical Review*, 1975, 80, 1244-76
268. Larkin, E., *The Roman Catholic Church and the Creation of the Modern Irish State*, Philadelphia 1975
269. Larkin, E., 'Communication', *Economic and Social Review*, 1978, 10, 1, 59 ff.
270. Larkin, E., *The Roman Catholic Church and the Plan of Campaign in Ireland 1886-1888*, Cork 1978
271. Larkin, E., *The Roman Catholic Church in Ireland and the Fall of Parnell 1888-1891*, Liverpool 1979
272. Latimer, W. T., *A History of the Irish Presbyterians*, Belfast 1902
273. de Latocnaye, H., *A Frenchman's Walk Through Ireland 1796-97*, trans. J. Stevenson, Belfast 1917
274. Latourette, K. S., *Christianity in a Revolutionary Age*, London 1959
275. Lauchert, F., 'Pietism', *Catholic Encyclopedia*, XII, New York 1911, 80-82
276. Lecky, W., *A History of Ireland in the Eighteenth Century*, abridged edition, Chicago 1972
277. Leclercq, J., 'From Saint Gregory to Saint Bernard' in *The Spirituality of the Middle Ages*, L. Bouyer et al (eds), London 1968
278. Lee, J., 'Money and Beer In Ireland 1790-1875', I, *Economic History Review*, 2nd series, 1966, 19, 183-90
279. Lee, J., 'The Dual Economy in Ireland 1800-1850, *Historical Studies*, 1969, 8, 191-201
280. Leetham, C., *Luigi Gentili*, London 1965
281. Le Fanu, W. R., *Seventy Years of Irish Life*, 1914
282. Le Fevre, S., *Peel and O'Connell*, London 1887
283. Leonard, H., 'Ethnic Conflict and Episcopal Power: The Diocese of Cleveland 1847-1870', *Catholic Historical Review*, 1976, 62, 3, 388-407
284. Lever, C., *The O'Donoghue*, London 1872
285. Lever, C., *The Martins of Cro' Martin*, London 1872
286. Lever, C., *Jack Hinton*, London 1901
287. Lewins, F., 'Continuity and Change in a Religious Organization: Some Aspects of the Australian Catholic Church', *Journal for the Scientific Study of Religion*, 1977, 16, 5, 371-82
288. Lewis, G. C., *On Local Disturbances in Ireland*, London 1836
289. Lewis, O., 'Tepoztlan Re-Studied, A critique of the Folk-Urban

Conceptualization of Social Change', *Rural Sociology*, 1953, 18, 121-34; reprinted in *Sociology: The Progress of a Decade*, S. M. Lipset and N. J. Smelser (eds.), Englewood Cliffs, NJ 1961, 623-35

290. Lockington, W. J., *The Soul of Ireland*, London 1919

291. Lombard, F., 'Confraternities and Arch Confraternities', *New Catholic Encyclopedia*, Vol. IV, New York 1966, 154

292. Lover, S., 'The Couple Beggar', *Irish Penny Magazine*, 2 February 1833

293. Lover, S., *Handy Andy*, Belfast 1842

294. Lover, S., *Rory O'More*, London 1898

295. Lover, S., *Further Stories of Ireland*, London 1899

296. Lover, S., *Legends and Stories of Ireland*, London n.d.

297. Lynch, P. and Vaizey, J., *Guinness's Brewery in the Irish Economy, 1759-1878*, Cambridge 1960

298. Lynch, P. and Vaizey, J., 'Money and Beer in Ireland 1790-1875', II, *Economic History Review*, 2nd series, 1966, 190-94

299. Lyne, G. J., 'Daniel O'Connell, Intimidation and the Kerry Elections of 1835', *Journal of the Kerry Archaeological and Historical Society*, 1971, 4, 74-97

300. Lyons, F. S. L., *Ireland Since the Famine*, London 1973

301. Lyons, F. S. L., *John Dillon*, London 1968

302. Macourt, M., 'The Nature of Religion in Ireland', *A Sociological Yearbook of Religion in Britain*, 1974, 7, 26-45

303. Madden, D. O., *The Revelations of Ireland*, Dublin 1848

304. Magee, W., *A Charge Delivered to the Clergy in the Diocese of Raphoe*, Dublin 1821

305. Magee, W., *A Charge Delivered at His Primary Visitation in St Patrick's Cathedral, Dublin 1822*, Dublin 1822

306. Magee, W., *A Charge Delivered at His Triennial and Metropolitan Visitation in St Patrick's Cathedral, Dublin 1826*, Dublin 1826

307. Magee, W., *The Evidence of His Grace the Archbishop of Dublin Before the Select Committee of the House of Lords on The State of Ireland*, Dublin n.d.

308. Magee/Anon., *An Answer to a Letter Written by a Dignitary of the Roman Catholic Church* by a clergyman of the Established Church, Dublin 1822

309. Maguire, J. F., *Father Mathew*, Dublin n.d.

310. Maguire, J. F., *Pius the Ninth*, London 1878

311. Malone, S., *A Church History of Ireland*, Dublin 1863

312. Mannin, E., *Two Studies in Integrity*, London 1954

313. Manning, D. J., *The Mind of Jeremy Bentham*, London 1968

314. Mansi, J. D. (ed.), *Sacrorum Conciliorum Nova el Amplissima Collectio*, Tomus 36us, 38us, 39us, Arnhem 1925

315. Mant, R., *History of the Church of Ireland*, London 1875

316. Mant, W. B., *Memoirs of Rt. Rev. Richard Mant*, Dublin 1857

317. Martin, D., 'The Denomination', *British Journal of Sociology*, 1962, 13, 1-14

318. Martin, D., 'Church, Denomination and Society', *A Sociological Yearbook of Religion in Britain*, 1972, 5, 184-91
319. Martin, R. M., *Ireland Before and After the Union*, London 1843
320. Marx, K., *Selected Works*, Moscow 1950
321. Mason, W. S., *A Statistical Account or Parochial Survey of Ireland*, Dublin 1819
322. Mathew, P., *Lord Acton and His Times*, London 1968
323. Maxwell, C., *Ireland Under the Georges, 1714-1830*, London 1836
324. Meagher, W., *Notices on the Life and Character of Most Rev. Daniel Murray*, Dublin 1853
325. Messenger, J. C., *Inis Beg*, Isle of Ireland, Cambridge 1970
326. Miller, D., *Church, State and Nation in Ireland, 1898-1921*, Dublin 1973
327. Miller, D., 'Irish Catholicism and the Great Famine', *Journal of Social History*, 1975, 9, 1, 81-98
328. Millet, B., 'Survival and Reorganization 1650-95' (P. J. Corish, ed., *History of Irish Catholicism*, III, 7), Dublin 1968
329. Milward, A. S., and Saul, S. B., *The Economic Development of Continental Europe, 1780-1870*, London 1973
330. Miner, H., 'The Folk-Urban Continuum', *American Journal of Sociology*, 1952, 17, 529-37
331. (A Missioner), *Missions in Ireland*, Dublin 1855
332. Monahan, J., *Records Relating to the Dioceses of Ardagh and Clonmacnoise*, Dublin 1886
333. Moody, T. W. and Beckett, J. C., *Queen's, Belfast, 1845-1949*, 2 vols, London 1959
334. Mould, D. D. C. Pochin, *The Irish Dominicans*, Dublin 1957
335. Mould, D. D. C. Pochin, *The Monasteries of Ireland*, London 1976
336. Mowinckel, S., *He That Cometh*, trans. G. Anderson, Oxford 1956
337. Mulhern, P. F., 'Devotions, Religious', *New Catholic Encyclopedia*, IV, New York 1966, 833 ff.
338. Mundy, J. H. and Woody, K. M. (eds.), *The Council of Constance*, New York 1961
339. Murphy, I., 'Primary Education', *Catholic Education* (P. J. Corish, ed., *History of Irish Catholicism*, V, 6), Dublin 1971
340. Murphy, J. A., 'The Support of the Catholic Clergy in Ireland 1750-1850', *Historical Studies*, V, 103-21
341. Murphy, J. A., 'Priests and People in Modern Irish History', *Christus Rex*, 1969, 22, 4, 235-59
342. Murphy, R. J., 'Primate (Canon Law)', *New Catholic Encyclopedia*, IX, New York 1967, 780ff.
343. Murray, D., *Sermons of the Late Most Rev. Dr. Murray*, Dublin 1859
344. Murray, P., *The Irish Annual Miscellany*, Dublin 1850
345. Macaulay, J., *Ireland in 1872*, London 1873

346. McAvoy, T., 'The Irish Clergyman', *The United States of America* (P. J. Corish, ed., *History of Irish Catholicism*, VI, 2), Dublin 1970

347. McCaffrey, J., *History of the Catholic Church in the Nineteenth Century*, Dublin 1909

348. McCabe, J., *Life in a Modern Monastery*, London 1898

349. McCarthy, M. J., *Priests and People in Ireland*, Dublin 1902

350. MacCormack, A., *Cardinal Vaughan*, London 1966

351. MacDonagh, O., 'The Politicization of the Irish Catholic Bishops 1800-1850', *Historical Journal*, 1975, 17, 1, 37-53

352. MacDonald, W., *Reminiscences of a Maynooth Professor*, D. Gwynn (ed.), London 1925

353. MacDowell, R. B., 'Ireland on the Eve of the Famine' in *The Great Famine*, Edwards and Williams (eds.), Dublin 1956

354. MacDowell, R. B., *The Irish Administration 1801-1914*, London 1964

355. MacGiolla Choille, J., 'Fenians, Rice, and Ribbonmen in County Monaghan 1864-67', *Clogher Record*, VI, 2, 221-52

356. MacGiolla Phadraig, B., 'Dr. John Carpenter, Archbishop of Dublin, 1760-1786', *Dublin Historical Record*, 1976, 30, 1, 1-17

357. McGovern, J. J. and O'Farrell, P., 'Australia' (P. J. Corish, ed., *History of Irish Catholicism*, VI, 6), Dublin 1971

358. McGrath, F., 'The University Question', *Catholic Education* (P. J. Corish, ed., *History of Irish Catholicism*, V, 6), Dublin 1971

359. MacGregor, G., *The Vatican Revolution*, London 1958

360. MacHale, J., *The Letters of Most Rev. John MacHale, D.D.*, Dublin 1888

361. McHenry, J., *The Hearts of Steel*, Dublin 1839

362. McKenna, J. E., *Parishes of Clogher*, Vol. I, Enniskillen 1920

363. McKenna, L., *Fr James Cullen S.J.*, London 1924

364. MacKnight, T., *Ulster As It Is*, London 1896

365. McLaughlin, J., *Brief Memoirs of the Bishops of Derry*, Dublin 1879

366. McNamee, J. J., *History of the Diocese of Ardagh*, Dublin 1954

367. MacSuibhne, P., *Paul Cullen and His Contemporaries*, Naas 1961

368. Newmann, W. M., *The Social Meaning of Religion*, Chicago 1974

369. New Testament, *The Greek New Testament*, K. Aland et al (eds.), Stuttgart 1966

370. Nicholson, A., *The Bible in Ireland*, London n.d.

371. Niebuhr, R., *The Social Sources of Denominationalism*, Cleveland 1962

372. Nolan, H. J., *Francis Patrick Kenrick*, Philadelphia 1948

373. Nolan, P., 'Religious Statistics', *Irish Times*, 3 December 1976

374. Norman, E., *The Catholic Church and Ireland in the Age of Rebellion*, New York 1965

375. Norman, E., *A History of Modern Ireland*, Penguin Press 1971

376. Nowlan, K. B., *The Politics of Repeal*, London 1965
377. Ó Cathaoir, B., 'The Kerry "Home-Rule" By-Election 1872', *Journal of the Kerry Archaeological and Historical Society*, 1970, 3, 354-70
378. O'Connell, M., 'Daniel O'Connell: Income, Expenditure and Despair', *Irish Historical Studies*, 1970-71, 17, 200-20
379. O'Connell, P., *The Diocese of Kilmore*, Dublin 1937
380. O'Connor, J., *History of Ireland 1798-1924*, London 1925
381. O'Crohan, T., *The Islandman*, trans. R. Flower, Oxford 1937
382. O'Donnell, P., *The Irish Faction Fighters*, Tralee 1975
383. O'Donoghue, D. J., *Life of William Carleton* including *Autobiography*, Introduction by F. C. Hoey, London 1896
384. O'Donoghoe, J., 'Incardination', *New Catholic Encyclopedia*, VII, New York 1966, 409 ff.
385. Ó Dufaigh, S., 'James Murphy, Bishop of Clogher, 1801-21', *Clogher Record*, 1968, 6, 3, 419-92
386. Ó Faolain, S., *King of the Beggars*, London 1938
387. O'Farrell, P., *England and Ireland Since 1800*, Oxford 1975
388. O'Farrell, P., *Ireland's English Question*, London 1971
389. Ó Gallachair, P., 'Clogherici', *Clogher Record*, 1966, 6, 1: 126-36; 1969, 6, 2: 379-87; 1968, 6, 3: 578-96
390. O'Gallagher, J., *Sermons in Irish-Gaelic*, Dublin 1881
391. Ó hAinle, C., 'Irish Spirituality', *The Furrow*, 1976, 583-96
392. O'Hegerty, P. S., *A History of Ireland Under the Union*, London 1952, Krause reprint 1969
393. O'Laverty, J., *An Historical Account of Down and Connor*, Vol. V. Dublin 1895
394. O'Leary, P., *My Story*, trans. C. Ó Ceirin, Cork 1970
395. Ó Muirgeasa, E., *Dánta Diadha Uladh*, Dublin 1936
396. Ó Muirithe, D., *A Seat Behind the Coachman*, Dublin 1972
397. O'Neill Daunt, W. J., *A Life Spent for Ireland*, London 1896
398. O'Rahilly, A., *Fr William Doyle*, London 1935
399. O'Reilly, B., *John MacHale*, New York 1890
400. O'Reilly, B., *Life of Leo XIII*, Glasgow 1887
401. O'Riordan, M., *Catholicity and Progress in Ireland*, Dublin n.d.
402. O'Shea, K., 'David Moriarty', *Journal of the Kerry Archaeological and Historical Society*, 1970, 3, 84-98; 1971, 4, 107-26; 1972, 5, 86-102; 1973, 6, 131-42
403. Ó Suilleabhain, P., OFM, 'A Letter of Nicholas Slevin 1817', *Clogher Record*, 1968, 6, 3: 493-9
404. Ó Suilleabhain, S. V., 'Secondary Education', *Catholic Education* (P. J. Corish, ed., *History of Irish Catholicism*, V, 6), Dublin 1971
405. O'Sullivan, W., 'William Molyneux's Geographical Collections of Kerry', *Journal of the Kerry Archaeological and Historical Society*, 1970, 4, 28-47
406. Otto, R., *The Idea of the Holy*, English translation, Oxford University Press 1931
407. Ó Tuathaigh, G., *Ireland Before the Famine 1798-1845*, Dublin 1972

408. Parker, C. S., *Sir Robert Peel*, 3 vols, London 1899
409. Parsons, T., *The Social System*, London 1952
410. Parsons, T., *Theories of Society*, Glencoe 1961
411. Parsons, T., *Sociological Theory and Modern Society*, New York 1967
412. Pastor, Ludwig Von, *History of the Popes*, Vol. 38, trans. E. F. Peeler, London 1951
413. Peel, R., *Memoirs of Sir Robert Peel*, London 1856
414. Philips, W. A. (ed.), *History of the Church of Ireland*, Oxford 1933
415. Pollard, H., *The Secret Societies of Ireland*, London 1922
416. Pollard, W. H., 'Rosminians', *Catholic Encyclopedia*, XII, New York 1912, 198-201
417. Popper, K., *The Poverty of Historicism*, London 1957
418. Popper, K., *Conjectures and Refutations*, London 1963
419. Porter, J. L., *The Life and Times of Henry Cooke*, London 1871
420. Potvin, R. H., 'Sociology', *New Catholic Encyclopedia*, XIII, New York 1966, 400-06
421. Power, P., *Parochial History of Waterford and Lismore*, Waterford 1912
422. Power, P., *Waterford and Lismore* (1937 enlarged ed.), Cork 1937
423. Pseudo-Dionysius, *Peri Tes Ouranias Hierarchias* and *Peri Tes Ekklesiastikes Hierarchias*, *Patrologia Series Graeca*, Vol. 3, J. P. Migne (ed.), Paris 1889
424. Purcell, M., *Matt Talbot and His Times*, Dublin 1964
425. Purcell, M., *The Story of the Vincentians*, Dublin 1973
426. Purcell, M., *A Time for Sowing*, Dublin
427. Rafferty, J., 'Local Administration in the Irish Counties Prior to 1800', unpublished QUB thesis, Belfast
428. Randolf, B., 'Congregation of Priests of the Mission', *Catholic Encyclopedia*, X, New York 1911, 357-67
429. Rapport, A., 'General Systems Theory', *International Encyclopedia of the Social Sciences*, New York 1968, 15, 452 ff.
430. Redfield, R., 'The Folk Society', *American Journal of Sociology*, 1949, 52, 293 ff.
431. Reeves, W., *Ecclesiastical Antiquities of Down, Connor, Dromore*, Dublin 1847
432. *Report of the Committee for the Relief of Distressed Districts in Ireland, 1822*, London 1822
433. Reynolds, J. D., *The Catholic Emancipation Crisis 1823-1829*, Westport, Conn. 1954
434. Riepe, C., 'Parish', *New Catholic Encyclopedia*, X, New York 1966, 1017
435. Riordan, E. J., *Modern Irish Trade and Industry*, London 1920
436. Robertson, R., *The Sociological Interpretation of Religion*, Oxford 1970
437. Robertson, R., 'On the Analysis of Mysticism', *Sociological Analysis*, 1975, 36, 3, 241-66

438. Robertson, R., 'Church, Sect, and Rationality: Reply to Swatos', *Journal for the Scientific Study of Religion*, 1977, 16, 2, 197-200
439. Roche, K., 'The Relations of the Catholic Church and the State in England and Ireland 1800-52', *Historical Studies*, 1961, 3, 9-24
440. Rodriguez, A., *The Practice of Christian and Religious Perfection*, trans. anon, Kilkenny 1806
441. Rogers, E., *Diffusion of Innovation*, New York 1962
442. Rogers, P., *Father Theobald Mathew*, Dublin 1943
443. Ronan, M., *An Apostle of Catholic Dublin*, Dublin 1944
444. Ronan, M., 'Archbishop Murray 1768-1852', *Irish Ecclesiastical Record*, 1952, 241-9
445. Rudge, P. F., *Ministry and Management*, London 1968
446. Rushe, J., *Carmel in Ireland*, Dublin 1903
447. Russell, D. S., *The Methods and Message of Jewish Apocalyptic*, SCM Press 1964
448. Ryan, D., *The Fenian Chief*, Dublin 1967
449. de Sales, Francis (Saint), *Introduction to the Devout Life*, trans. M. Day, London 1961
450. Savage, R. Burke, *A Valiant Dublin Woman*, Dublin 1940
451. Savage, R. Burke, *Catharine McAuley*, Dublin 1949
452. Schmidt, W., *The Origin and Growth of Religion*, trans. H. Rose, London 1931
453. Schnackenburg, R., *The Moral Teaching of the New Testament*, London 1965
454. Schnackenburg, R., *The Church in the New Testament*, London 1965
455. Schrier, A., *Ireland and the American Emigration, 1850-1900*, New York 1958
456. Schroeder, H. J., *Canons and Decrees of the Council of Trent*, New York 1941
457. Schroeder, J., 'Catholic Parochial Missions', *Catholic Encyclopedia*, X, New York 1911, 391-434
458. (An Seabhac, *Jimín, Eagrán Scoile de Jimín Mháire Thaidgh*, Dublin n.d.
459. Selznick, P., *Leadership in Administration*, New York 1957
460. Semmel, B., *The Methodist Revolution*, London 1974
461. Senior, N. W., *Journals, Conversations, and Essays Relating to Ireland*, 2 vols, London 1868
462. Shanin, T. (ed.), *Peasants and Peasant Societies*, Penguin Books 1971
463. Sheehan, P. A., *My New Curate*, Boston 1900
464. Sheehan, P. A., *Geoffrey Austin, Student*, Dublin 1899
465. Sheehan, P. A., *The Blindness of Dr. Gray*, London 1914
466. Sheehan, P. A., *Under the Cedars and the Stars*, Dublin 1903
467. Sheehan, P. A., *Glenanaar*, London 1914
468. Shepperson, G., 'The Comparative Study of Millenarian Movements', *Millennial Dreams in Action*, S. Thrupp (ed.), The Hague 1962, 44-52

469. Silke, J. 'The Roman Catholic Church In Ireland 1800-1922', *Studia Hibernica*, No. 16, Dublin 1975
470. Silvermann, D., *The Theory of Organizations*, London 1970
471. Smith, R. F., 'Religious Orders', *New Catholic Encyclopedia*, XII, New York 1966, 287 ff.
472. Snead-Cox, J., *The Life of Cardinal Vaughan*, London 1910
473. Southern, R. W., *Western Society and the Church in the Middle Ages, Pelican History of the Church*, Vol. II, London 1970
474. Spencer, P., *Politics of Belief in Nineteenth Century France*, London 1953
475. Staehle, H., 'Statistical Notes on the Economic History of Irish Agriculture 1847-1913', *Journal of the Statistical and Social Enquiry Society of Ireland*, 1950-51, 18, 444-71
476. Stark, W., *The Sociology of Religion*, London 1967
477. Steele, E. D., 'Cardinal Cullen and Irish Nationality', *Irish Historical Studies*, 1974, 19, 239-60
478. Steenman, T. M., 'Church, Sect, Mysticism, Denomination', *Sociological Analysis*, 1975, 36, 3, 181-204
479. Sullivan, A. M., *New Ireland*, London 1878
480. Swatos, W. H., 'Weber or Troeltsch? Methodology, Syndrome, and the Development of Church-Sect Theory', *Journal for the Scientific Study of Religion*, 1976, 15, 2, 129-44
481. Swayne, S., 'The Future of Old Churches', *The Furrow*, May 1976
482. Symondson, A. (ed.), *The Victorian Crisis of Faith*, London 1970
483. Tackett, T., *Priest and Parish in Eighteenth Century France*, Princeton 1977
484. Tawney, R. H., *Religion and the Rise of Capitalism*, London 1936
485. *Thom's Irish Almanack and Official Directory*, Dublin 1844
486. Thomas Aquinas (Saint), *Summa Theologiae*, Omnia Opera, Parma 1853
487. Thompson, A. H., *The English Clergy and Their Organization in The Later Middle Ages*, Oxford 1947
488. Thompson, D. M., *Nonconformity in the Nineteenth Century*, London 1972
489. Thompson, K., 'Bureaucracy and the Church', *A Sociological Yearbook of Religion in Britain*, 1968, 1, 32-46
490. Thompson, K., *Bureaucracy and Church Reform*, Oxford 1970
491. Thompson, R., *Statistical Survey of the County of Meath*, Dublin 1802
492. Thrupp, S., 'A Report on the Conference Discussion', *Millennial Dreams in Action*, S. Thrupp (ed.), The Hague 1962, 11-27
493. Thurles, Decreta 1850, *Decreta Synodi Plenariae Episcoporum Hiberniae MDCCCL*, Dublin 1851
494. Tierney, B., *Foundations of the Conciliar Theory*, Cambridge 1955
495. Tierney, M., *Murroe and Boher*, Dublin 1965

496. Tierney, M., *Croke of Cashel*, Dublin 1976
497. Tönnies, F., *Community and Association*, London 1955
498. Towlson, C. W., *Moravian and Methodist*, London 1957
499. Townsend, H., *Statistical Survey of the County of Cork*, Dublin 1810
500. Trench, W. S., *Realities of Irish Life*, London 1870
501. Trevelyan, G. M., *English Social History*, London 1946
502. Trevor, M., *Newman, Light in Winter*, London 1962
503. Trochu, F., *The Curé D'Ars*, London 1930
504. Troeltsch, E., *The Social Teaching of the Christian Churches*, London 1931
505. Tuam, 1817 *Statuta, Decreta Synodi Tuamensis 1817*, Tuam 1855
506. Tynan, K., *Twenty Five Years: Reminiscences*, London 1913
507. Tynan, M., 'The End of an Era', *The Furrow*, December 1974
508. Twiss, H., *Life of Lord Chancellor Eldon*, London 1844
509. *Ursuline Manual*, Dublin 1841
510. Vane, C., *Memoirs and Correspondence of Viscount Castlereagh*, Vol. IV, London 1849
511. Vandenbroucke, F., 'From the Twelfth to the Sixteenth Century' in *The Spirituality of the Middle Ages*, L. Bouyer et al. (eds.), London 1968
512. Wall, M., 'The Rise of the Catholic Middle Class in Eighteenth Century Ireland', *Irish Historical Studies*, 1958, 91-115
513. Wall, T., *The Sign of Dr. Hay's Head*, Dublin 1958
514. Wallis, R., *The Road to Total Freedom*, London 1976
515. Walpole, S., *The Life of Lord John Russell*, reprint, New York 1969
516. Walsh, K., *Dom Vincent of Mount Melleray*, Dublin 1962
517. Walsh, P. J., *William J. Walsh*, London 1928
518. Walsh, W., *The Irish University Question*, Dublin 1897
519. Walsh, W., *O'Connell, Archbishop Murray and the Board of Charitable Bequests*, Dublin 1916
520. Ward, W. R., *Religion and Society in England 1790-1850*, London 1972
521. Ware, T., *The Orthodox Church*, Pelican Books 1963
522. Watt, J. A., *The Church and the Two Nations In Medieval Ireland*, Cambridge 1970
523. Weber, M., *The Protestant Ethic and the Spirit of Capitalism*, London 1930
524. Weber, M., *The Theory of Social and Economic Organization*, trans. A. M. Henderson and T. Parsons, Glencoe 1947
525. Weber, M., *The Sociology of Religion*, Boston 1964
526. Weber, M., *Economy and Society*, New York 1968
527. Webster, C., *The Foreign Policy of Castlereagh*, London 1963
528. Weld, C. R., *Vacations in Ireland*, London 1857
529. Westhues, K., 'Curses Versus Blows: Tactics in Church-State Conflict', *Sociological Analysis*, 1975, 36, 1, 1-16

530. Westhues, K., 'The Church in Opposition', *Sociological Analysis*, 1976, 37, 4, 299-314
531. Whitty, M. J., *Tales of Irish Life*, London 1824
532. Whithworth, J. McKelvie, *God's Blue Prints*, London 1975
533. Whyte, J. H., *The Independent Irish Party*, Oxford 1958
534. Whyte, J. H., 'The Influence of the Catholic Clergy on Elections in Nineteenth Century Ireland', *English Historical Review*, 1960, 239-59
535. Whyte, J. H., 'The Appointment of Catholic Bishops in 19th Century Ireland', *Catholic Historical Review*, 1962, 12-32
536. Whyte, J. H., 'Landord Influence at Elections in Ireland 1760-1885', *English Historical Review*, 1965, 740-60
537. Whyte, J. H., 'Political Problems 1850-1860' (P. J. Corish, ed., *History of Irish Catholicism*, V, 2), Dublin 1967
538. Whyte, J. H., *Church and State in Modern Ireland 1923-1970*, Dublin 1971
539. Wilson, A., *Blessed Dominic Barberi*, London 1967
540. Wilson, B., 'Religious Organization', *International Encyclopedia of the Social Sciences*, XIII, New York 1968, 428-37
541. Wilson, B., *Magic and the Millennium*, London 1973
542. Wiseman, N., *Recollections of the Four Last Popes*, London and New York n.d.
543. Woodham-Smith, C., *The Great Hunger*, London 1962
544. Woolf, B. L., *Reformation Writings of Martin Luther*, 2 vols, New York 1953
545. Wyse, T., *Historical Sketch of the Catholic Association*, London 1829
546. Yinger, J. Milton, *The Scientific Study of Religion*, New York 1970
547. Zeller, R., *Lacordaire*, Paris 1929

Archival Sources

548. *Acta*, Propaganda Archives, *Acta*, 192, NLI
549. Bishops' Minute Book, Meetings of the Irish Bishops, Minute Book 1829-51, Dublin Diocesan Archives 5/1
550. Blake Papers, Church Notices and Announcements, Dromore Diocesan Archives
551. Blake Papers, Convents etc., Dromore Diocesan Archives
552. Blake Papers, Letters etc. relating to Dromore Diocese, Dromore Diocesan Archives
553. Blake Papers, Dr Blake Files, Letters from Irish Bishops, Dromore Diocesan Archives
554. Blake Papers, Dr Blake Files, Letter from Daniel O'Connell, Dromore Diocesan Archives
555. Blake Papers, Dr Blake Files, Loose Papers, Dromore Diocesan Archives
556. Blake Papers, *Memoir of the Most Rev. Dr. Blake, Freeman's Journal* offprint, Dublin 1890, Dromore Diocesan Archives

557. Blake Papers, Rescripts, Briefs etc. of Dr Blake, Dromore Diocesan Archives
558. Clogher Chapter Papers, Chapter Papers Dio (RC) 1/12, Clogher Diocesan Archives, PRONI
559. Cullen Papers, Cullen Financial Papers 66/1, Dublin Diocesan Archives
560. Curtis Papers, Curtis Archive (Calendar), Armagh Diocesan Archives
561. Delahogue Papers, Papers of the Abbé Delahogue, Clogher Diocesan Archives Dio (RC) I, II, III, PRONI
562. Donnelly Papers, Papers of Dr Donnelly, Clogher Diocesan Archives Dio (RC) 1/11, PRONI
563. Hamilton Papers, Letters to Dr Hamilton, Dublin Diocesan Archives, 35/1
564. Hamilton Papers, Hamilton's Accounts and Receipts, Dublin Diocesan Archives, 65/1
565. Hill Papers, Letter of Sir George Hill, October 1826, 622/208, PRONI
566. Hugh Kelly Papers, Rescripts of Dr Hugh Kelly, Dromore Diocesan Archives
567. Thomas Kelly Papers, Dr Thomas Kelly Archive, Armagh Diocesan Archives
568. Thomas Kelly Papers, Dr Thomas Kelly File, Dromore Diocesan Archives
569. Kieran Papers, Kieran Archive, I, Folder 4, Folder 1, Folder 3, Armagh Diocesan Archives
570. Leahy Papers, Papers of Dr Leahy, Cashel Diocesan Archives, Microfilm, p. 6006, NLI
571. MacDermott Papers, MacDermott Papers, Dio (RC) 1/6, Clogher Diocesan Archives, PRONI
572. Kernan Papers, Papers of Dr Edward Kernan Dio (RC) 1/5, Clogher Diocesan Archives, PRONI
573. McNally Papers, Papers of Dr McNally, Dio (RC) 1/10, Clogher Diocesan Archives, PRONI
574. MacParland, E., Note on Churches in Dublin, Dublin Civic Museum
575. Maher Papers, Memoranda by J. Maher P.P. Carlow Graigue, Dublin Diocesan Archives 66/1
576. Massereene Papers, D207/50 PRONI
577. Murphy Papers, Papers of Dr Murphy Dio (RC) 1/4, Clogher Diocesan Archives, PRONI
578. Murray Papers, Letters to Dr Troy and Dr Murray, Dublin Diocesan Archives, 30/7
579. Murray Papers, Property of Warrenmount Convent, Dublin Diocesan Archives, 30/7
580. Murray Papers, Murray Files 32/5 and 32/6, Dublin Diocesan Archives
581. Murray Papers, Visitations of Bray Parish, 1834, Dublin Diocesan Archives 24/5

582. Murray Papers, Official Return (By R. C. Clergyman) on Schools in Parish of Wicklow, 1825, Dublin Diocesan Archives, 34/5

583. Murray Papers, Murray's Visitations, Dublin Diocesan Archives, 35/4

584. Murray Papers, Murray's Financial Papers, Dublin Diocesan Archives, 39/1

585. Ordnance Survey, Ordnance Survey Memoirs, printed excerpts by Parish: Ballymoney (1935) Mic 6/13; Ballyscullion Mic 6/210; Boleran Mic 6/210, Antrim Mic 6/4; Ardclinis (1832) Mic 6/5; Glynn Mic 6/45; Killeavy Cal. 103/3A Box 18 XIII; Loughall Box 18 XVI; Seagoe (1837) Box 18 XVI; Lurgan, Box 18 XVI; Maghera, Cal. 103/60; Dromore (Tyrone) Cal. 103/7; Clogherney, Cal. 103/7, PRONI

586. Parliamentary Papers, 1822 (14) *Papers Relative to the Disturbed State of Ireland*

587. Parliamentary Papers, 1825(3) *A Bill to Make Provision for the Relief of the Poor in Ireland*

588. Parliamentary Papers, 1825 (8) *Report from the Committee Enquiring into the State of Ireland*

589. Parliamentary Papers, 1826-7 (13) *Eighth Report of the Commissions of Irish Education Enquiry*

590. Parliamentary Papers, 1831-2 (30) *Report on the Roman Catholic Marriage Act*

591. Parliamentary Papers, 1833 (17) *Commissioners Reports. Appendix to Eleventh Report of Inspectors General*

592. Parliamentary Papers, 1835 (32) *Report of the Royal Commission on the Condition of the Poor Classes*

593. Parliamentary Papers, 1835 (33) *Report From The Commissioners of Public Instruction*

594. Parliamentary Papers, 1835 (35) *Second Report of the Commissioners of National Education. Appendix No. 3, Fourteenth Report of the Commissioners for Enquiring into the State of All Schools*

595. Parliamentary Papers, 1835 (40) *Returns Respecting National Education*

596. Parliamentary Papers, 1836 (30 and 31) *Third Report of the Commissioners for Enquiry into the Condition of the Poorer Classes in Ireland*

597. Parliamentary Papers, 1839 (11 pt 1) *Report on the State of Ireland*

598. Poor Clares, Papers, Archives of Poor Clares Newry T1461, PRONI

599. Richard Reilly Papers, Archive of Richard Reilly, Armagh Diocesan Archives

600. Roden Papers, Papers and Correspondence of the 3rd Earl of Roden 1820-34, Mic 127, PRONI

601. *Scritture Referite Nei Congressi Irlanda*, Vols 24, 25, 29, 30, Propaganda Archives, NLI

Sessional Papers: see Parliamentary Papers

602. Slattery Papers, Papers of Dr Slattery, Mic p6003, Cashel Diocesan Archives, NLI

603. Troy Papers, 30/7 — Clerical Conferences 1823, Dublin Diocesan Archives

604. St Vincent de Paul Papers, Minutes of the Society of St Vincent de Paul, Mic 186, PRONI

NLI: National Library of Ireland
PRONI: Public Record Office of Northern Ireland

Index